Neil Jeffries

# BON JOVI

SIDGWICK & JACKSON

First published 1996 by Sidgwick & Jackson

an imprint of Macmillan Publishers Ltd
25 Eccleston Place, London SW1W 9NF
and Basingstoke

Associated companies throughout the world

ISBN 0 283 06281 9

1 3 5 7 9 8 6 4 2

A CIP catalogue record for this book is available from
the British Library

Typeset by CentraCet Limited, Cambridge
Printed and bound in Great Britain by
Mackays of Chatham plc, Chatham, Kent

*To Michelle*
*Good girls don't always wear white . . .*

# Acknowledgements

I would like to offer sincere and grateful thanks to all those writers of the articles and books that have proved invaluable in my research. In particular, thanks is due to the archives of *Kerrang!* – the weekly British institution that has followed Bon Jovi from Day One and enjoys a unique and privileged relationship with Jon and the band. Bon Jovi's whole story has been told in its pages and I was there to watch it unfold during the ten years I worked for that title.

Cheers also to *The Guinness Book Of Hit Singles*, *The Warner Guide To UK And US Hit Albums*, *The MusicMaster Metal Catalogue*, *The International Encyclopedia Of Hard Rock And Heavy Metal*, *Halliwell's* and the *Virgin Film Guide* and the Bon Jovi books by Malcolm Dome, Mick Wall, and Dave Bowler and Bryan Dray. Oh, and my *W. H. Smith World Atlas* and *Chambers Twentieth Century Dictionary* came in quite useful, too . . .

In addition to my own interviews with Jon and Richie, I have made use of quotes obtained from sources I have tried to credit at the end of each chapter. I wish to especially thank all those named there. Many thanks also to Geoff Barton and Scarlet Smith. To Dawn Bartlett, Julie Quirke and Kas Mercer at PolyGram. To Ingrid Connell for commissioning the book. And to Mick Wall for his encouragement and support.

Finally, thanks beyond words to the staff of the Norfolk and Norwich Hospital for making sure my dad is here to read this. Even though he almost certainly won't want to . . .

# Contents

# The Definite Article

*'You've just got to have guts. If you want anything, you can do it. If there's a way, you find out what it is. It's not too hard. If you want it, you better go out and run for it . . . That is the truth – there's no doubt.'*
Jon Bon Jovi, 1984

*'We sweat every night, and that's the pressure we put on ourselves – to put on a good show. If you can't take two hours out of your day to do that, then you're not doin' your job.'* Jon Bon Jovi, 1988

FROM THE BACK of the stage, about a quarter of a mile away, some uninteresting support band can just be heard. But the crowd gathered here in the drizzle, around a man-made grassy knoll near the parking area, ignore it. Instead, gazing aloft, they watch a helicopter grow larger and larger in the dull grey sky as it swoops noisily down towards them. Steadily, the rhythmic beat of the engine grows louder until it drowns out the far off band. The noise reaches its peak as the craft's nose first rises and then levels when the helicopter's landing skids meet the grass. There is a whine as the pilot releases the throttle and returns the engine to an idle, then a cheer as a perspex-windowed door is thrown open and a star jumps down, ducking needlessly beneath the whirling rotors above his head as he jogs to a nearby Range Rover, its motor running. Its passenger on board, the vehicle immediately makes its way gingerly down the bank and onto the gravelly track whilst anxious policemen watch the crowd and marshal them away from the roadside. Necks crane and eyes stare as the vehicle approaches and all too suddenly flashes by. Its important cargo, hiding behind shades, cocks the middle finger of his left hand and points it at the rain-soaked onlookers. His adoring public.

It's not a pretty sight. A joke, maybe. Insulting, for sure. But that's what you might have come to expect of Guns N' Roses singer Axl Rose.

A couple of months later the scene is repeated. Except that this time it's not raining and the crowd is a little larger. Except that this time the star doesn't wear shades and is called Jon Bon Jovi. And this time as the car drives past it goes just a little slower and its important cargo smiles, looks all around and *waves*.

Nothing fancy, just a little human touch.

Both the above episodes happened within four months of each other in 1993 at the Milton Keynes Bowl in England. But either could have happened anywhere in the world and serve perfectly to illustrate why, although Axl Rose might be more infamous and get bigger/more controversial headlines, it is Jon Bon Jovi who will be around longest and ultimately get the better notices. In an industry full of fakers and posers, that incident serves to illustrate that Jon Bon Jovi is the real McCoy, the definite article . . .

Maybe only a couple of hundred watched him fly into Milton Keynes that day, but over sixty million of his records have been sold because almost as many believe in what he offers. Long before Jon could ever afford to travel in helicopters, when he worked as a 'gofor' in a New York recording studio, he met many famous stars. Almost every one of them gave him the time of day and very often some good advice, too. He has often recalled the experiences by commenting: 'The bigger the star, the nicer the person. I hope I've not forgotten that . . .' All the evidence would suggest that he never has.

Jon may never draw as big a crowd as the Pope, the US president or Princess Diana, but he's coming closer each year and besides, his crowds are just as diverse. Hurrying along to Bon Jovi gigs all over the world these days can be seen teenage girls and young women, teenage guys and thirtysomething guys, married couples and courting couples. And significantly, there are mothers with daughters and fathers with sons. Join the tens of thousands at a Bon Jovi show and you'll not fail to notice the incredible kaleidoscope of human life that surrounds you. In these days, when the outdoor stadium gig is supposed to be a dying institution, with people staying at home to log on and read about it on the Internet, a Bon Jovi outdoor stadium gig is still a sight to see – if *only* for its audience, a microcosm of society that illustrates so graphically how one man from New Jersey has built a personal dream into something millions have shared a piece of.

Jon Bon Jovi will never enjoy the kind of artistic credibility of Bruce Springsteen or Bono, Neil Young or Tom Petty, for example, nor should he. But much of Jon's best work has been overlooked because of the perception of him as an entertainer, an escapist pretty-boy pin-up.

Although he is now taking more notice of the real world, his earlier denials still hang around his neck. In the late eighties, he excused himself from taking any moral or political stance in his songs by telling an interviewer: 'Little Steven once said to me, "I'll save the world, you save the kids . . ."'. Escaping that mould to emerge as a serious artist could take many more years. His past has painted him into a good-time radio-friendly corner.

He will now move steadily away from that, slipping in

more serious songs among what everyone else is expecting. His fans will grow with him. It's up to the critics to discern, to pick the wheat from the chaff. The media, he would have to admit, have been kind to him – when he's most needed it. For sure, he's been ridiculed often enough but latterly, because the media have at least grown to appreciate his success and tenacity, he gets a better 'press' than ever. But by now he has learned that he must take the rough with the smooth.

'I've read the good and the bad about us, and you can't believe one if you don't believe the other. I guess I just never really was one to believe my own press . . .'

But still he dutifully works at courting the media, knowing it is a part of his job that is almost as important as singing and writing songs. He is fully cognisant of the promotional value of an interview for a magazine's cover story, a thirty-second slot on a radio station, or just ten seconds on MTV, but the man who talks to the media is very different from the one behind closed doors. He carefully tells the story he wants his interviewer to hear, and makes them think they've got the story they wanted to write. He'll be polite and friendly, but once the interview is completed, he'll not waste time on goodbyes and small talk.

With a fan he will be different. He'll far more happily sign an autograph for a fan because he knows what it means when people stop asking. But the fans have kept on asking, and show no sign of stopping.

The reasons why are simple. Being in the right place at the right time was important, but not as important as Jon's own ambition and tireless dedication.

He has an inbuilt belief that if he is to establish himself it has to be at the peak . . . or not at all. Jon Bon Jovi is unable to accept silver when gold is within his grasp. 'You've just got to have guts,' he said in one of his earliest interviews. 'If you want anything, you can do it. If there's a way, you find out what it is. It's not too hard. If you want it, you better go out and run for it . . . That is the truth – there's no doubt.'

That ambition has driven him since teenage days to the point where, even in his mid-thirties he still has goals to achieve and targets to reach. Throughout his career he has been a supremely shrewd operator, steering Bon Jovi along the course he has plotted. By and large he has avoided the trap of appealing to contemporary tastes, instead creating rather than following any musical fashions. The group's image, like its music, has changed almost imperceptibly album-by-album, tour-by-tour. And on those tours the quality of the performance has always been paramount.

'I never go out there and say, "Fuck it! I wanna get this over with", because I'd be cheating myself more than the kids,' said Jon in 1988. 'We sweat every night, and that's the pressure we put on ourselves – to put on a good show. If you can't take two hours out of your day to do that, then you're not doin' your job.'

And yet the job does sometimes prompt him to contradict himself. In 1989, as the *New Jersey* tour began, he offered this view of what he did for a living to Q magazine: 'People think, "That Bon Jovi is such an energetic performer . . ." Man, I'm scared to shit up there. The only reason I can't stand still is because if I did there'd be shit coming out of my ass!'

And yet talking to the same magazine six years later he reckoned: 'I'm not nervous before I go on. I take the mental position that there's no question I know how to do this. I just go out there and do the one thing I know I can do as well as anybody . . .'

So has he now lost all trace of stage fright and nerves? Or is he just prone to saying whatever comes into his head? A little of both, almost certainly. Although without doubt one of the world's most accomplished performers, he isn't a natural.

'It's more a case of watching, seeing, learning and stealing,' he recently admitted. 'Everything I do on stage is Southside Johnny. It's his fault I can't dance, because he never learned.'

And so to watch Jon Bon Jovi on stage when he's not singing his lines at the mic, is to see a man shadow boxing, skipping and bouncing like someone who really doesn't have too much of an ear for the music his band is playing. Adrenaline brought on by pure terror, as he once observed, is an important component. But is it an act?

Again, in 1989 he said: 'Sometimes I'd like to come out on stage like Willy DeVille [the lounge lizard frontman of Mink DeVille] used to. He'd come out real cool smoking a cigarette, then he'd take it out of his mouth, look at the fucker, stub it out and start the song. Part of me wants to do that but the other half is split between being Eddie Murphy and Mick Jagger.'

But six years later he was telling a different story: 'When the house lights go down, I don't change. I've never felt that I became a character, even if it was a good, bad or indifferent one. I never felt that I went out there and became "him".'

All this teaches us much and nothing at all about Jon Bon Jovi. It teaches us that he likes a smoke or two. (Except that he doesn't, anymore.) It teaches us that he swears more than his mother would like. Which probably means Jon Bon Jovi really *is* close to being the wealthier and far more successful version of the guy next door that so many people perceive him as. Mind you, he's a lot better looking . . .


In Bon Jovi's wake have come a host of similar bands, and while imitation may be the sincerest form of flattery, it rarely pays any royalties. And for every Poison and every Europe, there are a hundred more bands dressing like Jon Bon Jovi, posing and moving like him, maybe even including one of his songs in a heartfelt set delivered on a wet Tuesday night to an apathetic audience of three men and the barman's dog. If we've got anything to curse Jon Bon Jovi for, it is inspiring others to copy rather than improve upon his example.

Aerosmith were once the kind of band whose success and status Bon Jovi aspired too, inviting Steven Tyler and Joe Perry to get up and join them for an encore. These days, despite all Aerosmith have achieved since their 1987 rebirth, their best shots at hit singles too often sound like the reworking of a ballad they first heard on a Bon Jovi record. The wheel turns full circle and now Bon Jovi are up there.

In fact, they are *way* up there and snapping at the heels of legends like The Rolling Stones. When Jon cheekily faxed Mick Jagger and asked if Bon Jovi could support the Stones in Paris in June 1995, Jagger said yes out of respect. He would never expect that billing to be reversed, but he knows that these days Bon Jovi sells around six times as many records as his band.

Increasingly, Jon looks to The Rolling Stones as a benchmark. When he was nineteen, he saw them play for the first time during what was then perceived as an ambitious and unlikely comeback tour to promote their *Tattoo You* album. The dates were dubbed, with no small amount of irony, the 'Still Life' tour, and saw the band set up stages using enough steel, cable and power to rival the consumption of many a small town, inside massive sports stadiums. Back then, such tours were groundbreaking events and the Stones were taking giant leaps both for rock'n'roll and in assuring their own future. Jon was overawed. He has even mentioned the show in the same breath as his first Springsteen gig. And the Stones show has played a big part in shaping Jon's ambition.

Above all, it proved that however much people would complain about the loss of intimacy involved in watching a band on a video screen from a hundred yards away or more, they would come because it was an event. Jon has always appreciated that presentation and projection are the keys to success and has learned these lessons well. In the UK in 1995, his band matched the Rolling Stones ticket for ticket, both acts playing an unprecedented three nights at Wembley Stadium.

But whereas the Stones have got this far surrounded by drugs, death and controversy, bookmakers would offer pretty long odds against one of Bon Jovi dying from self-inflicted wounds or excesses. They'd take your money but don't expect any of the band to, as Kurt Cobain's mother put it, 'go and join the stupid club'. Nor is any one of them likely to become a drug or alcohol casualty. Even when the thrill of success with *Slippery When Wet* was at its greatest and, as Jon admitted, 'there were bouts of alcoholism and drugs, dope, certainly a lot of bad money blown', the band still kept it to themselves and cured themselves. There is no potential Jimi Hendrix, Keith Moon, Brian Jones or Sid Vicious in Bon Jovi and Jon himself is about as likely to do a Jim Morrison as the band are to rework The Doors' 'LA Woman'.

Even in the mid eighties, long before it became fashionable for rock stars to go teetotal and get up before midday and head straight for the gym, Jon basked in an image so clean he almost squeaked when he walked. 'I guess I still do have that image, to an extent. It's funny that you have to defend yourself and go, "I'm sorry I don't do heroin. I'm sorry I didn't kill anybody again today . . ."'

So if it's rock 'n' roll excess you're looking for the legend of Bon Jovi is not the best place to start. But if you're a parent wondering if your young offspring's idols are about to lead him astray, to paint his bedroom walls black or start scrawling pentagrams on the garage door, you can rest easy.

In over fifteen years, the most controversial thing Jon Bon Jovi has ever done is part company with his bass player. And he was just about drawn into a slanging match with Sebastian Bach of his one-time protégé hard rock band, Skid Row, over some strange goings-on in the world of royalties. Oh . . . and he and guitarist Richie Sambora stopped talking for about three months.

But none of this would mean diddly squat if Bon Jovi didn't have the songs. To those who buy the albums and go to the shows, all that really matters is that the songs touch a nerve. Bon Jovi songs are usually the ideas of two people that somehow millions of total strangers can't get out of their heads. It's a remarkable process if you think about it. Bon Jovi don't have to have gone through all the joy and fulfilment, pain and heartache they project, they merely have to express it sincerely enough for millions to believe they are enjoying a shared experience. Very few musicians are able to do this. Even fewer rock bands come close.

Charisma will sell so many records, technical brilliance will impress others and sell a few more, but if a band's songs can't conjure that all-important spark of raw emotion that unites them with a mass audience, they are forever going to be among the also-rans. Jon has never been an also-ran. He has enjoyed well over a decade of being odds-on favourite front-runner. Simply because he is the definite article. He can write songs.

'The greatest joy I have in music – more than playing, more than making records – is writing a song,' he insists. 'I know how to do whatever it is I do and that's all I know how to do . . .'

Quotes gratefully taken from:

Shelly Harris, *Kerrang!* 65, 5–18 April 1984; Alison Joy, *Kerrang!* 205, 17 September 1988; Adrian Deevoy, *Q* 28 January 1989; Steffan Chirazi, *Rip*, April 1994; Sylvie Simmons, *Kerrang!* 500, 25 June 1994; Andrew Collins, *Q* 98, November 1994; Steffan Chirazi, *Kerrang!* 543, 29 April 1995; John Aizlewood, *Q* 106, July 1995.

# CHAPTER ONE

# The Beginning

*'I'm not kidding, I broke out in a sweat. He killed me . . .*
*Watching Bruce Springsteen was when I got the point.'*
Jon Bon Jovi, 1990

*'Mick Jagger was very nice to me . . . 'You keeping up those*
*demos? You keep on it.' I never forgot that. Maybe that's part of*
*the reason I'm here today. That was a buzz because I was just a*
*shithead little gofor with a tape.'*
Jon Bon Jovi, 1990

*'I could never think of the idea of not getting signed,*
*not making records. I've always believed in it that much.'*
Jon Bon Jovi, 1984

JON BON JOVI was born Jonathan Francis Bongiovi on 2
March, 1962 in Perth Amboy, New Jersey, less than twenty
miles from where he now has a house at Rumson. His father,
Jonathan (John) Bongiovi Snr was a hairdresser of Italian
descent, as his own father had been. His mother, Carol, was a
sometime beauty queen and Playboy bunny-girl. The couple
met when they were both working for the US Marine Corps.
After leaving the service John Snr worked for a time as a professional singer, but earned his pay chiefly from his skill with

1

scissors. Carol later sold flowers and brooms to raise the money to buy their son his first guitar when he was seven. Junior was unimpressed and impatient and threw the instrument down the basement steps. But such petulance was tolerated within the Bongiovi family – whose name translates, approximately, as 'good life' – producing a happy home for Jon and his two younger brothers Anthony (Tony) and Matthew.

His father would be the man responsible for Jon's trademark permed haircut and most of his subsequent stylings, but Jon is most grateful to him for his inherited sense of ease. His mother, whose genes Jon believes gave him his drive, would eventually immerse herself in his fan club, running the busy operation like the labour of flesh and love it so obviously was. She still runs it today.

Jon grew up in the small New Jersey town of Sayreville, where the family moved when he was four. Initially he was educated at a Roman Catholic school but hated both the doctrine and the discipline. His rejection of both has troubled him ever since and landed him with a weight of guilt shared with so many lapsed Catholics.

Located south of the mouth of the Hudson River, Sayreville is about a thirty mile drive from the Staten Island Ferry and the bright lights of New York's Manhattan Island.

South of Sayreville, in the coastal town of Long Branch, thirteen years earlier Bruce Springsteen was born. Not far from there, in the town of Asbury Park, 'Southside' Johnny Lyon and 'Little/Sugar/Miami' Steve Van Zandt grew up and cut their musical teeth. All three would have a profound influence on the Bongiovi family's most famous son. (Although another crooner of some renown, one Francis Albert Sinatra, hailed from the New Jersey town of Hoboken, the state has always been more associated with blue collars than blue eyes, be they old or new.)

Jersey might be known as the Garden State but its central

eastern portion is, above all, home to one of America's largest industrial areas. Neighbouring Long Island and New York State can boast much in the way of Old English charm, but the landscapes inland from Sayreville are not usually the kind found on picture postcards: swamps, giant Exxon signs, smoke-belching chemical refineries, sprawling automobile factories and mile upon mile of black-top highways. It's the kind of place even other Americans make fun of. 'Noo Joisey' is the one accent just about everyone can mimic and some would suggest it is the only state in the union that really is 'worse than Detroit'.

'Jersey's not a place, it's an attitude' explained the singer much later, when he had named his band's third album after the state. Those landscapes make a particular mark on the population, give the people that 'attitude' they carry around with them till the day they die, however far from home they might eventually wander. 'It's something you're born into. An attitude that a lot of people from there seem to have. There's a lot of camaraderie, a lot of loyalty. There's a certain sense of truth when you see another guy from New Jersey. It's a little bit of grease, and a little bit of muscle and a little bit of spit. It's a working man's place.'


Jon Bongiovi Jnr was just nineteen months old when President Kennedy was assassinated in 1963. He was only seven when Neil Armstrong took one small step for a man. Eight when Jimi Hendrix died. When the first *Dirty Harry* movie and Francis Ford Coppola's masterpiece *The Godfather* were first exhib-ited, he was aged ten and eleven respectively. The significance of these events would shape his life only in retrospect.

'My age bracket was the last of the Kennedy era who believed in the dream and the white picket fence,' he has reflected. 'I'll admit it, I voted for Ronald Reagan in 1980. He was the first person I was old enough to vote for and he looked like someone's grandad and he said it'd be okay. He sold me the dream . . .'

But politics was always a faraway thought for the teenage Bongiovi, far less interesting than pursuits and ambitions closer to home. Things like following the progress of the New York Giants American football team. But he was never built to be an NFL quarterback. Instead he was a bright and lively – if introspective – kid who for a while entertained fantasies of being a cop. It was one of the few ambitions that he didn't go on to realize.

He forsook it around the time that he reached thirteen, discovering – like most other healthy heterosexual males – women and rock'n'roll and beer and cars. Whether in that order he has declined to specify, but his virginity was something he relinquished around the age of fourteen. The experience was, as far as he can recall, 'terrible', but whether that was a comment on his own performance or his personal satisfaction he has again declined to elucidate.

Around the same time, as a result of peer pressure, he started smoking a lot of dope. He recalls smoking 'way too much' once while at home and scaring his parents. He was very stoned throughout his first ever gig – watching Rush, Heart and the Doobie Brothers at Eyrie, Pennsylvania, in 1976. And he recalls that from there he progressed to the odd tab of acid – or perhaps only the one. But his tolerance levels were low and drugs were not a big part of his youth. In fact, they were really only there at all as part of the small-time gang life he was drifting into.

In reality Jon was a loner from a happy home and gang life was never going to be a full time pursuit for him. Although not truly shy, he was an introverted youth who never needed others as much as they needed him. As in his later life, he liked to be the centre of attention but as the gang grew older and the risks more serious, he retreated from it. Many of those he knew in the gangs died young, he once said.

It was around this time that he met Dorothea Hurley, his long-time girlfriend and now wife. They struck up a friendship at school after he sat next to her and asked if he could copy her history homework. In spite of her help, his schoolwork suffered as he steadily lost interest in studying the books before him, prefering to gaze out of the window, daydreaming about being in a rock'n'roll band. Lousy grades followed just as predictably as nights spent hanging around in bars or practising guitar, but just before this starts to read a little too much like a script for the remake of James Dean's *Rebel Without A Cause*, the reality was less desperate.

Along with a few friends, Jon Bongiovi took guitar lessons and made his first public performance at a talent show aged twelve or thirteen – he can't remember precisely. Perhaps, since he came last, he's been trying to forget as much as possible. Clearer in his mind is that his band played covers by Kiss, Bachman-Turner Overdrive and Chuck Berry, which probably places his first crack at stardom in 1975, making him thirteen.

BTO, you understand, were unknown outside their native Canada until November of 1975 when they had their first hit, 'You Ain't Seen Nothing Yet'. Kiss, from New York, had been around a while longer but in '75 were almost certainly America's biggest rock act, having just released their epochal *Alive* double album. And Chuck Berry? Well, anybody who couldn't fill their set out with a Chuck Berry riff shouldn't be up there in the first place. Twenty years later a painting of Chuck would be seen behind the band – along with portraits of Elvis Presley and Little Richard – when they began the *Cross Road* world tour . . .

But that almost forgotten talent contest notwithstanding, his thirteenth year was one in which his whole life and sense of ambition changed. Because when Jon Bongiovi was thirteen, another New Jersey guy called Bruce Springsteen released an album called *Born To Run*. 'That's when I first got into rock 'n' roll. That was one of the first albums I ever bought . . .'

Although nicknamed 'The Boss', Springsteen's first couple of albums had been only moderate sellers, establishing him in New Jersey but never setting the world on fire. But with *Born To Run* Springsteen struck gold – quadruple platinum, even, with the disc going on to sell four million copies in the US that year. Jon steadily fell under its spell as he gave it more time on his turntable than his previous favourite, that year's Elton John album, *Captain Fantastic And The Brown Dirt Cowboy*.

Springsteen's impassioned lyrics, mixed with smouldering arrangements and the richly textured efforts of a stunning backing band, reached into the hearts and souls of youngsters the world over. Closer to home, many of his fans were in awe, taking incredible pride in the then 24-year-old's enormous success, just as you would when an elder brother captained the local football team.

As indicated, until *Born To Run*, Jon's big hero was Elton John. Elton's landmark double album *Goodbye Yellow Brick Road*, released in 1973, and *Caribou*, out the following year, had a great influence on him. 'When he was on the cover of *Time* in '74 or '75, I remember as a class project I made a red, white and blue guitar and wrote "Elton" on it. That whole era, he was the biggest to me. I listened to him religiously.'

He would later become a big fan of The Babys (launched in 1976, a California-based English band, fronted by singer John Waite who would achieve further success when his debut solo was released in 1983) and he also collected works by Irish rockers Thin Lizzy (fronted by the charismatic Phil Lynott) and England's 1960s heroes The Animals (both artists almost unknown among his peers in New Jersey). The impact of all these bands – particularly The Babys – can be heard in Bon

Jovi's style but it was *Born To Run* that would play the greatest part in shaping Jon's ambition and Bon Jovi's future. His biggest heroes were Southside Johnny And The Asbury Jukes, yet it was the example of Bruce that turned him from a kid who liked music to a young man who needed to play it. After seeing just how good local boy Bruce was making, the teenage Bongiovi was – as he never tires of telling audiences today – a man on a mission.

'I'd have given any finger to sell a million records. All I ever wanted to be was an Asbury Juke. They weren't a big band [but] they played regional gigs and that was what I aspired to. That was what a rock star was to me. The concept of selling 40 million records was totally beyond me,' he said, when the reality hit him in the early nineties.

New Jersey is a heavily populated state but not all its denizens become rock stars. It's not a birthright. But those that did, have retained something the state has given them and many of those that did were vital to the Jon Bongiovi as he grew up. In particular, Bruce Springsteen, but also the whole Jersey scene that spawned him.

'It was because of those guys I played guitar. It wasn't because of The Beatles. I was only three years old when they came to America. My mother listened to The Beatles . . .'

The guitar, note, remained the thing. His voice was acceptable but not the main weapon in his arsenal. Or so he thought.

His first band had been started with the kid across the street who played guitar. Together with a drummer who couldn't drum and a bassist who couldn't play they would jam along to Beatles tapes. Regional gigs and one million records were well beyond him at that point. But after *Born To Run* he started to get more serious, and claims to have carried his guitar into any bar that would let him play. 'I was dead set on being in a rock'n'roll band. And it's like anything else, you've got to want it bad enough. If you want it that bad, you'll get it.'

In 1978, indeed, he was so dead set on getting in to see Springsteen play, that he and a friend sold bootleg posters outside Bruce and the E Street Band's gig at New York's Madison Square Garden. 'I didn't have enough money to buy a ticket and the only way I could get in was by selling these posters. I got arrested [but when] they realized that I didn't do it for a living they let me out in time to get back to the show. But we still didn't have enough money for a ticket . . .'

But find the money he did, eventually, and the ticket gave the sixteen-year-old access to something he has never forgotten.

'I'm not kidding, I broke out in a sweat. He killed me . . . Watching Bruce Springsteen was when I got the point.'


His parents, satisfied that at least they knew what he was up to while he was playing the clubs, would on occasion go along to watch and encourage him. He always enjoyed a good relationship with his parents, even when he dropped out of his Catholic school. Later, when he became hugely successful, he remained very close to them, buying them tickets for their (first ever) visit to Italy for Christmas 1987 and trying desperately to get them to retire and live off his earnings.

For years he tried to persuade them: 'I told them, "I'll buy the businesses you work in if you'll just stop." But they just told me to shut up and remember where I was from . . .'

When not under their watchful eye he would race around in his Camero. Once, on the way to his favourite bar, he picked the wrong guys to race with and ended getting pulled over by some cops who were chasing them too. Not for the first time, his grin got him off with a caution. Not for the last time, a couple of tickets to the gig that night got him two new fans.

Summers, predictably for one growing up so close to the coast, were spent on or around the beach on the Jersey shore. Living on junk food, getting a tan, chasing girls, cruising around in cars, a simple story he told later in the *New Jersey* album's '99 In The Shade'. Beaches have always exercised a special draw for him. 'Life Is A Beach – Y Ain't I On It . . .' he scrawled on a guitar once, and both his East and West Coast homes are very close to one.

Back on the Atlantic shores, a decade earlier, when he was still a teenager, the beach was the place he would go to pick up girls – except that his winning smile and unblemished features seemed to attract so many he hardly needed to try. 'I was a little gigolo when I was seventeen. I'd had older women picking me up when I was fifteen. I've been round the block a time or two . . .' He has complained that he sometimes felt like little more than a 'play toy' for women, but seemed happy enough to accept the role.

On the rock'n'roll front, things were a little less glamorous. He and a schoolfriend who played keyboards, David Rashbaum – known better today as David Bryan – were in a band together even at sixteen, below the state's legal drinking age. Another guy from school was Dave 'Snake' Sabo, who would later come to fame as a member of fellow New Jersey band Skid Row.

'We used to go to school and classes would start at 8:00 in the morning,' Jon recalled. We'd get there at 8:30, but the teachers would still let us in 'cause they knew we'd been hitting the club scene all night . . .'

If they weren't playing, then they'd be watching, catching British bands such as Squeeze and U2 in their formative years. But most local bands in the area then were very R'n'B/Motown influenced, playing covers as tradition – or, more specifically, bar-owners who want their places full of dancing or at least thirsty customers – dictates. Jon, though, was already writing songs of his own and would play them to audiences whenever he could.

The bands he played in were short-lived affairs, with names like Johnny And The Leeches or Raze, and sidemen – including Rashbaum – who came and went, but Jon's ambition burned unabated. Somehow, as he claims, he knew what he wanted and understood that the people he needed were not available yet. So instead, fired by that much celebrated New Jersey attitude, he saw opportunities and went for them with both hands, playing with whoever was around just to learn his chops and get his name known. And besides, it was a whole lot better than his shortlived stint working in a shoe store.

While other kids his age were either up to no good or only up to watching television, Jon was spending as many of his evenings as possible watching or opening for acts that worked in or passed through the New Jersey area. By the time he'd gained enough of a reputation to front a ten-piece outfit, named after a local highway, Atlantic City Expressway (or ACE) – an R'n'B band with a horn section heavily influenced by Southside Johnny and Rashbaum in the line-up – he was able to rub shoulders with some of the bigger names at clubs like the Stone Pony and The Fast Lane. 'I supported everyone and anyone who came to Asbury Park. The local band got the slot supporting Joe Blow as he came through town. Everyone played in Asbury: U2 to Elvis Costello, Ian Hunter, Pat Benatar, you name it, they came through there and I supported a lot of those people.'

This was no idle boast. In ACE, he supported Edgar and Johnny Winter, Southside, even Bruce Springsteen. Often he would be invited up to jam with the band at the end of the evening on their encores. 'Bruce would come down and play. No big deal – he'd play with anybody. Southside Johnny, Little Steven, the Jukes played with us all the time . . .'

In this way he formed an early friendship with Southside and in particular with Spingsteen's E Street Band guitarist Little Steven (as he came to be best known). The Fast Lane proved a musical education in more ways than one. 'It was there that Southside Johnny told me all about Sam Cooke and Springsteen gave me a copy of The Raspberries' *Greatest Hits* and said, "You'll love this!" I was 16 or 17, still at school, and I knew Aerosmith . . .'

It would be years before the R'n'B influences he picked up around these times stood out in Bon Jovi's music as clearly as those he gained from Aerosmith and their ilk, but it was all grist to the mill.

First, though, came a move to a hard rock outfit called The Rest, an already established club band based largely on the songwriting talents of guitarist Jack Ponti. With The Rest, Jon was able to perform original material to packed bars and develop a stage persona that wasn't constricted by the parameters of R'n'B. In 1979, The Rest opened the show for Hall & Oates (with Southside Johnny playing between them as special guests) at an open air gig in New Jersey's Freehold Raceway. The bill attracted 20,000 people and The Rest were able to bask in some of the reflected glory. But, despite the interest of some major record labels, The Rest's demos – or their live performances – couldn't convince any A&R man to sign them. Ponti grew disillusioned and Jon found himself out of a job.

Looking back he would be able to see these times through glasses of an exaggeratingly rosier hue: 'By the time I was eighteen I was used to playing 10,000 seaters with Southside Johnny, Hall & Oates – I just opened for a million people, without a record deal.'

Speaking of his lack of a deal in that way is typical of his determination. Rather than see it as a failing – which to him, at the time, it clearly was – he chose to accentuate the positive, maybe even underline the irony.

But for one so ambitious, these were not wholly good times for the teenage Bongiovi. He'd come into close contact with many of his heroes but had been unable to come close to emulating them. The bands he had been in were unprofessional, their demos unimpressive. He knew that with an outfit like ACE he could play all the college parties or bars he ever wanted but he still hoped for something more.

It was around this point, when aged just seventeen, in the summer of 1980, that he got a different kind of job – courtesy of his second cousin, Tony Bongiovi – at the Power Station recording studio in New York, where disco stars Chic recorded so many hits and the band's Nile Rodgers and Bernard Edwards were making a name for themselves as producers. Following the massive worldwide success of Chic during the late seventies, the Power Station, in downtown Manhattan, became much in demand and a number of top artists from all areas of music kept the studio busy. Tony had seen his distant relative performing with The Rest and made some mental notes. When Jon's parents asked if there was anything he could do to help their son fulfil his seemingly insatiable ambition, Tony reckoned he was busy enough to create a vacancy. He made a phonecall and offered Jon $52.50 a week.

Once he had his foot in the door, Jon turned up the heat a little more. In truth, he was a long way from the glamour he sought but he wasn't too proud to get his hands dirty on the way up. Tony had plans to nurture Jon's talents and employed him as the studio's 'artist in development', but really Jon was working for himself. The teenager at the Power Station quickly got himself noticed, doing anything to win friends and make contacts. His job was in reality little more than the studio 'gofor' and as such he would be expected to sweep dirty floors, change dud lightbulbs, fetch sandwiches and make endless cups of coffee. He would run any errands the other staff or customers demanded.

One of the Power Station's lesser-known customers was a Canadian guitarist-cum-multi-instrumentalist called Aldo Nova. Recently signed to Portrait Records, he was in Studio A cutting his eponymous first album with Tony Bongiovi employed to mix the recordings. Jon took his number and didn't lose it.

Away from the Power Station, Jon – with the help of Tony – got together a pick-up band of a number of similarly disenchanted and freelance musicians and formed The Lechers, who played the clubs and bars of Manhattan. Once more he grew disillusioned as members came and went and the band was never able to establish itself. Later, in frustration, he knocked The Lechers on the head and started another band, this time called The Wild Ones. He also put in a call to David Rashbaum, who had quit rock'n'roll a while back to study classical music at New York's Juilliard School. Luckily for Jon, Rashbaum had grown bored with this diversion and decided to give rock'n'roll another shot.

Back at the Power Station, Jon would watch Chic and Kiss and Queen and all these other big name bands, soon coming to realize that he couldn't make it to their level in The Wild Ones. As much as he respected Rashbaum, the rest of the line-up didn't gel, the oft-quoted chemistry was not present. He would bide his time with The Wild Ones but he knew that he was going to need a group as committed to the cause as he. That determination kept him going, as always.

'Some kids say, "I want to do it, I want to do it", but they wait for it to come in the mail to their house. They might sit in their room and actually get told by society – society being their parents, their teachers, their friends – "It'll never happen". They're wrong! It *can* happen!'

Eventually it would, but for the time being, Jon continued to be inspired by the Power Station's customers. Bruce Springsteen, David Bowie and others all used the studio and Jon vividly recalls a time in 1980 just after John Lennon had been shot.

'I'm paying off a cab driver and I looked up and suddenly I

saw this *flash-flash-flash!* Then I saw Mick Jagger and a couple of guys standing there looking pretty stunned because this photographer had just jumped out of this garbage can. Two of my guys just jumped on the photographer and smashed him up against the wall and busted up his camera pretty bad. Now Mick obviously knew this photographer but he still didn't want his picture taken. The photographer was still going, "Mick, please let me have a picture of the Stones", so Mick put his arms around me and my guys and said, "This is the new Rolling Stones" and called us the Fabulous Frogs, or something, and we had our pictures taken with him. I was eighteen years old and I was blown away.'

Jagger used the studio again during the mixing of The Rolling Stones' live *Still Life* album released in 1982, whereon one Barry Bongiovi earned himself an assistant engineer's credit. Barry later did the same job on Bon Jovi's first album.

'Mick Jagger was very nice to me. The second time he came in he remembered me enough to say, "You keeping up those demos? You keep on it." I never forgot that. Maybe that's part of the reason I'm here today. That was a buzz because I was just a shithead little gofor with a tape. It was very nice of him . . . you don't forget.'

But celebrity chaperoning was not high on his list of goals. Writing and recording his own songs was. As part of the Power Station staff he was allowed a limited freedom to record in the studio at nights. It was a time-honoured tradition. If you were a big shot you got up at midday, sauntered into the studio and went home when you got bored. If you were on your way up, you got up a little quicker and worked a little harder, mindful of the price of studio time. If you were a nobody with a broom in your hand and a guitar case slung in the corner, you worked on down-time when no one else wanted to, carefully making use of whatever instruments the big boys left lying around. Significantly, though, Jon has always claimed he paid Tony for the studio time he needed – which even at the wrong end of the working day almost certainly meant he was sometimes running up bills of more than he could afford. But with the tapes in hand he at least had the benefit of a number of small but captive audiences to act as guinea pigs and sounding boards.

'I was pushing a broom and I used to play my stuff for people, at maybe three or four in the morning when all the sessions were done. The first person to [help me] record a demo was Billy Squier and the second was Southside Johnny.'

Billy Squier had been in a band called Piper but released his first solo album, a melodic hard rock collection, *Tale Of The Tape*, on Capitol Records in 1980 but didn't really make a name for himself until the single 'The Stroke' off his follow-up *Don't Say No*, a year later. By the time Jon Bongiovi put out a record of his own three years later, Squier was unsuccessfully trying to reinvent himself and appeal to an older, soft rock audience. A decade later, his own career on the backfoot, the example of his former protégé would ironically overshadow him.

Southside Johnny, of course, was already something of a role model. A talented artist, by 1980 he was a veteran of five albums backed by his band The Asbury Jukes. His own music leant far more towards Memphis/Phil Spector/R'n'B/soul than rock but he was nevertheless impressed by both the enthusiasm and the demos played to him by the youngster from Sayreville. Maybe, too, he was moved by the memory of his big break five years earlier when Miami Steve produced a demo for him which led to his first recording deal, with Capitol. (Four years down the road, Southside was signed to Mercury Records and his support could not have gone unnoticed when the same label ultimately signed Bongiovi himself, another four years on.) Southside invited Jon to bring his band to open some shows for him and The Jukes.

As simple as it sounds, this shouldn't be underestimated.

The world is full of aspiring stars, and some of them don't even get to play the bars, but here was Jon getting his name, face and voice into the conciousness of a lot of very influential people on America's East Coast music scene. It was all giving Jon the confidence to keep on keeping on . . . 'If you believe from the beginning, you know it's going to happen, there's no doubt in your mind. I could never think of the idea of not getting signed, not making records. I've always believed in it that much.'

Whether he truly believed in a Tony Bongiovi-produced project called *The Star Wars Christmas Album* was less likely. Nevertheless, he did record vocals for the song 'R2D2 I Wish You A Merry Christmas'. He got paid $180 for his trouble but any copies of this less-than-bestselling opus that may be gathering dust in your roof space, are worth a dollar or two more – if not actually worth listening to . . .

Jon, meanwhile, was pretty much on his own. Although Bruce Springsteen himself was impressed enough with one of Jon's songs, 'Don't Leave Me Tonight', to encourage Gary 'US' Bonds to record it, The Wild Ones had amounted to little more than a continuous revolving door of friends, acquaintances and rivals who would join in for a month, a week, or a one-night stand. Although he knew that without a record deal he couldn't pay enough to tempt anyone to give up their jobs in lucrative cover bands, Jon was keeping his eyes wide open. Watching those he played with, watching those who played with others, looking for the guys who would suit him best. If he was frustrated at not being able to pin down the right backing band, he didn't let that frustration spoil his ambition by settling for second best.

For all the constructive criticism and encouragement he received from Power Station staff and customers, getting record companies to appreciate his demo tapes was another matter entirely. Their A&R departments were no easier to reach then than they are today. Unanswered letters, phonecalls and knocked doors was the dead-end route taken by almost nobody who ever went on to be a star. With his day job allowing him to grow in confidence through talking to so many of the people who already had not just a foot in the door, but the key to it, Jon could see that an up-front personal approach would almost certainly get him much further. But first he needed his best demo yet to hawk around.

That demo turned out to be a four song recording credited to 'Johnny B' that featured a song called 'Runaway', co-written by him and George Karakoglou whom history has chosen to confine to just this briefest moment of glory. Backing Jon on the song (recorded after two years at the Power Station) were keyboard maestro Roy Bittan – from Springsteen's E Street Band, session man Hugh McDonald on bass, plus guitarist Tim Pierce and drummer Frankie La Rocka who had just joined ex-Babys singer John Waite's new solo band. It was an impressive line-up of talent for anyone, let alone a kid with no record deal.

The tape garnered no response when mailed to record labels on the East Coast, so Jon and Rashbaum flew with it to LA hoping to generate some interest there – but they returned only poorer and wiser. Next, with the tape in hand, Jon decided to doorstep a DJ at one of his favourite rock radio stations, WAPP, north of New York on Long Island.

'I thought, this guy sits in a room all day and just listens to records so he must really love music. It was the new station in town, I figured, instead of NEWW in New York who were all pompous and wouldn't let you in to play them anything. So I went to the new kid in town and said, "Listen, does this sound like it could be on the radio?" because I ain't having any luck.'

The DJ told him, yes, it did sound like the kind of thing that would be good on the radio and began to play it, sandwiched between the likes of Led Zeppelin and Rush, Thin

Lizzy and Aerosmith. When the station organized a 'Rock To Riches' new talent contest Jon's 'Runaway' demo was an obvious candidate. WAPP contacted Jon to say that they wanted to include the track on their planned promotional *Home Grown* compilation. Jon was not over-enamoured with the plan, concerned that he would be selling himself short by donating the track for free. Moreover, he feared that he would waste what seemed like a pretty good shot on a risky first chance that could prove to be his last. One-off single or EP deals were then commonplace and, although they seemed like a pot of gold to those who could see no other light at the end of the tunnel, Jon's sights were set a good deal higher – if only to pay off the substantial debts that he had been amassing by supporting his ambition.

Today he reflects on the irony: 'I never wanted to be a part of it, this little thing, but three bands got record deals off it.' (The others being Twisted Sister – as notorious for their heavy make-up as their heavy metal – and a band called Zebra who 'sounded kinda like Led Zeppelin'.)

Syndication of WAPP's *Home Grown* sampler followed. WAPP was just one of a chain of radio stations owned by the Doubleday corporation and circulation of the sampler led to airplay for the song on stations in states far from New Jersey. 'Runaway' was arguably the most radio-friendly track on the disc and the ripples it made did not go unnoticed. Sceptical and worried though he had been when he finally took the plunge and agreed to the deal, it was a decision Jon has never regretted. But in 1982, deep in debt and with no band to speak of, he had little choice and signed up for the WAPP compilation. Then, all of a sudden, the big record companies started coming to *him*.

Two front-runners emerged in the battle for Jon's signature: Atlantic and PolyGram. At this stage, Jon's debts were considerable – 'three, four hundred thousand dollars' – but he wanted not merely to settle these but to sign to the company that would support him the best. He spoke to both labels and prefered PolyGram, but just to be on the safe side, when Atlantic offered him a sum he was happy with he took their offer to Derek Shulman at PolyGram and asked him to better it. He did and Jon signed to PolyGram's subsidiary label, Mercury, on 1 July 1983. Until three years earlier, A&R man Shulman had himself been a professional musician, having made nearly a dozen albums in a decade as a member of the progressive rock outfit Gentle Giant. Jon hit it off immediately with Shulman and looked forward to sharing the benefit of his considerable experience. Others in PolyGram weren't quite on the same wavelength, however.

Jon had been signed as a solo artist, and although the name Johnny B attached to 'Runaway' was merely a shorthand convenience, many were none too enamoured of his real moniker. Some suggested his given name was a little too Italian. They tried to get him to opt for something else. 'People came up with names that made no sense to me at all. They wanted me to be, like, Johnny Fury, Johnny Lightning or Johnny London.'

No, he insisted, he would form a band. Great, they said, let's call it Victory . . . 'And I said, "Wrong! Let's do this!" And they went with it.'

Not for the last time, he emerged from a compromise with something that suited him far better than those who had raised the issue in the first place. Dropping an 'h' from his adopted Christian name and re-spelling his family name may seem like a betrayal of his Italian-American roots, but it has always been perceived more as a corruption rather than a denial of his heritage. (On the 1995 tour, he reminded audiences of it by having the stage-right drape painted with a storefront that read 'Joviani's'.) Moreover, it was a deceptively clever way of making a band's name point the spotlight at its frontman. 'Bon Jovi', synonymous today with the man as much as the band, offered him the best of both worlds: a name to thrust down people's throats and a band to shelter in. Except right then, there wasn't any band . . .

Quotes gratefully taken from:

Shelly Harris, *Kerrang!* 65, 5–18 April 1984; Adrian Deevoy, *Q* 14, November 1987; Paul Elliott, *Sounds*, 10 September 1988; Alison Joy, *Kerrang!* 204, 10 September, 1988; Mick Wall, *Kerrang!* 217 10 December, 1988; Adrian Deevoy, *Q* 28 January 1989; Howard Johnson, *Kerrang!* 271, 6 January 1990; Mick Wall, *Kerrang!* 300, 28 July, 1990; Mick Wall, *Kerrang!* 301, 4 August 1990; Casey Clark, *Kerrang!* 336, 13 April 1991; Neil Jeffries, Raw 131, September 1–13 1993; *Q* Questionnaire, *Q* 92, May 1994; Steffan Chirazi, *Kerrang!* 513, 24 September 1994; Steffan Chirazi, *Kerrang!* 543, 29 April 1995; John Aizlewood, *Q* 106, July 1995; David Hochman, *US*, August 1995.

# CHAPTER TWO

# The Learning Curve

*'I wanted to write three-and-a-half minute songs. I know that the hook has to be there for it to be played on the radio, to sell records, so we can make enough money to make more records . . .'*
Jon Bon Jovi on his ambition, 1983

*'Our songs are about lust, not about love'*
Jon Bon Jovi on his manifesto, 1984

*'You look back at pictures and you cringe a little bit. But at least I've never put on a dress . . .'*
Jon Bon Jovi on his image, circa 1984

As 1983 DREW to a close, Jon Bon Jovi was a solo artist with a recording contract but no band. His immediate debts had been taken care of by PolyGram, and now he was faced only with the task of earning enough to cover recoupable expenses like most professional musicians. Better yet, he was signed to a label that was prepared to advance him the funds that would finance four good musicians in what he hoped would be the ultimate band. The price for that would not be measured in numbers, however, but responsibility. Jon would have to shoulder the blame and the credit for his decisions from now on. As the only one of them under direct contract to PolyGram, he would become both the leader and the figurehead of his band; the paymaster, hirer and firer. He could, if he chose, have hired musicians on a purely short term basis but this appears to have been an option he never considered. Instead, Jon wanted a band of ambitious and like-minded souls – four guys who would stand by him as much as brothers would. Picking them would be among the most important decisions he had ever had to make. As history has proved, he was a shrewd judge of character and within three years people all over the world would know his band and the newly adopted name of Bon Jovi.

Having met all the likely candidates during his time gigging around Manhattan with The Lechers and The Wild Ones, Jon was convinced that in order to get a permanent band of people who would exhibit his own level of determination, he needed to go back to the bars and clubs of the New Jersey shoreline. He didn't need to look for a keyboard player. The first name on the Bon Jovi team sheet had to be that of his old school friend David Rashbaum. Jon had played with him often enough to know he was good and, having forsaken his course at Juilliard, Rashbaum's commitment was hardly in doubt. Next in was bassist Alec John Such (born 14 November 1952 – although until only recently he always claimed to be four years younger). Such gave up a lucrative place in a covers band called Phantom's Opera for the promise of something a little more challenging – if not immediately more rewarding than his share of the $3,000 Phantom's Opera could earn for a Friday or Saturday night gig.

'I watched Alec for years, from an audience viewpoint, when he was on the East Coast cover circuit, but he knew he was going nowhere fast, explained Jon. 'He's a great singer and a great bass player. He's got a heart of gold.'

Alec recommended and introduced him to a drummer named Hector 'Tico' Torres (like Alec, around ten years older than Jon, having been born 7 October 1953) who had just played on the third Frankie And The Knockouts album. More significantly, as far as Jon was concerned, Torres had once replaced Vinny 'Mad Dog' Lopez (who would later join the E Street Band prior to the *Born To Run* album) in a band called Lord Gunner.

'I'd seen him when I was about sixteen so when Alec suggested [him] I thought, great, despite having been pretty pissed off that he'd replaced Vinny Lopez.'

Frankie And The Knockouts weren't really going anywhere (despite being managed by one Burt Ward, the man who had played Robin in the 1960s TV version of *Batman*) and so Torres had little hesitation in joining Bon Jovi.

PolyGram, however, were less keen. They tried to persuade Jon that both Such and Torres were too old for the band and told him that he should shop around for a younger and better-looking rhythm section. Jon refused their advice, insisted on his right of way and continued with his search for a lead guitarist.

His choice was crucial to the band's future. He knew they would not survive without the services of a top flight lead guitarist. Jon realized that his own guitar playing was never going to be strong enough, especially as his songwriting was steadily drifting towards a heavier, hard rock style. He wanted a lead guitarist to share his vision and as luck would have it he had already found one a few months earlier, while playing a gig on the back of the 'Runaway' hit. More accurately, as Jon recalled, the guitarist found *him*.

'I was playing in a four-piece and Richie Sambora was in the audience when I was playing the WAPP radio *Home Grown* album vocal shows. There were about 1500 or 1600 kids there and he came in from the audience after we went off, started making small talk and said, "Look, I want to be your guitar player". I didn't know who he was. Kids come up to you like that all the time. So I just sorta laughed, said, "Oh yeah, yeah, yeah . . ." walked away, got my hundred bucks for the night, paid everybody and split.

'Later we got together and I realized what a really nice guy he was. When I heard him play, I liked the way he played. I thought he was good. Then we sat down to write and that seemed to be creative. It was exciting to me, that here was somebody I could write with that I liked as a person. Having done it by myself for three, four years, without the rock of having a band, this was a real refreshing breath, then the relationship went on from there.'

Given Jon's longstanding friendship with Dave 'Snake' Sabo (later of Skid Row), it's perhaps interesting to note that Snake was actually playing in the band that night when Richie introduced himself. Jon is adamant, however, that just as he only expected his band at the time to last three weeks ('Then we'd all go back to doing our own things and I'd go back to banging on record company doors') so Snake was merely helping Jon out on a short term basis. 'I didn't want Snake in the band – it wasn't that he was ever gonna do [Bon Jovi].'

His style just wasn't what Jon had in mind. Richie's, on the other hand, turned out to be exactly what he was looking for. The guitarist was formerly a member of a band called Mercy who had been signed to Led Zeppelin's Swan Song label in the US but when he met Jon he was hungry for a real shot at success. With Richie (born 11 July 1957), Jon was convinced he had the perfect recipe for that success. From the others he would expect no caution or half-hearted gestures and so, linked by a common commitment and hunger, Bon Jovi threw themselves heart-and-soul into their new career. Years later, with platinum discs and plaudits galore, Richie would still stress: 'Bon Jovi is a real band, not a corporate machine. We were just a bunch of kids who got together and made it in this business out of hard work and good music.'

Hard work, good music and – initially at least – the tireless dedication of their manager Daniel 'Doc' McGhee. The relationship went sour and came to an end in 1991, but to begin with McGhee and Bon Jovi were a formidable team.

Doc McGhee was also instrumental in the hell-raising rise to infamy of LA band Mötley Crüe, taking over control of them in early 1983 – from their original manager and financial backer Allan Coffman – after their independently-released first album and subsequent signing by Elektra. At the time, McGhee was managing Canadian solo artist Pat Travers, whose career direction he had taken over in 1982. But Travers had passed his commercial peak and Mötley Crüe offered McGhee a far more attractive prospect. In February 1983, McGhee convinced the party-hearty Mötley Crüe of his credentials by flying them from LA to Las Vegas in his private plane. Almost immediately afterwards, he signed them to McGhee Enterprises Inc. – in effect himself and Doug Thaler. Thaler was another man who had worked with Travers but had first met McGhee while cutting his teeth with the hugely successful Leber-Krebs team of the 1970s that had backed Aerosmith, Ted Nugent, et al.

A few months after snapping up the Crüe, McGhee got the dream ticket every manager prays for. For Jon, there was the relatively small matter of a two-year management contract he had signed with a New Jersey club owner on his eighteenth birthday, but by the time the band came to record their debut album, he was free to be solely represented by the manager of his choice. And so Doc McGhee got in at day one on a band that was going all the way to the top.

He and the band first met in 1983, and in McGhee Jon saw much of the force that drove himself and a friendship as much as a business relationship began to blossom. McGhee was, like Such and Torres, around a decade older than Jon but more importantly, just like the band, he seemed prepared to give everything for the cause. And so, despite the lack of a major success in McGhee's track record, Jon gave him the task of masterminding Bon Jovi. At the offices of McGhee Enterprises Inc. in New York, a second floor suite on Central Park South, he and Bon Jovi toasted their plans for future success. The office had a basketball hoop on the back of the door and a balcony overlooking the park. As Jon has put it: 'Back then the band didn't have the price of a cup of coffee between us.' Even so, he was thinking bigger and looking further. McGhee could supply them with coffee – and more – and was impressed not only by Jon's songs but also that the band's work ethic matched his. He taunted them: 'You guys would play a pay-toilet and use your own change!' But it was an ethic he and the band would employ to the limit.

Initially, of course, pay-toilets would have been suitable venues. The first club gigs together were less than awe-inspiring. In fact, recalled Tico, 'it sounded like shit. Everyone was trying to do their own thing but there was definitely a feel there, so we thought we'd persevere and see how things turned out.'

Early shows were poorly attended, a crowd of just six girls reputed to have been their smallest ever draw, whilst the worst gig they ever played – according to Richie – was at Xanadu's in New Jersey on Thanksgiving Day, November 1983. The guitarist blamed the band's failure that night on the most original excuse in the history of rock'n'roll. 'About thirty people turned up and this isn't a well-known fact but there's this enzyme in turkey called Tyagaline and it puts people to sleep. It's a relaxant, a pacifier ... Those people who came that night must have eaten some big turkeys because there were very few signs of life.'

Fortunately, there were plenty more signs on the stage itself. The band were steadily finding their feet and learning how to play off each other. Jon and McGhee gave the band around six months to learn enough to record together and so at the tail end of 1983, Jon led them into the familiar (for him) surroundings of the Power Station studios to start work on their debut album.

Pride of place on the record, made under the working title of 'Tough Talk' but eventually eponymously titled, was given to 'Runaway' but rather than re-record it with the new band, Jon elected to retain the original June 1982 demo version that had served him so well, the sleevenotes crediting it to 'The All-Star Review'. An even older solo demo, 'She Don't Know Me', dating from 1980, was included too and features drummer Chuck Burgi (then playing with Hall & Oates, later of Ritchie Blackmore's Rainbow), Aldo Nova and Hugh McDonald again on bass. The bassist, in particular, would play further parts in the Bon Jovi story ...

The album's other seven tracks were recorded from scratch, with Tony Bongiovi sharing production duties alongside Lance Quinn. The pair had worked together at the Power Station before, most notably producing Talking Heads' classic *Psycho Killer*, but Quinn's most recent (and relevant) qualification was taking the helm of Bon Jovi's then label-mate Lita Ford's *Dancing On The Edge* album. (A record which, ironically, also featured contributions from Aldo Nova and Hugh McDonald.)

Quinn and Bongiovi employed the very latest glossy techniques but the prime driving force was, predictably, Jon himself. The songs slipped comfortably into a melodic rock vein with Richie's guitar only occasionally threatening to pull them over into harder and heavier territory. Jon had a clear vision of the sound he wanted, though: 'I wanted to write three-and-a-half minute songs. I know that the hook has to be there for it to be played on the radio, to sell records, so we can make enough money to make more records . . .'

If Richie, a self-confessed Led Zeppelin fan who idolised their guitarist Jimmy Page, wanted it any different, Jon must have spelt it out to him as he did to *Sounds* magazine: 'Our music leans towards more melodic rock because I had that upbringing within the industry as opposed to sitting in my room listening to Led Zeppelin records.'

After the album was completed, one of the first things Bon Jovi did was open for ZZ Top at Madison Square Garden. 'There used to be this promoter who was desperate to do business with us,' recalled Jon. 'In order to convince us, he got us this gig. After it they offered us a contract for the entire tour. We ended up following their coaches in our cars.' Back at the Madison Square show, bassist Alec John Such was hauled away by police for wearing a gun on stage. Quite a gig for a band whose debut album hadn't even been released yet.

Bon Jovi introduced themselves to the UK press in March 1984 with a one-sided biography and a three track white label 12″. Copies of the former are far less sought after than the latter, which is currently fetching anything upwards of five times the price of a regular single. But the disc – featuring 'Runaway', 'Shot Through The Heart' and 'Breakout', all from the first album – says a lot less about the band's state of mind than the press release. Printed on unfortunately pink paper in ink apparently laced with testosterone, it introduced the band and Jon Bon Jovi himself with the immortal quote: 'Our songs are about lust, not about love.' It was a worrying start.

But those were worrying times, when heavy metal as invented by Black Sabbath was on the wane and the first rumblings of Thrash Metal, that adrenaline-fuelled beast that would not so much kick rock music up its backside as bite off and spit out large chunks, were but a dark cloud on the horizon. Heavy metal's Class Of '84 were doing their best but Jon was here to suggest that Bon Jovi's best would be even better. And however much the press release suggested this was 'non-stop melodic hard rock' telling 'real life escapades' in 'quintessentially rock'n'roll terms', behind the hyperbole there was no escaping the fact that Bon Jovi were really rather good.

Back then, however, they looked fairly horrendous. It must be understood that brightly-coloured skin-tight satin or leather-look trousers, any number of studded belts (worn obliquely from waist to the hip rather than through any belt-loops), ripped vests or cap-sleeve T-shirts, scarves, headbands and cheap costume jewellery were what passed for haute couture among, it has to be said, far too many sections of the heavy metal fraternity.

At the time, Jon was understandably eager to divert attention from the image of the band. 'If you look on the album cover, we're just wearing what we're wearing on the street. We're image-conscious, but in a different way, and I certainly play down any looks that the band has.' Jon must have had his fingers crossed behind his back. He was closer to the truth when he suggested that he'd rather not be playing than be in a band that relied *solely* on image, because at least in terms of music, he could reasonably claim to have maintained his self respect.

On the release of Bon Jovi's debut album, *Kerrang!* – in particular – raved effusively about its merits whilst comparing them to melodic rock supremos Journey and Night Ranger, harping (ironically) on the presence of Aldo Nova – then a bigger star than Jon – and concluding that it was 'truly an excellent package ... already in the running for album of the year'. Also in the UK, *Sounds*, while accepting that the record contained 'nothing earth-stoppingly inventive' recognized its potential and urged readers to 'get a piece of the action'. *Soundcheck*, too, tipped the band for the top, pronouncing them 'tight as a sumo wrestler's G-string' while comparing them very favourably to The Babys.

Bon Jovi's music was, Jon maintained, 'American rock'n'roll' but Europe was clearly equally impressed by it, setting a pattern that would ensure the band's longevity. In the States, on the back of the album's release, the re-promoted 'Runaway' climbed into the *Billboard* top forty (the album itself would peak at forty-three) and the band took the first steps along the road to stardom. Initially, Bon Jovi gained their most fervent support from sectors of the heavy metal following and its media. But uppermost in Jon's mind was the knowledge that however loud they played, Bon Jovi did not sit comfortably with their heavy metal contemporaries. Over the following years he would gradually, and very subtly, ease Bon Jovi away from that pigeonhole. To begin with, though, heavy metal was a gravy train they could hitch a ride on.

To be successful in such a field, Jon had to tread a razor's edge during interviews, trying to deflect attention from the fact that Bon Jovi *had* been manufactured. In fact, they had grown up fast and grown up together and he was rarely perceived as a solo artist with a band of merely faceless session men – a perception that would almost certainly have led the metal and hard rock media to ignore him. Instead, he and Bon Jovi won a useful first footing on the ladder which would not only gain them worldwide attention, but also secure a loyal and relatively young fanbase that, by and large, would grow and mature with the band over the years to come. Jon would, however, refuse to do interviews with the pop music magazines for fear of losing the rock credibility he was so keen to foster.

Instead, back in 1984, both Bon Jovi and their following were reading the same magazines – *Hit Parader* and *RIP* in the

States, *Kerrang!* and *Metal Hammer* in the UK and Europe, *Burrn* and *Music Life* in Japan. They were seeing countless bands with the same image again and again. Bon Jovi themselves were at the bottom of a learning curve, looking up to a lot of these established bands which they would soon be in competition with. To put Bon Jovi in the same ballpark – and often, literally, on the same stages – Bon Jovi could *not* dress as they would in the street. They had to cultivate the fashionable image no matter how awful it looked in retrospect.

And so the band grew up in a glossy magazine spotlight that illuminated each one of their sartorial mistakes all too painfully. An image isn't something you can perfect in a rehearsal studio, and although God only knows what clothes they might have tried on and rejected in private, what they finally wore in public – on stage, at a photo session – was something they would have to live with for ever. Four or five years later, although knowing that at the time it was something he had done willingly, Jon was clearly prepared to recognize that this had all been a ghastly mistake.

'In the early days we were trying to find ourselves. We were from New Jersey – all we ever had was a pair of jeans and a leather jacket. Then all those bands came out, that whole LA thing. I remember seeing bands like Mötley Crüe and Ratt [whom they, respectively, shared management with and supported on an American tour in 1985] and whoever, in all these magazines. They were all doing huge business and we couldn't get arrested. I remember thinking, we gotta go out and rip our clothes up, we gotta go out and wear make-up, and we gotta go out and get fake jewellery. This'll make us big . . .'

Their early image was something they had to work long and hard to shed, the memory of it denting their credibility long after they had wised-up, dressed-down and moved on. Other bands from that era made similar errors of judgement, but most of those would fall by the wayside.

'It took a long while to find ourselves, that's all. I mean, you walk down the street in Jersey [wearing an] earring, make-up, man, you're gonna get your ass kicked! None of that stuff was really us.'

For the next couple of years, though, they would be not so much hiding behind it as parading it like a neon sign. The image would lead to more adult sections of the music industry and media branding Bon Jovi 'pretty boys', 'glam rockers', 'a hair band' . . . and much worse. Each of those labels were, in many ways, a worse stigma than the heavy metal tag they would much more quickly outgrow. 'Hair bands' were by implication shallow with only youthful appeal, hardly aspirational stuff. It even stigmatized them to sections of the heavy metal audience who henceforth viewed them with suspicion, scepticism and scorn.

To begin with, they fielded the questions about their image graciously, wearing the latest jibe about as comfortably as any millstone designed to discredit their every move. Later, with no small amount of success behind him, Jon could afford to be more philosophical, claiming that he didn't mind if people were into the band because of his looks. 'Muhammad Ali was still the champion of the world but he was bold enough and vain enough to say, "I'm the prettiest, but I'm the baddest". We just go around saying we're the baddest.'

It was a nice try. Better still was Jon's frequent habit of appearing to deflect attention from himself and onto the rest of the band and the music. He was very obviously aware of the value of his looks but always tried to dismiss the idea that he exploited them. He did exploit them, of course, pouting for the camera in countless photo sessions, but he would have been foolish to admit it. 'We had to out to fight against that image thing. We purposefully put ourselves up against the heaviest bands on earth to prove that we could stand up to them. We showed everyone that we were a rock'n'roll band, that we meant what we were doing.'

Indeed. Bon Jovi began their touring life by supporting bigger, and heavier, name bands – the first of these being German heavy metal band The Scorpions, touring the States to promote their *Love At First Sting* album which coincided with the release of Bon Jovi's debut. It was a perfect opportunity.

Jon and McGhee had already decided that going out on their own, playing to club and bar audiences was never really an option. A band without a major deal would have had no choice and for Bon Jovi this would have meant slogging around the New York/New Jersey area then venturing further into states where fewer rock fans had heard of their name, notwithstanding the 'Runaway' single. But PolyGram were prepared to spend money pushing Bon Jovi to audiences far larger than they could ever hope to draw on their own.

Supporting slots are the lifeblood of any new band, introducing them to the fans of a similar group on a two-for-one basis. And while theatres and arenas are rarely full at eight in the evening when a support band takes the stage, they usually have enough people in them to help spread by word of mouth that here was a band that was well worth checking out – or that totally sucked. The reaction earned was in the hands of not only the bands themselves, but their headliners. A headline act could make or break their openers, and while some merely grab the buy-on fee and run, others take an active interest in nurturing the openers, ensuring them use of a fair proportion of the stage, PA and lighting rig. Jon remembers that The Scorpions, in particular, fell into the latter category ('they were very good to us') although other reports suggest that Bon Jovi went the whole four-and-a-half month tour regarding soundchecks as something of a luxury.

Live, supporting The Scorpions (or Judas Priest as they also

briefly did) the relatively lightweight songs of the album were
delivered with suitably increased power and commitment. By
putting them to work before potentially hostile crowds not
necessarily familiar with or receptive to Bon Jovi's music, Jon
knew that he was toughening up the band, making them work
harder and become more versatile. He also knew that for the
next album he needed more than anything else to be able to
write killer songs and have a killer band with him every step of
the way. He was the man in charge but he was constantly
trying to promote Bon Jovi the band.

'I'm not that egotistical,' he told Sylvie Simmons. 'I mean,
I'm confident about everything, but to have just sidemen you
lack a vital ingredient. My guys put out one hundred per cent
every night, too. We really are a band, on and off stage. We
hang out together, we're always around each other. A lot of
bands, they don't talk unless they're on stage together. I
couldn't have a band like that. We are truly a family. My
mother thinks she has four more sons called Bongiovi, because
it's very much a team.'

He offered brief pen portraits of the four of them, describing Richie as a 'guy with a heart of gold who never complains
and works for the cause'. Jon saw David as an Indiana Jones-
type character, part adventurer, part clown with Alec just 'out
there' living the rock'n'roll lifestyle. Tico Torres Jon looked up
to. He was, after all, the only one of the band who had made
records before and offered advice and opinions Jon was keen
to take on board. He was also a man, as Jon observed, who as
well as being the last guy to leave the hotel bar of an evening,
would also be the first one up in the morning.

It was a band, a team, a family that would last longer than
most. Elsewhere in 1984, at the more melodic end of Bon Jovi's
heavy metal fraternity, numerous cracks were showing: Van
Halen were about to part company with lead singer Dave Lee
Roth (a man Jon much admired for his outrageous larger-than-

life on-stage persona); Aerosmith were enduring private drug-induced hells and not even speaking to, much less performing with, each other; Def Leppard were in a largely self-induced studio hell that would see them take four years to follow-up 1983's multi-platinum *Hysteria* album; Foreigner singer Lou Gramm and guitarist Mick Jones were finding each other increasingly impossible to work with, forcing a lay-off; and David Coverdale was moving heaven, earth and all of his long-term band members to assemble a new Whitesnake to tackle the lucrative American rock market.

For a unified band like Bon Jovi, such cracks among their most respected and successful peers could only serve to enhance the impact they would make with their own debut album. As *Bon Jovi* found its way into record shops around the world, it was only a year after Thin Lizzy had bade farewell, UFO had seemingly given up the ghost and even the once omnipotent Kiss had failed to make the same impact without their grease-paint as they once had done with it. The throne of melodic rock was an easy prize for any well-equipped troupe of young pretenders that fancied storming the castle. Easier still for a band who would eschew the mediaeval fantasy imagery that was being peddled by other heavy metal newcomers.

Whatever their stylistic shortcomings, their promise was clearly evident when they took to the stage. Bon Jovi were a band that worked very hard and exploited their allotted forty-five minute slots to the full. Content in the knowledge that, in many ways, opening a show offered great rewards and very little responsibility, the band threw themselves into the task.

Once they left the stage they found no shortage of admirers hanging around by their dressing room or tour bus doors. Being a bunch of (reasonably) young men high on adrenaline and whatever else may have crept onto their backstage rider, they weren't shy about exploiting their admirers. 'It never surprises me how forward some of the girls are.' Jon observed as he pushed his relationship with Dorothea to – and beyond – the limit. Others in the band found long term relationships foundering on the rocks of touring – Such and Torres were both divorced soon after returning home.

Jon and Dorothea would, within less than a couple of years, be able to rekindle their relationship, but in 1984, he was more looking forward to Bon Jovi's European debut as the opening act on the Kiss tour. The very first night was in Brighton on 30 September. 'I remember walking in and there's Gene [Simmons] and Paul [Stanley] building the set, literally, spray cans and hammers and nails – what a way to meet Kiss!' he recalled later with some amusement. 'It was our first time in Europe and we didn't know shit from Cheyenne. Gene Simmons was a classy-ass guy. He was all right with me.'

And so Jon listened and learned from an old pro who knew the ropes. In fact, even as little more than a wet-behind-the-ears wide-eyed kid he looked, listened and learned from all that went on around him. He partied, for sure, but even at the age of twenty-two was smart enough to pick up at least a few tips that would serve him for the rest of his career. Without a doubt, McGhee's plan to bring the young band to Europe was to prove a masterstroke in their long term development.

'He always thought of things on a global basis,' Jon reflected when he was both older and wiser. 'Great American bands like Journey and Van Halen never really went global. They never really toured too many places other than America, whereas we always thought of going around the world.'

Back in 1984, though, Jon's perspectives seemed rather narrower as, in full-on self-promotional mode, he spoke about what he saw as his band's driving force: passion. 'The passion that I sing in the lyrics and the passion we play with. We've got a raw energy. When you're up there it just comes from the heart, a hundred miles an hour. I'm up there giving one hundred per cent all the time.

'We love to play live,' he stressed. 'You get in a different frame of mind when you're in the studio compared to being on the road. On the road you get that forty-five minutes a night on stage, and the rest of the day they can just shut you off. That concentrated time on stage is everything.'

It was a sentiment he would echo many times in countless interviews in the years to come. And while their time on stage would increase from forty-five minute slots to seventy minutes and beyond, right up to the two-and-a-half hours they would ultimately enjoy as stadium headliners, there was seldom any doubting Bon Jovi's on-stage passion and commitment. Away from the spotlights, the singer would dutifully speak to the media, rarely without a smile on his face but always with his mind's eye focused on his ultimate goal: those minutes on stage where the dumb-ass questions, the cynical interrogators and the otherwise endless round of self-promotion could be put to one side and he could do what he had always dreamed of.

Early reviews of how he did it had been mixed. *Kerrang!*, ironically the first European magazine to champion the band, ran a less than flattering Malcolm Dome review after he saw the band support The Scorpions in Costa Mesa, California. 'The art of formula manipulation has rarely been reduced to such a mundane level with such spectacularly profitable results,' reckoned Dome. 'If Bon Jovi are to reinforce their rapid rise to prominence and earn long term recognition they'll have to . . . perform with a lot more verve and vitality.'

Eager to create a good impression first time out, Jon took this criticism to heart. He particularly objected to the idea of 'formula manipulation'. The support of the UK press was very important to Bon Jovi and if the idea got around that they were just another formula rock band – heaven knows, enough would follow in their wake – then their career could take some substantial steps in the wrong direction almost before it had begun. Even a year later, the review still bothered Jon, then at pains to explain it away while admitting it wasn't one of the band's better nights

'I agreed with him,' Jon told another *Kerrang!* writer. 'I was wearing this pair of pants that I always wore if I had less than two feet of room on the stage so I couldn't slide around on my knees. It was outdoors, no soundcheck, it was about the fourth date on The Scorpions' tour.'

Come the Kiss dates, the band had clearly improved. But what everyone had completely failed to criticize was the way the band looked. This was once again more a sign of the times rather than the result of a lapse in reviewers' visual or critical facilities. Besides, in Japan, their image was the band's main advantage. Odd as it may seem, Japan has always been a hotbed of heavy metal fanaticism and a lucrative market. Youngsters there, in particular the girls, have long been attracted to any pretty face that could wield a guitar and Bon Jovi were greeted with open arms and screaming voices.

Encouraging album sales and the enormous popularity of Bon Jovi in magazine polls meant a first visit to Japan followed the European tour. All this was impressive for a young band fresh 'out of the box', but small beer compared to what was to follow. Years later Jon could put it in a better perspective: 'The first record sold 350,000. We thought that was cool because it was as many records as the Jukes sold and we got to go around the world, to Europe, Japan and America. I thought that was as big as it got. I didn't fathom the concept that you could make money out of this.'

Indeed, money was the last thing on their minds, even if the thrill of having a little of it to throw around was still hugely entertaining to them. Bon Jovi's state of mind during their first year together as a band can be summed up from one of the first 'breaks' they enjoyed together.

'We got our first tour bus in January 1984 and we rode on it to a gig in our home town,' recalled Jon. 'We got it at four o'clock in the afternoon, pulled into the Holiday Inn parking lot, hung out there until midnight when we went on stage and then jumped straight back on it after ... I'd made it! I was Mick Jagger that night!'

Touring with Bon Jovi brought many thrills but this remains one of the most endearing memories, coming at a time when Jon still lived at home with his parents. But the dream could, and would, get a lot better than this ...

Instigating a pattern that would become all too familiar over the next few years, Bon Jovi appeared to drive direct from the last gig of the tour, park the tour bus outside a rehearsal studio, and dash inside to set about writing material for their second album. Okay, so pre-production may not have been quite that rushed, but it wasn't exactly undertaken over a period that would enable a young band room for much manoeuvring should the creative juices not flow immediately and quickly. If the band felt under pressure at the time they certainly weren't in a position to complain. Young, ambitious and excited, new bands tend to do what they are told – until youth is replaced by experience and excitement by caution. At the time, Jon claimed that the situation was actually ideal because the five of them, having spent no more than a week apart since the release of the first album, had developed a unity that gave them a renewed strength of purpose and the desire to make an even better record than their debut.

The writing schedule allowed them roughly a month and a half before they were due in The Warehouse studio in Philadelphia – less than two hours drive to the south and west – to record. Like the first album, production duties fell to Lance Quinn but, as suggested by the move away from the Power Station, Tony Bongiovi was in no way involved.

After two years working at the Power Station for a little over fifty dollars a week, Jon's relationship with his second cousin had never been a sparkling one. In 1985 it broke down completely following disagreements over the publishing deal the pair had entered into at the time of the 'Runaway' hit. McGhee worked hard to free his charge of the contract but in doing so created a rift that would mean Jon and Tony would not even speak to each other for ten years. The details of their disagreement have never been made public, but Tony Bongiovi's name was absent from the thanks list on the sleeve of *7800° Fahrenheit* and Jon didn't even telephone the man until 1993 during the American leg of the *Keep The Faith* tour.

With Tony Bongiovi out of the picture and a working relationship with Lance Quinn already established, Jon got himself far more involved in the second album's production than he had on the debut. The experience would serve him well for the future but the two rarely saw eye-to-eye during the process and Quinn would not work with the band again. Although in later interviews to promote the album Jon tactfully stressed Quinn's qualities as a producer, this was little more than a professional courtesy, a smoke screen to hide a clash of professional opinions. The album bore an additional 'mixed by David Thoener' credit.

Because someone suggested keyboard player David Rashbaum ought to abandon his surname and adopt the more easily pronounced short form of David 'Bryan' – his middle name – he did just that. Around the same time, someone else told the band that 7800° Fahrenheit was the temperature at which rock would melt (a piece of trivia frequently untrue, but who's holding the thermometer?) That temperature became the title of Bon Jovi's second album. Fired (no pun intended) by the promise of the debut and encouraged by PolyGram's predictions for its successor, *Kerrang!* agreed to grant the band its first front cover. The immediate impact of the band and their music seemed to guarantee that when *7800° Fahrenheit* was released in May 1985, it was going to be big news. And so the magazine duly dispatched a writer and photographer to New

Jersey to write and shoot the story, due to run just before the album's release.

With the album mixed and at the pressing plants, Bon Jovi had retired to their familiar New Jersey haunt of Perth Amboy to rehearse in The Seven Arches, a bordello-like venue of crimson velvet upholstery, chandeliers and ornate stucco. While the band ran through their next set, PolyGram pondered on the choice of first single. Jon's favourite was 'Only Lonely' but the label plumped for 'The Hardest Part Is The Night'.

That *Kerrang!*'s writer was more impressed by the setting and devoted less than five per cent of his copy to the interview (and that his editor let him get away with it) made little difference to Bon Jovi. Far more important was the fact that Jon's face was staring out from newstands all over the UK (and thence to parts of Europe and the States). No matter, either, that the chosen shot inexplicably depicted Jon pinning a black Fender Stratocaster guitar to a pool table rather as an aggressive lover might pin a partner to a bed ... This bizarre image aside, the arrival of the band on such a prime slot in the UK media was a significant step forward. In 1985 *Kerrang!* was the only UK magazine wholly dedicated to heavy metal and hard rock music and its cover was seen as a vote of confidence by both the readership and the music business. Unfortunately, a fortnight later when the magazine ran its review of the album, the prognosis was not looking quite so healthy.

To this day, *7800° Fahrenheit* has remained a thorn in Jon's side, giving birth to many more excuses than hit singles. Primarily, the modern verdict is that Bon Jovi at the time were still growing up and certainly weren't the first band to fail to match a promising debut at the very next attempt.

'You have your whole life to write your first album, and then you have six weeks to write the second one. When we made [it], there were five of us sleeping together in a two-bedroom apartment. My dad would come down every couple of weeks with a big pot of spaghetti and some mattresses – it was like *The Godfather* . . .'

In an attempt to deflect some of the criticism Jon would also hark back to his conflicts with the producer, Quinn. 'Lance did over-complicate matters just a little. I still believe that we could have had a hit with something like 'Hardest Part Is The Night' [one of *7800* . . .'s few standout tracks] with a different production and on the next tour we'll be doing an acoustic arrangement of the song that, I think, brings out its strong points and proved what I'm saying. I like that second album of ours, but when I listen to it now, I honestly can't justify why Lance Quinn did certain things on the production front, like multiple harmonies or doubling up on the guitars at every opportunity . . .'

But these were relatively minor sonic indiscretions that would have been overlooked had just one of the songs – on which any album must ultimately rest or fall – become the hit that would have enabled the *7800° Fahrenheit* album to meet expectations.

'Within the band and our label [in 1985] there was a feeling that *7800° Fahrenheit* would be a massive seller, doing about five hit singles and selling in excess of 3 million albums in the USA alone, but I was always more realistic about what would please me. I said from the day it was released that I'd be happy if it went gold and I'm therefore certainly not despondent that we'd somehow failed to meet a specific target, because to my mind things went well.'

Most American and European reviewers were smart enough to see the band were at best treading water but overlooked any shortcomings out of genuine enthusiasm based on memories of the live act. But the *Kerrang!* review – describing the record as 'a pale imitation of the Bon Jovi we have got to know and love' while awarding three Ks (the magazine's equivalent of a three-out-of-five star rating) would have made sobering reading for the band even as they basked in the glory of adulation in Japan, where the reviews were kinder and the band's world tour began on 18 April.

In 1985, Jon was second only to the some time UFO guitarist Michael Schenker, then ploughing a furrow with his own outfit, MSG, in the popularity/pin-up polls. Happily for Jon, Schenker's star was in only a temporary high as, having released an album called, rather pitifully with hindsight, *Rock Will Never Die* the year before, Schenker's band headed straight for the graveyard as Bon Jovi overtook them on their way to the top.

In 1985, though, Bon Jovi were about to find themselves a little stretched after being booked into Tokyo's premier rock venue, the 12,000 capacity Budokan. Selling it out would have been a tall order for any band never mind relative newcomers like Bon Jovi. Jon, ever with one eye on the business affairs, was anxious to know about advance ticket sales.

When told it was only fifty per cent sold, Jon was horrified. The thought of playing such a prestigious gig in a half-full hall appalled him and he set about taking steps to rectify the situation.

'I rode the train from Osaka to Tokyo on my own and told the record company that I would talk to anyone and everyone to make that gig happen.'

That kind of task is not normally what one might associate with lead singers. Many managers wouldn't work that hard. But the story is typical of Jon's single-minded determination and a perfect example of why the band were never likely to be just a flash in the pan. Jon won a lot of friends with his efforts that day and although the gig never did sell out, he helped raise the attendance to a more respectable 9,000. The band would come back on subsequent tours and sell out the Budokan with ease. No one in Japan ever doubted his commitment or potential again.

Japanese fans were also honoured that the new album contained a song called 'Tokyo Road' (although any of them familiar with Doc McGhee's former client Pat Travers, would doubtless have recognized the line about 'snorting whiskey, drinking coke') and were once again impressed with the band's image, revamped this time around in a mistaken attempt to bring the band closer to the visual appeal of LA bands like Mötley Crüe and Ratt. Jon was still the focal point (his face appearing, albeit heavily disguised, on the album's front cover) but the back of *7800° Fahrenheit* showed that the rest of the band had been given a Hollywood rock makeover. The man responsible for the teased and back-combed barnets ('Hair Design' in the credits) was none other than Mr Bongiovi Snr but far more worrying was a namecheck for Modern Girls under 'Wardrobe'. Closer inspection of the shot on the back cover showed Alec Jon Such chewing a cheroot and thereby drawing attention to a minuscule beard perched, like a dribble of soup, just beneath his lower lip. Said 'beard' would hang around there for years, remaining in favour far longer than even the most sober of the clothes.

Ah, but those clothes . . . Jon will admit now, of course: 'You look back at pictures that are ten, twelve, fourteen years old and you cringe a little bit. But that's the way it was. You can put it into perspective when you realise that others you looked at were the same way – Jagger, Bowie, whoever. At least I've never put on a dress . . .'

When it came to touring, Bon Jovi once again started out as a support act in the States on a big tour. The 1985 tour deemed most suitable was the lengthy trek headlined by Ratt and beginning in the summer.

Ratt's 1984 album, *Out Of the Cellar*, may have outsold

Bon Jovi's debut six to one, but its follow-up, *Invasion Of Your Privacy*, failed to match it and things got worse when their support act came close to upstaging them every night.

Ratt singer Stephen Pearcy believed, quite rightly as it turned out, that Jon was a threat and the atmosphere between the bands backstage was never good. Ironic, really, considering that Ratt actually opened for Bon Jovi in 1984 and then moved up to headliners when their 'Round And Round' single became a US hit and Bon Jovi's 'Runaway' failed to match it. Ratt, however, never lasted the course, fragmenting in the early nineties having, with hindsight, peaked in 1984 followed by a series of less than successful albums and tours.

The problem in 1985 was that Jon was insatiably ambitious and Ratt were hugely jealous. Whatever limitations the nervous headliners tried to impose on him, he ignored. '[They] hated me,' he admitted. 'If they said, "Don't climb that ladder", I'd climb it. If they said, "Don't go into the crowd" I'd jump in . . .'

While he may not have done this to every band he supported, he certainly did it to Ratt, frequently antagonizing them enough for fistfights to result.

After the Ratt tour, the band – encouraged by their A&R man Derek Shulman – returned to the UK to play their first headline show at the London Dominion. Proud of the landmark this represented, Jon flew his parents over to London to watch and introduced them to the crowd, encouraging the Dominion to make a lot of noise and convince his parents that Bon Jovi were really famous. Then, when the PA tripped out after 'Tokyo Road', they got a clue as to just how famous he would one day become. He filled the potentially embarrassing interlude with an acoustic version of 'Roulette' until the problem was fixed then led the band to a triumphal finish. Jon's years of experience and inbred cool paid off. Keeping his head in a crisis, he made a lot of friends that night. *Kerrang!* enthused:

'The man held the show and the audience together superbly and fully deserved the rapturous response he was afforded by the patient and receptive Dominion crowd.'

Jon later looked back on the hiccup gratefully: 'Chances are, had the juice not blown three or four times that night, it probably wouldn't have been such a wonderful, historic gig.'

The live performances aside, however, sales of *7800° Fahrenheit* weren't going anywhere near as well as Jon had hoped. In Europe the previous year, Canadian singer-songwriter Bryan Adams had broken through with his *Reckless* album (5 million plus copies sold) and singles like 'Run To You' and 'Summer Of '69'. Jon noted that Adams' blend of punchy guitar rock and radio-friendly hooklines was not a million miles removed from Bon Jovi's and still felt hopeful about the prospects of *7800° Fahrenheit* – but the record was a long way from making the same kind of impact as recent releases like *Agent Provocateur* by Foreigner (double platinum) or ZZ Top's techno-boogie classic *Eliminator*. Even the faltering Ratt's *Invasion Of Privacy* was certified platinum.

All these (relatively mainstream) records were selling on both sides of the Atlantic but *7800° Fahrenheit* left Bon Jovi a long way from even knocking on the door of that kind of big league release. They were still firmly rooted in amongst the commercial end of the heavy metal spectrum and could only dream of the fourteen million copies Bruce Springsteen's *Born In The USA* had sold. In Europe that meant they were just another one of countless US imports. The encouraging news, however, was that many of these bands were old enough to be viewed as less of an attractive prospect by any youngsters turning on to the music.

In 1985 Van Halen had been around the block five or six times and were replacing 'Diamond' Dave Lee Roth with Sammy Hagar, no spring chicken. Kiss' tenth anniversary party had long since faded in the memory. Ditto other big selling rock rivals like Journey and Judas Priest. Even relative new-comers Def Leppard had already made three albums and were in the middle of a four year wait for the fourth.

In what was perhaps a thinly veiled reference to the likes of Deep Purple (who had recently reformed) and Black Sabbath (who were carrying on regardless) Jon observed: 'We're not forty-year-old guys with toupees that pretend to believe in the kids and tell them, oh everything can be all right! What do they know, driving around in their Ferraris, living in mansions? They don't know what it's like to touch the kids in the first row because they don't do it anymore . . . but we do!'

But did Bon Jovi have a message for the kids, a blinding flash of enlightenment and ultimate truth to share in those intimate moments? Actually, no. But in 1985 the idea of telling the audience to forget the world and party down was good enough. Jon himself was twenty-three years old and living his life to the full, like it was a roller-coaster that never stopped. Once upon a time, he'd thought a tour bus was a status symbol, now he was travelling the world.

In the August, Bon Jovi were booked to play at the UK's sixth Monsters Of Rock festival at Castle Donington and even though the band were only third on a bill of six (followed by Marillion and headliners ZZ Top, preceded by Magnum, their old buddies Ratt and the fast-rising Metallica) they felt like they'd come further than they'd dared hope. Before a crowd of 50,000 they played what many believed to be the best set of the day and, with remarkable prescience, promised they would one day return as headliners.

But the thrill of it all superseded all thoughts of ambition, as Jon recalled: 'We made sure we had a photographer on stage, behind us, to take our picture so we could hold onto that memory later . . . There was an innocence there. We didn't know what we were writing for, there was nothing to worry about. We had no idea of the market place, or the radio or MTV. We were just writing and hoping people would like it.'

Generally, people did. But looking around at his US contemporaries preaching a similar 'message' – the likes of Mötley Crüe, Ratt and Dokken – Jon was at a loss to explain why these were all faring better, that is selling more records, than his band. Bon Jovi spent much of their time off during 1985 hanging out in Hollywood hoping that a little of the magic might rub off on them, but really all they got was more bad clothes and to sleep with too many of the Hollywood hangers-on.

By his own admission, Jon tried the movie star girlfriend (Dianne Lane, star of *Rumblefish*, *Streets Of Fire* et al, later to marry Christopher Lambert) and went to all the big parties, but he didn't like it. He wasn't suited to it. Eventually, the whole band learnt their lesson, that the best thing they had going for them was their strength as a unit, 'the brotherhood' of five unrelated guys all sharing a similar ambition. Hanging out in Hollywood offered them fast flash cars and all the 'wild parties and reckless abandon' that they could handle but they came to realize that, unlike so many of the bands they were looking up to, to Bon Jovi the music was more important.

'It just gets boring,' Jon told Carol Clerk. 'I had my share of fucking my way through Hollywood. There's nothing wrong with that. I had my share of it and I probably limited it because I could have had some more. But to tell you the truth, I realized that wasn't for me. I'm just not comfortable there.'

Publicly, Bon Jovi continued to hide behind a more confident front. Richie explained, 'This album is a bit harder, a little bit of a stronger statement on where we're coming from. It's more positive.' Jon was more succinct: 'The first album was written from the point of view of five guys from New Jersey.

Then we toured the world and talked to kids and saw who our audience was and saw what the band was.'

Contact with the young fans who came to watch them was to prove a critical factor. Those converted at an early age would remain loyal to the band for many years to come. Even if, as Dave Bryan suggested, whilst on tour the band 'lost a lot of respect for women'. Such macho posturing apart, the band got on so well with audiences because at the time they were very close to the same age. They were still upstarts, younger than the bands they were opening shows for.

Yet no amount of promotional bluff and bluster could hide the fact that with their second album, but for some sterling live work, Bon Jovi could easily have nose-dived to obscurity. The record sold well enough to gain a gold disc (500,000 sales) in America, earn an increase in interest in the UK and cement the adulation in Japan, but this had to count as a disappointment. Eighteen months later, with their third album sales eclipsing the first two combined, Jon could afford to be realistic.

'I really can't complain about that album. It was a rushed job but that was my fault,' he later admitted, adding ruefully that in a way, such a faltering attempt had at least proved to be the perfect second step to a more certain future. By then, of course, he could afford to care less.

But back in 1985, Jon was already attempting to distance himself from the hard rock bracket many saw the band as occupying, citing the influence of singers like U2's Bono – listen to his vocals on 'Pride (In The Name Of Love)' and reflect on Jon's growing maturity as a singer, for example – and 'my hero' Little Steven (then two albums into a post Bruce Springsteen And The E Street Band solo career with his Disciples Of Soul outfit). And with these thoughts in the background, Jon could rationalize the whole experience with what would become his customary head for figures.

'I look at events this way: Bon Jovi has sold about 3 million albums and singles worldwide in just three years of being in the business and that's good going for anyone!'

Finally, in 1992, he came clean. When asked to name the most embarrassing record in his collection Jon answered without hesitation: *7800° Fahrenheit*.

Quotes gratefully taken from:

Shelly Harris, *Kerrang!* 65, 5–18 April 1984; Dee Tracey, *Soundcheck*, April 1984; Jay Williams, *Sounds*, 21 April 1984 Malcolm Dome, *Kerrang!* 69, May 31– 13 June 1984; Robbi Millar, *Sounds*, 7 July 1984; Sylvie Simmons, *Kerrang!* 78, 4–17 October 1984; Dave Dickson, *Kerrang!* 92, 18 April–1 May 1985; Howard Johnson, *Kerrang!* 93, 2–15 May 1985; Dave Dickson, *Kerrang!* 96, 13–26 June 1985; Malcolm Dome, *Kerrang!* 128, 4–17 September 1986; Carol Clerk, *Melody Maker*, 13 September 1986; Howard Johnson, *Kerrang!* 132, 30 October–12 November 1986; Adrian Deevoy, *Q* 14, November 1987; Mick Wall, *Kerrang!* 217, 10 December 1988; Stuart Maconie, *NME*, 2 September 1989; Howard Johnson, *Kerrang!* 271, 6 January 1990; Mark Putterford, *Select*, September 1990; Casey Clark, *Kerrang!* 336, 13 April 1991; Dave Reynolds, *Kerrang!* 412, 3 October 1992; Toby Jepson, *Metal Hammer*, September 1993; Sylvie Simmons, *Kerrang!* 500, 25 June 1994; David Cavanagh, *Q* 101, February 1995; Paul Henderson, *Metal Hammer*, July 1995; John Aizlewood, *Q* 106, July 1995.

AN INTERLUDE

# The Godfather

*'I worked my whole life, I don't apologize, to take care of my family.'*
Marlon Brando as Don Corleone in Francis Ford Coppola's movie
*The Godfather*, 1972

*'I was always grateful to them for that help. Now I am in a
position to help others I would be neglecting my beliefs if I didn't
do what I can for them.'*
Jon Bon Jovi thanks Southside Johnny in 1986

JON BON JOVI was only seven when Mario Puzo published his novel *The Godfather*, and had just turned ten when Francis Ford Coppola brought his vision of the bestseller to the big screen, but being an American of Italian stock, the chronicling of one family's rise to power has captured his imagination ever since. Impressed by the twin concepts of loyalty and family, the romance of the story has inspired him in many ways, not least, his professional life wherein he has tried to surround himself with what he calls a 'brotherhood' made up of professional colleagues he can look (and rely) upon as friends and blood brothers.

Jon symbolizes the concept by giving to his very closest supporters a diamond-encrusted gold pendant. He first bought a batch of these, one of which he himself often wears, when

**51**

*Slippery When Wet* went platinum. The pendants are shaped like the Superman badge but have the slewed tyre track pattern of the 'S' in the *Slippery . . .* logo and to be given one you have to have worked for Jon for at least a couple of tours and have shown true dedication and fraternity. Legend has it that Jon only presents one (or sometimes two) of these pendants each year – each an expensive token and symbol of not only brotherhood, but success.

This is not to suggest Bon Jovi's rise to prominence has had anything to do with any Mafia-like stranglehold on the corridors of power in PolyGram Records, or that any reign of terror by use of force has enabled them to secure headline dates. Far from it, but Jon is a sensitive individual and above all a family man. He may once have cultivated the image of a leather-trousered Lothario but in reality his long and (excepting 1985's rockier moments) steady relationship with Dorothea shows where his real strength lies. He has been fiercely loyal to his family – insisting on employing them when and wherever possible – and the extended family that is his band.

Equally as significant, however, is his support of those not directly linked with the Bon Jovi brotherhood. Whilst working at the Power Station, he remained steady in his belief that he had the talent, but was stymied by the failure of anyone else around him to recognize and allow him to exploit it. Inspired by the memories of the frustration this caused, and the relief brought by the friendly advice and assistance he received from Mick Jagger, Southside Johnny et al, Jon has taken it upon himself to offer similar favours to those who remind him of his former predicament.

Whether inspired by his love for *The Godfather* or, more realistically, inheriting such principles from his Italian/Catholic roots, Jon has worked hard to build up and support his perceived family. Like Don Corleone distributing favours while outside his daughter's wedding is in full swing, Jon has since made time for those less fortunate than himself whenever it is in his power to do so. Sometimes such gestures have appeared to be the acts of a Good Samaritan – on other occasions there may have been more than a streak of self-interest involved. But what is not in doubt is that such gestures are uncommon among the rock fraternity.

Everyone makes friends, of course, but it's a cut-throat business and those who don't step on a few toes as they move through it don't tend to be the ones at the top of the heap. Plenty know the truism that it pays to be nice to everyone you meet on the way up (because you'll meet them all again on the way down), but nevertheless few can point to a litany of goodwill gestures like Jon's.

While recording the second Bon Jovi album in 1984, still relatively wet behind the ears with only one moderately successful album under his belt, Jon came across a kindred spirit when during a break from recording he walked into the Empire Club in Philadelphia. Playing the club that night was one of the city's better rock bands, Cinderella.

At the time, the band were known only on the local circuit. Jon hadn't gone along to check out a band that was enjoying any widespread media support. But once inside, he saw enough to know that Cinderella, in particular their lead singer, Tom Keifer, was a man after his own heart – a talent deserving a break. The quartet had been locked into the East Coast bar and club rock scene for a couple of years when Jon wandered in for a beer but stumbled upon something with a much longer-lasting aftertaste.

'There were only about fifty people in the club, about fifteen of them paying attention,' remembers Jon, 'and Tommy was singing like he was playing Madison Square Garden, pouring out his heart.

'Tommy was decked out in this long coat and scarves and was leaning over the mic stand delivering some pretty nifty, growling vocals. I was impressed. Then he whipped out a Les Paul guitar that had been previously hidden behind his back . . . The guy struck me as a star right there and then.'

A few of Tom's tricks – like the long coat and the guitar slung over his back – Jon would adopt a few years later, but right there and then he was inspired enough to go backstage and meet the man.

'He had a different guitar player and a different drummer [then] and I told him they stunk. I asked him if he had a manager and he said, "Nah". Then I set about calling people I knew at record companies and getting them to check them out.'

Kiss' Gene Simmons had reputedly tried to persuade others to sign the band some months earlier but his pleas fell on deaf ears. Jon's word received a more sympathetic hearing, not least from his A&R man at PolyGram. Derek Shulman had not heard of the band but trusted Jon's ear enough to see for himself just how amazing the singer was. He didn't regret the journey and six months later Keifer and a suitably revamped Cinderella line-up were signed to the same label as Bon Jovi. Jon and Keifer had begun a firm friendship that endures to this day. The release of Cinderella's debut album, *Night Songs*, coincided with that of *Slippery When Wet* and so, as would become his wont, Jon invited the band out on the road as tour support. In 1988, Shulman and PolyGram's faith in Jon's opinion was repaid as Cinderella's second album, *Long Cold Winter*, was released and sold over a million copies.

Back in 1986, while Bon Jovi were ensconced in Vancouver's Little Mountain studios at work on *Slippery . . .*, Southside

Johnny And The Asbury Jukes played their tenth anniversary show at the Stone Pony Club in New Jersey. Predictably, as a long term fan, Jon was desperate to go, but had to miss it because recording schedules and the physical distance prevented him. But ever mindful of the start that Southside had given to him when he produced his demo at the Power Station, Jon couldn't let the occasion pass without saying thanks and marking his respect. Bon Jovi's first two albums had recently been certified as selling over 500,000 copies in the States and Jon had PolyGram make up gold discs for both of these and ship them to Vancouver so he and the band could sign them. From Vancouver Jon then sent them on to the Jukes in New Jersey. Southside immediately called Jon to thank and congratulate him. Ironically, the gifts were the first gold discs Southside Johnny had ever received.

'I was amazed that none of his albums have ever sold well enough for him to get such a plaque. Southside actually phoned me up and asked me to come down to another gig and play on stage with the band. It was a fabulous honour to play with people who've been your heroes for so long!'

Jon, who had just seen his first two records sell 3 million copies worldwide, was humbled and took the news as a timely reminder of just how far he had come. It was a reminder, too, of how perverted the music business could be, placing Southside – then eight albums into his career – in Bon Jovi's commercial shadow. Jon was, of course, about to leave Southside even further behind . . .

But even as his junior, Jon still exercised that almost Godfatherly care and looked around for others he might help out of what he believed was a sense of duty – again inspired by his own experiences.

'I got help from people like Southside Johnny when I was starting out – and I was always grateful to them for that help.

Now I am in a position to help others I would be neglecting my beliefs if I didn't do what I can for them.'

The album Jon was working on was about to change his life for ever, but those beliefs would survive . . .

(To be continued . . . )

CHAPTER THREE

# The Explosion

*'The girls are in the shower soaping up to these songs . . . We were sitting there yapping and one thing led to the other and the shower became why the album was called* Slippery When Wet.*'*
Jon Bon Jovi on his inspirations in 1986

*'Something just happened when we met in Vancouver to do Slippery . . . It was like a comic strip phenomenon: KAPOW! We became these "rock stars".'*
Jon Bon Jovi reflecting on the explosion in 1992

*'I was ready to die. We shouldn't have been there. I was really too physically ill . . . I couldn't sing and we looked like death.'*
Jon Bon Jovi at the end of the *Slippery When Wet* tour in 1987

AS THE BAND began working up songs for their third album, the record which would finally be christened *Slippery When Wet*, Jon was under no illusions. The band had made a great start with the debut but had done little more than tread water with the second. Admittedly, there were gold discs on the office wall to remind him of the fact that all disappointments were relative and already Bon Jovi had come further than most bands, but his ambition was pushing him to deliver more.

He faced an element of financial pressure, too. Combined

worldwide sales approaching the 3 million mark may have kept their record label content but Jon and the band would not see the real benefits until their advances and recording costs had been recouped by PolyGram. When the accountants added and subtracted all the relevant figures the balance was on the red side of rosy – despite all the plaudits and the gold discs, Bon Jovi were still around $2 million in the hole. 'Everything in life,' as Jon quipped ironically with the weight of experience sitting heavily on every syllable, 'is recoupable.'

Bon Jovi were by no means the first or last band to learn that kind of lesson. It's a financial fact of life that major record labels are well prepared to make an investment of that scale if they believe their protégés will (soon) be in a position to repay their advance. Although their A&R man, Derek Shulman, has always denied it, a number of contemporary rumours suggested that PolyGram were beginning to doubt whether Bon Jovi would ever be in such a position. The label's initial confidence in the band had waned and had *Slippery When Wet* not been such a success, the label would have dropped the band from its roster . . .

In order for Bon Jovi to start clawing their way back out of the hole, Jon needed to be certain that this time around they took more care with their songwriting and was determined to get every member of the band working as hard as he was to make that happen.

Looking around him, Jon reckoned one member of the band was not pulling his weight and pointed the finger at David Bryan.

'Richie and I would spend ages in the rehearsal studio working on material and David would take the blasé attitude that, "Okay, I'm going home now". His heart didn't seem to be into working as hard as us, which is why he only co-wrote one track on the album. So I just told him that unless he started to pull his weight I'd have to think about where he stood in this band.

'People may find this strange, but I care about the musicians in this band. We've all worked together for so long that we're really good friends. In fact, we all live so close to each other that being in Bon Jovi is like being in a small community.'

Even when the pressure on Jon was at its greatest – he was, after all, solely responsible for the debts the band had run up – he still wanted to maintain that community rather than sacking a weak link and bringing in someone stronger. The sense of brotherhood once more served Jon well as Bryan took the criticisms on board, looked at the options and made the not unpredictable decision to buckle down. Jon defended his criticism of his long-time friend by insisting that, above all, he remained a music fan and therefore cared about the quality of what his band produced.

But having given the warning to Dave Bryan and re-established his relationship with Dorothea (the two reconciled their differences and rented an apartment together on the Jersey shoreline) the most significant steps forward for Jon were two connections made during pre-production of *Slippery . . .*, which combined to turn Bon Jovi from contenders into champions. Those connections were with a producer called Bruce Fairbairn and a songwriter named Desmond Child.


Choosing Bruce Fairbairn to produce *Slippery When Wet* was certainly one of the better decisions Jon has made during his career. Jon decided that another record made with Lance Quinn at the faders was not likely to be the best recipe for megastar status. But even if the inspiration for Jon's choice still had its roots in Quinn's work on Bon Jovi's disappointing second album, chiefly it was down to the magic of serendipity.

'I was on the road listening to a compact disc version of *7800° Fahrenheit*', trying to pick the next single to be taken off the album. At the time I went for 'Silent Night' so I put this onto a tape I was making of various tracks from different records. I had the second Black 'N Blue LP with me . . .' [the otherwise unremarkable and long-forgotten *Without Love*]. By accident, I began to compare the way our compact disc sounded alongside the ordinary cut of *Without Love*. And I was stunned by how much better the latter sounded. It was quite incredible. So I called up their producer . . .'

Black 'N Blue's debut album had been produced by Kiss' Gene Simmons but the man behind their second was Bruce Fairbairn, who had gained a production credit with the mercurial Blue Öyster Cult but whose best claim to fame was as producer and sometime co-writer with Canadian band Loverboy, a faceless act virtually unknown outside of North America who nonetheless had a priceless talent for churning out radio-friendly pop rock hit singles. It was the perfect background for the hugely aspirational Bon Jovi.

Jon wasted little time in sending Fairbairn a cassette of about eight or nine demos for *Slippery* . . . and inviting him to make notes then fly from his home in Vancouver to meet the band in pre-production. On arrival, Fairbairn's response surprised Jon. The would-be producer said he liked the demos just as they were. Hearing the band run through these and other numbers in a rehearsal studio, again he commented that all the material sounded fine to him. Jon was surprised, and not a little concerned because he was not used to such a laissez-faire attitude.

'Lance [Quinn] would always suggest quite a number of changes to arrangements and I began to feel that if there was nothing he could contribute then I might as well produce the record myself. But this was where Bruce really showed how clever he is, because he got to know the band and the way we liked working before making production in-roads.'

Jon and the band eventually warmed to Fairbairn's new approach, and in particular the sense of simplicity with which he approached song arrangements and recording. In retrospect, he could see that perhaps the previous two albums had been unnecessarily complicated. Better still, there was the added bonus of Fairbairn's right hand man, Bob Rock, the engineer responsible for setting up and capturing sounds within the studio.

With *Slippery* . . . in the can, Jon was moved to describe Rock as 'quite brilliant and probably second only to Bob Clearmountain' (a man they would employ many years later). Richie was equally uninhibited in his praise adding that Rock 'knew instinctively what we wanted and he got it with the minimum of fuss all round, which was an enormous help.'

Jon clearly hoped to work with Rock again, and in a couple of years, he would. But until then, most of the plaudits not aimed at Bon Jovi themselves would be headed in the direction of producer Fairbairn – and one Desmond Child.

When the young Bongiovi was sweeping the floors at the Power Station, Desmond Child was living almost penniless in a commune and sleeping in a car. A lucky seven years later, the two men with stars in their eyes crossed paths and put noughts on the end of their respective bank balances.

The combination of Bon Jovi and the hitherto almost unknown songwriter was like a marriage made in heaven. On the sleeve of *Slippery When Wet*, where his name first made the connection by appearing in that album's 'The Hundred Heroes Column' of thanks, it could have belonged to any unsung hero. But added alongside the names of J. Bon Jovi and R. Sambora in the credits to 'You Give Love A Bad Name', 'Livin' On A Prayer' and 'Without Love', it catapulted Bon Jovi into charts all over the world.

When Bon Jovi latched onto him, the only other band apparently aware of his prowess were Kiss. He had co-written their freak disco smash 'I Was Made For Lovin' You' in 1979, and then in 1984, their 'Heaven's On Fire' hit, among others. It was Kiss guitarist Paul Stanley who recommended Child to Jon.

Like many artistic types, the songwriter was, it has to be said, an odd character. He gave much of the income from his first Kiss hit to The Akwenasa Community, a US cult he had become part of. With friends' help, he left Akwenasa, albeit acrimoniously, and only then turned his hand again to writing songs.

The qualities Kiss had been quick to recognize, Bon Jovi were eager to turn to their own advantage. Desmond Child was what had come to be known as a 'song doctor', a professional songwriter who, given the bare bones of a work in progress, could by nipping and tucking fold it into a made-to-measure masterpiece. In the 50s and 60s dozens of such talents were to be found beavering away under the roof of the Brill Building on New York's so-called Tin Pan Alley. These writers worked, initially at least, exclusively on behalf of others, but by the 80s this tradition had largely died out and if anyone believed they could write, they were out there fronting, or sheltering in, a band.

Child, too, had tried his hand at this as Desmond Child And Rouge (the latter being an all-female trio), making two albums – *Desmond Child And Rouge* and *Runners In The Night* – for Capitol in 1979. Each featured a host of session musicians and each met with a conspicuous lack of success. But it wasn't long before Child was part of a growing body of faceless talent called upon by a variety of stars to shorten the odds of chart success – people like Jim Vallance, Holly Knight and the most successful female songwriter of all time, Diane

Warren, whose names even today are largely unknown to all but those who read the very small print on CD sleeves.

The services of such a man or woman might be requested by a band or their manager up front, or they could be called upon when an A&R man, hearing rough mixes – or even hitherto finished tracks – could tell that his act was on the verge of something very successful, but in need of expert guidance. Child was nothing if not expert. Two of the three songs he worked on for *Slippery . . .* would go on to become major hits and, although as they worked together Jon did not know this, he quickly became a huge fan of his talents and was convinced that Child had taught him a master class in the art of songwriting.

But while Jon has often acknowledged the band's debt to Child he has also – usually when answering the charge that they could not have succeeded without him – been uncommonly dismissive. 'There are those who believe that Desmond played an important part in breaking Bon Jovi, but they forget that at the time, he wasn't established. In all honesty, we helped him as much as he helped us.'

It had been a while since the songwriter's hit with Kiss, for sure, but Child's master class unquestionably offered Jon the key to a door that had hitherto hidden a level of success he could not have imagined – and Child would be invited to work with the band again on every subsequent album. But first they had to finish the one they were working on . . .

All the time they were recording it, Bon Jovi were convinced that the album would bear the title of its most potent track, 'Wanted Dead Or Alive'. But fate and young men's minds being what they are, this plan evaporated after a series of visits to a bar at Number Five Orange Street. To many, the city of

Vancouver is the jewel in western Canada's crown, a mini San Francisco set by the bay at the gateway to the unspoilt wilds of British Colombia, but to Bon Jovi and many of the bands who have followed them to Little Mountain Sound studios, it was the strip-club capital of the North West. The bar never got named in the album's 'The Hundred Heroes Column' but probably only because the band wanted to keep it to themselves and keep it unspoilt for their next visit to the city, as Jon hinted.

'It was a really great place for us to hang out because it wasn't a big bar, it was a small rather intimate bar, the entertainment was great mind you, and the atmosphere around it was great. I liked to go there, to chill out.'

Other than the beer, the main attraction of the bar was a shower stall in which dancing girls could, er, freshen up as they livened up the passing trade.

'We went in there with these pictures when the album was going to be called "Wanted Dead Or Alive" and the pictures looked terrible and we weren't happy with that as an album cover,' Jon told Johnny Walker. 'But sitting in there over a pint of beer, one thing leads to another, and the girls are in the shower soaping up to these songs . . . We were sitting there yapping and the shower – that was once famous and wasn't duplicated by every other bar – became why the album was called 'Slippery When Wet'. That turned it around . . .'

The band organized a fresh cover shoot, and plumped for a close-up shot of a girl in a torn, but not noticeably wet or transparent, yellow 'Slippery When Wet' T-shirt and the original album cover sessions were history. Vancouver at the time was far enough away from PolyGram's offices in New York to need two or three connecting flights and the band were pretty much left to their own devices while working there. But at the eleventh hour, when PolyGram did see the artwork – a pink-bordered photograph showing the girl from her bottom lip down to midriff with only the merest amount of naked breast peeping through one of the shirt's rips – they refused to sanction its use. Even in these more politically correct times one might be surprised that PolyGram rejected such artwork on the grounds of sexism, but back in 1986 it was far more of a surprise that the cover wasn't rejected simply on the grounds that it was awful. Neither risqué nor titillating, it was instead merely tacky.

Although unimpressed at the time, Jon later reckoned PolyGram's last minute change of heart actually helped the record. It was released with the wet T-shirt artwork in Japan but other territories had the album adorned by a dark photo of what looks like misted glass into which a finger (Jon always claimed it was his) had written the album's title.

'That sleeve's greatest attribute was that it left it all to your imagination. *Slippery* . . . would be anything it wanted to be to you,' Jon said. But years later (and significantly after the *This Is Spinal Tap* movie had turned black album artwork into the art of high comedy) he had revised this estimation: 'The black album cover was a garbage bag.'

In truth, the sleeve's greatest attribute was that once seen it was completely forgotten and left its purchaser free to concentrate on the music. But before any paying customers got that opportunity, Jon had an unfinished version of the work-in-progress road-tested in the grand tradition of Hollywood studios who pre-release early cuts of movies to a selected audience to gain an idea of how well it might be received. This being a Bon Jovi album and not a blockbuster movie, however, material for *Slippery* . . . was premiered at their New Jersey rehearsal studio to an audience roped in from the local pizza parlour.

'Once the new songs had been arranged and worked out, we invited in a lot of local kids we'd met in there to listen to them and asked what they thought of the numbers to get some form of feedback from those who'll buy the record,' Jon explained.

It's hard to imagine, given the eventual runaway roller coaster success of *Slippery . . .*, that Jon could have had much in the way of doubt about the material. Perhaps he was merely anxious to show as many people as soon as possible that he wasn't about to release another relative lame duck like *7800° Fahrenheit*. His younger brother Anthony, then still at school, was seconded to the pre-release campaign also. Jon gave him a tape of the finished – but unsequenced – album and told him to play it for all his friends at school to get their reaction.

'To me, it's always important to know what the fans think; sometimes their choice of songs can radically differ from your own and we certainly took their preferences into account when the final order of tracks was decided. I've become rather adept at playing the record company game and it's important that any aspiring muso does exactly this – but no one should ever lose track of what, and who, really counts at the end of the day.'

By this Jon almost certainly meant his own satisfaction. For no matter how many hearts the record eventually touched, it needed first to have come direct from the one beating in Jon Bon Jovi. Cornball philosophy, maybe, but it was still the force driving him and the band – his singular vision and a desire to move onward and upwards with each step he took.

One of the things he was keen to improve was his lyrics. Few would have argued that there was plenty of scope. This time out, he aimed to imbue his songs with a sense of character – something he had wanted to do on *7800° Fahrenheit*, but never quite achieved. In truth, he was still a handful of albums and several more years away from writing anything like, say, Springsteen's 'Thunder Road' or 'The River' but at least with *Slippery . . .*'s 'Wanted Dead Or Alive' he was getting closer.

Springsteen's lyrics were a constant source of inspiration to him even if he was never able to match their standard.

'[His] writing and imagery moved me,' said Jon in 1995. 'He's a wonderful storyteller and to me that's the greatest compliment . . . There's nothing phoney, I believe he believes it.' That honesty was a quality Jon tried to add to the lyrics of *Slippery* . . ., leaving behind the naive (or tongue-in-cheek) hedonism and almost cartoon clichés which had populated the first two albums. Jon's greatest strengths as a songwriter were melodies, hooklines and choruses . . . but he was clearly working hard on his weaker suit.

Today, 'Wanted Dead Or Alive' is widely viewed as something of a masterpiece and has since acted as a template for a plethora of atmospheric, cowboy-flavoured odes to the road. Hell, even Jon himself has reworked it a couple of times.

'I've always wanted to do an acoustic track like this one with the Clint Eastwood approach,' explained Jon prior to its release. 'After all, rock'n'rollers do have a nomadic, cowboy-style existence. We come to a town to do a show, try to pick up women, take the money and you don't see us again. I'm especially proud of this number.'

His immodest guess that the song was 'likely to become a classic' has actually proved correct. Live, the number is a guaranteed crowd-pleaser almost always saved till the very last encore where its presence signals that, although politically correct thinking may have overtaken it, its impact on stadium-sized crowds remains undiminished.

The cowboy theme in its lyric would be a motif he'd never shake off. It and the lifestyle he alluded to has served him well, however, and he has never grown tired of explaining it.

'I feel that you ride into town. You don't know where the fuck you are. You're with your gang: stealing money; getting what you can off any girl that'll give it to you; drinking as much of the free alcohol as you can; and being gone before the law catches you ... Before someone wakes you from this wonderful dream and says, "You're an asshole, you're going to jail". Because it's not the real world I'm living in. It's a dream sequence, a big fucking wet dream.'

But interviewed prior to the album's release, Jon was keen to stress that there was more to his character than that. Not for the last time he tiptoed along a grubby chalk line separating Jon Bon Jovi the serious musician from Jon Bon Jovi the tongue-in-cheek rock'n'roller. The balancing act was in its infancy and not always convincing, but at least a picture was emerging of a singer and performer quite different to the man away from the spotlight. In heavy metal circles at least, this was not often the case, with frontmen's larger-than-life personas commonly maintained for the whole of their waking day.

As evidence of his own maturity, Jon cited the example of his appearance at the 1986 Farm Aid II (a charity concert put together by John Mellencamp, amongst others, to raise funds for American farmers driven to poverty by recent US government legislation). There, Jon jammed on stage with Willie Nelson and Kris Kristofferson. Unlike subsequent year's events (which included appearances by Guns N' Roses) or the previous year's Live Aid shows, the 1986 Farm Aid wasn't well publicized outside of the US and so in Europe and elsewhere Jon's support and attendance wasn't widely known. But with his charitable intentions taken as read, the event also provided him with the opportunity to be seen to be performing in something other than a hard rock environment. Speaking to the UK press he was keen to point this out. 'It was such a thrill and gave me the feeling that at last I was being accepted by these legends as a peer.'

And such acceptance was important to him, because despite their rapid and still burgeoning success, Bon Jovi had never been taken seriously as a musical force – except perhaps by their record company, who were probably more impressed by their commercial potential. Jon wanted more, he wanted respect. But in the immediate future he would at least see that commercial potential fulfilled in a way he hadn't even dared dream . . .

*Slippery When Wet* was released to the shops in September 1986. It came just 18 months after *7800° Fahrenheit*, but in terms of quality, was light years away.

'A Triumph of Artistry' proclaimed PolyGram's press ads. 'Includes the Rock Classic "You Give Love A Bad Name"' they suggested, modestly, beneath a picture of the band bedecked in drainpipe jeans, Cuban heels, tassles and back-combed hair. Alec, mysteriously, took centre stage in the line-up, his soup-dribble beard refusing to leave . . .

*Kerrang!*'s Malcolm Dome waxed lyrical on the record's virtues and let his four-and-a-half star review spill over into his feature in the next issue where he volunteered that *Slippery When Wet* was 'a strongly individual record that is a giant leap ahead' turning Bon Jovi into 'a world-class band'.

'You Give Love A Bad Name', released as a single one month ahead of the album, did indeed go on to gain something like 'Rock Classic' status. Moreover it kicked down doors Jon couldn't even get an answer from before. In short, radio stations everywhere went mad for it – and the successive singles 'Livin' On A Prayer', 'Wanted Dead Or Alive' and 'Never Say Goodbye'. Far more importantly, however, was the support of MTV. Seven years after The Buggles had had a hit with 'Video Killed The Radio Star' and two after Queen's 'Radio Ga Ga', the video for a single was now every bit as important as the music it was only supposed to accompany. If MTV liked the clip, and played it heavy rotation (once – or more – every hour of daytime programming) then, in the US at least, a record company could save itself the trouble of even pressing up singles and instead just sit back whilst thousands watched the clip then went out and bought the album. It was the easiest way to advertise a new product ever invented. And all in the name of entertainment.

Bon Jovi were the first to admit that their first five videos (those made for the first two albums) had been awful and had therefore been ignored by MTV. Making them, the band merely did what they were told – although they drew the line at taking instructions from the *Cats* choreographer who showed up for one of the shoots. That apart, as Richie stressed, the band 'had no control'. 'We were kids, we didn't know what to do anyway, and we certainly didn't know how to make videos. But after watching those five being made we were able to put our foot down . . .'

The videos were expensive, too, the bill for *7800° Fahrenheit*'s 'Only Lonely' coming in at a reputed $90,000. That would have been small beer if the video had taken off and produced the desired boost in album sales – but it didn't and that expense went down as a loss, recouped ultimately from the band's other earnings. Little wonder, then, that until *Slippery* . . . began to soar up the charts, the band were still only earning around $350 each a week.

The videos helped change all that and Torres recalls getting a pay cheque for $100,000 which he promptly held up before a camera for posterity then quickly cashed and bought a car with. It remains a particularly sweet memory as it happened soon after his first wife had divorced him due, he argues, to lack of income. Maybe she should have been more patient because the band members' incomes were about to go through the roof. This happened because the videos, once played on MTV, could do what radio couldn't – sell Bon Jovi to a massive audience that was traditionally only a very small part of rock's market: girls. One glance at their screen could show much of the female population of North America that here was a bunch of reasonably handsome hairy rock types backing one notably handsome variety of the species . . .

It would be a couple of years before MTV took off in Europe (around the release of *New Jersey*) but it was right there in America when Bon Jovi needed it most and the Wayne Isham-directed promos for 'You Give Love A Bad Name' and, especially, 'Wanted Dead Or Alive' played a vital part in catapulting Bon Jovi up the charts to *Billboard*'s top slot.

*Slippery* . . . would spend forty-six continuous weeks in *Billboard*'s top ten, a remarkable feat matched only by Springsteen's *Born In The USA* and Michael Jackson's epochal *Thriller*. The sales and predominance of *Slippery* . . . did almost as much for rock music in general as they did for Bon Jovi. Notwithstanding opening MTV to an avalanche of commercial rock, the album also completely redefined the attitude of commercial radio stations towards rock music. Hitherto, much of it had been viewed as just too damn loud for daytime mainstream consumption when listeners could skip to any number of alternative stations whenever anything even vaguely tough on the ears hit the airwaves.

'When *Slippery* . . . came into radio,' said Richie, 'it opened the door for rock music again. We made that mark. Actually, I shouldn't say "we" because really it was the kids that requested the songs. They made radio turn. People wanted rock music to come back.'

There was a lot of truth in the guitarist's observation, acknowledging as it did the American public's long wait for a successor to Def Leppard's 9 million-selling *Pyromania* album of 1983. A series of misfortunes and personal tragedies had delayed the English band's follow-up to the point where Bon Jovi were in the right place at the right time to fill the void on the airwaves with *Slippery* . . .

In the US there were hundreds of dedicated rock stations,

each broadcasting hard rock or heavy metal twenty-four hours a day (unlike much of Europe where stations ghettoize such programming to one or two-hour slots late at night). These stations, too, picked up on Bon Jovi – even though many of them believed the band's lighter, more song-driven, approach to be at the outer edges of their listener's musical tastes. The importance of stations such as these was very much secondary, however, as the crucial point about *Slippery* . . . was that it reached, and converted, fans outside rock's traditionally limited catchment.

Other contemporary albums that benefited from (and contributed to) this new level of popularity included Iron Maiden's *Somewhere In Time*, Queen's *A Kind Of Magic* and Cinderella's *Night Songs*. But it was the Bon Jovi singles 'Wanted Dead Or Alive', 'You Give Love A Bad Name' and (especially) 'Livin' On A Prayer' that really threw the airwaves open.

Record companies weren't slow to react, either, and in *Slippery* . . .'s wake came a host of releases by similarly poised, radio-friendly, young bands: Poison's debut *Look What The Cat Dragged In* was just a month behind the Swedish band called Europe released their biggest ever hit with *The Final Countdown* in November and the following twelve months would see big comeback records by Def Leppard, Whitesnake, Aerosmith and Boston – and Jon could take extra satisfaction when his hand-picked labelmates Cinderella's debut album *Night Songs* followed *Slippery* . . . into the US top ten.

These successful bands, however, were just the tip of an iceberg that Bon Jovi's rise to prominence gave birth to. 'In 1986 the funniest thing happened,' said Jon 'All these rock stars started having the same haircut. I'd be going, "Hey, that's pretty wild. That guy looks exactly like me!" '

And while Jon's scissor-shy father clearly had a lot of hirsute copycat crimes to answer for, it was as if something had turned full circle. Suddenly, far from being a minority interest and underground phenomenon, heavy metal (at least of the style which these bands purveyed) was high fashion – and Bon Jovi were the band leading them all down the musical catwalk.

'The first two albums went along nicely, then *Slippery* . . . came along. That third album is the make-or-break point in any band's career. Ours went way past that make point . . .' Amongst everything else, Jon had also apparently learned the art of the understatement, although he could attempt to rationalize the band's success when the need arose.

'When we met, Des[mond Child], Richie and myself, along with Bruce Fairbairn and Bob Rock, were all on separate journeys, all making a living. Des had got a little money from a Kiss song, whilst Fairbairn and Rock were doing okay with Loverboy and the likes . . . But something just happened when we met in Vancouver to do *Slippery* . . . It was like a comic strip phenomenon: KAPOW! We became these "rock stars" . . .'

The album went to number one in the States and number six in the UK, outselling Bruce Springsteen's *The River* six to one as it became the (then) fastest selling album of all time. It sold over 13 million copies worldwide, 11 million of those in the States in 1986 alone – beating Def Leppard's *Pyromania* by 2 million copies

'An absolute dream' were the best words Jon could use to describe his feelings at the news. '[Thirteen] million is beyond anyone's expectations. I was looking at the sales of Southside Johnny And The Asbury Jukes, who for me were *the* band . . . Their best selling albums only sold in the region of 240,000. Even Bruce, who was Jesus Christ to me, only sold around four million copies of *Born To Run* which was one of the best albums of all time . . .'

Although marketing techniques in the music industry had clearly improved considerably in the eleven years since the release of *Born To Run* (which has gone on to more than double its initial sales), the performance of *Slippery* . . . was still a remarkable achievement in comparison.

It was an achievement that was impossible to really put into perspective and sometimes Jon would prefer to belittle it.

'The success we're having now,' he told Carol Clerk, 'is not as romantic as it was growing up thinking, "Some day we'll get a record deal . . ." I don't pay any attention to what we've been told about our success. Our attitude is just that we made a record.' But the comic-strip *kapow!* of hindsight was far nearer the truth – and not just for Jon and the band. There was a knock on effect for Fairbairn and Rock who became stars in their own right. With *Slippery* . . . (and similarly spectacular success with their combined work on Aerosmith's 'Permanent Vacation' album – recorded almost directly after) the pair were able to work apart and both become hugely successful rock producers in a new super league, on a par with Robert John 'Mutt' Lange, the man responsible for the sound of The Cars, Def Leppard, AC/DC and Foreigner. Desmond Child, too, suddenly found himself in huge demand and rapidly went on to be one of the rock world's most lauded songwriters.

Aerosmith themselves were one of the first to follow Jon's example, moving into Little Mountain Sound almost as soon as Bon Jovi moved out and getting Child to co-write three songs for them (two of them, 'Dude (Looks Like A Lady)' and 'Angel', echoed the performance of 'You Give Love A Bad Name' and 'Livin' On A Prayer'). The long celebrated American rock heroes had been to the top of the mountain in the mid seventies but had slipped and fallen badly due to over-indulgences in drugs and alcohol. In 1987, safely on the 'de-tox' and comeback trail, they watched Bon Jovi rise to usurp their former crown. Reports even filtered out that Aerosmith, having heard the album's Bon Jovi/Sambora song 'Social Disease' before it was complete, had tried to persuade Bon Jovi to leave it off the finished cut: a perfect indication of how Bon Jovi were now rubbing shoulders with the kind of names they once only looked up to. For a starry-eyed singer with just four years' experience as a professional musician behind him, it meant more than any material rewards.

'I could easily afford a $400,000 house the way many other supposedly big name vocalists can,' Jon said, even as the album was released, 'but it's not my style. I'd rather live near the rest of the band, in the environment I love, rather than being "the star". I love music, rock'n'roll and what I do. It's my life. If someone gave me $5 million and told me that the condition of acceptance was that I could never work again, I'd be scared and lost.'

It was fitting that he should have been so keen to work, given the tour schedule that was about to unfold before him.


No one seems to remember exactly how long the *Slippery When Wet* tour lasted. For a band so adept at quoting figures and statistics, this seems quite remarkable – and also indicative of the fact that it was, by any stretch of the imagination, exactly *too* long.

Varying opinions by the band members themselves put it at anything between fourteen and eighteen months, taking in 'about 250 shows'. Which actually says more about the tour than any honest-to-god, written-in-stone, cold-blooded statistic could. Actually, it was more like sixteen-and-a-half months (in front of audiences that totalled around 4 million people) but really, all you need to know is that nobody remembers for sure. That and the fact that at the start of it, Bon Jovi were wide-eyed and bushy tailed and come its end they were sunken-eyed zombies. Even when the dust had settled, it took them a little while to think of the joke that has since become a rock'n'roll cliché: 'We were so tired that if you looked in the dictionary, under the word "burned" they had a picture of us . . .'

Ha-ha! It was all so much more fun when it started, though, setting out with the very best of intentions merely to revamp their image, as Richie predicted: 'This time when we tour we can't be trying to project an image that goes against our personality. There are too many bands either into the aggressive look or else the pretty-boy style. We wanna be ourselves, that's all.'

Checking into hotels on the *Slippery* . . . tour became something of a covert military-type operation, as well as a bit of a game. On the pretext of stopping his room number falling into the wrong hands – either ever-zealous female followers or maybe just other members of the entourage keen to run up a late night drinks bill on the singer's tab – Jon Bon Jovi checked into hotels under any number of pseudonyms. His favourite though, was 'Callaghan, H.' in honour of the Dirty Harry character of Clint Eastwood's perennial no-quarter cop series. How often it worked, and how often the less discreet among the world-weary profession of hotel receptionists merely passed it on anyway, is anyone's guess. Either way, it was a problem that would prove to be the least of the 24-year-old Jon Bon Jovi's worries.

He had already admitted to being bemused by the whole whirlwind of success the band were enjoying but could, privately at least, be pleased with what *Slippery* . . . represented in terms of a financially safe future. Musically it was clearly better than either of its predecessors, and although always claiming not to listen to the band's albums once they went on sale, in a private moment, once the hotel door behind him had shut, who would blame him if he allowed himself the not at all conceited pleasure of a smile while a tape played in his portable stereo.

Publicly, though, he was as gracious as ever, winning friends and influencing people by proclaiming: 'It's the kids who've broken this band, without a doubt. Radio is too fickle to bring you lasting success ... We really have come through the traditional way. We're not an overnight sensation, we're a hard working band with over 500 shows under our belts. We've never put on an elaborate show or gone out in make-up; it's always been a really honest thing and people have responded to that.'

It was a theme he would return to often and the band did have undeniably strong links with their audience. Meeting fans and signing autographs, as he would often say, was 'all part of the job' – as much as reaching out to touch their hands or establishing eye contact during the shows.

But Jon knew there was much more to it than that and would enter into the endless round of self-promotion with gusto. Radio stations worldwide were every bit as important. Their support in the States would fuel the album's rocket ride to the top of the *Billboard* chart.

Yet, ironically, the band began their *Slippery* ... tour cautiously, joining the latter stages of the US tour of radio-friendly Southern boogie merchants, .38 Special. Even as the support act, Bon Jovi's name on the posters had done exactly what the promoters had expected, boosted ticket sales at every venue the bill went to. Old pros, .38 Special were humble enough to be grateful rather than try to scupper the efforts of their openers as many a headliner might have done. 'They were real good to us . . . .38 Special were legitimately nice guys,' Jon later observed.

Despite an initial struggle to outsell Boston's comeback album *Third Stage* and then, ironically, Bruce Springsteen And The E Street Band's *Live 1975–1985* five-album box, Bon Jovi were the makers of a number one, million-selling album ... only this record wasn't going to stop anywhere near a million.

It wasn't until the autumn of 1986, however, that the band began their first ever headline tour – in Europe. That landmark was reached when around 1600 people cheered them onto the stage at the UK's sleepy Ipswich Gaumont on 9 November 1986. In support were British band FM, although Seattle's soon-to-be famous Queensrÿche took over at both shows in Hammersmith and at Bradford. When tickets went on sale in Britain, the tour sold out within hours and, as in territories all over the world, extra dates were swiftly added, making fourteen sell-outs in all. It was a statistic that gave an early indication of just what the album was going to do for the band's bank balance – if not their physical and mental health.

The first British dates came on the back of the 'You Give Love A Bad Name' hit, and Jon took the unprecedented demand for tickets as proof that the band had taken a giant leap forward – believing British audiences to be convinced purely by their music, rather than by their image. Or so he would maintain. But he did have his doubts, as English photographer Ray Palmer heard when Jon visited his studio at the time of those British dates.

'In keeping with the album's title, I photographed Jon with his shirt off in the shower and I always remember two things. One, he wanted to know if his make-up would run; and two, he asked me if I thought the album would do well. He seemed really nervous about that and not at all sure if it would . . .'

At that time, Bon Jovi's appeal was very much a combination of Jon's looks and the music, however much he might deny the former. His face appeared in magazines such as *Smash Hits* and *Just Seventeen* – aimed at young girls into pretty pictures and glamour – as well as those read by hard core rock fans. Any dreams Jon fostered of being recognized as a great songwriter rather than a sex symbol would have to be put on hold.

To his credit, though, he was trying to shake off some of

the limelight and its inherent pressure. Press interview duties were wherever possible shared by him and Richie – although 99 per cent of the time it was only his quotes that got used and, inevitably, his photograph that accompanied them or adorned the front cover . . .

Just prior to the British dates, on the tail-end of the .38 Special tour, Jon undertook a telephone interview with *Kerrang!* which underlined both his naiveté and current state of mind. Being on the road at that early stage of the tour was a thrilling experience and he clearly couldn't contain his enthusiasm: 'I love hotel rooms, man, so the fact this will be going on till April or May is great. I'm doing an instore [signing session] later today so I'll get three or four new albums and there's a note here by my bed saying: "We deliver pizza in thirty minutes!" I mean, hey, what could be better?'

The appeal of instores, free albums and readily available pizzas would, of course, pale once the tour reached and passed 'April or May' but such disappointments were a way off at that point.

On returning to the States the band were afforded the ultimate touring luxury: a private jet. It was something Jon had dreamed of – as the final proof he'd reached top dog status in the business – ever since he saw a photo of Led Zeppelin posing casually in 1973 in front of an aeroplane that bore their logo.

Jon was only ten at the time but the picture has been reprinted thousands of times since and when Jon finally saw it he identified with it immediately. Zeppelin broke the mould in so many ways and by having their own plane created a new benchmark that defined success. Jon remembered this and wanted it for himself. But as well as kudos, the plane (acquired from the then studio-bound Def Leppard) also brought freedom from commercial flight schedules. With it, Bon Jovi were free to leave the venue when they were ready and not when an airline dictated.

Moreover, it allowed them the opportunity to travel from city to city to play enough venues to maximize their earning potential. Planes are expensive and McGhee wouldn't have sanctioned one purely to fulfil Jon's childhood dream. Before they even considered painting their logo on the side of it, he had to be certain it would pay for itself. When a band only travels by road, its options regarding the next show are limited to how far a bus can roll overnight or from the hotel to the next venue in time for a late afternoon soundcheck. Within that distance there may not be a venue that is both available to play and large enough to warrant booking, given the size of the band's stageshow and support personnel. Since the eighties, private planes have ceased to be luxury status symbols and represent the only sensible logistical choice (Bon Jovi now have two). That they also allow a band to travel in greater comfort was not in doubt either, however uncomfortable Jon initially felt talking about it in interviews. He was anxious to rationalize the idea, aware that any perceived 'superstar' behaviour patterns could distance Bon Jovi from their mostly blue collar audience.

'If it wasn't for that jet I could never be out here. I couldn't be on a bus any more and singing two hours every night and running around and then getting on a bus to drive eight more hours. I've done it, I did it for a million miles, but I can't do it any more. So the plane is worth spending the money for, because you can go to bed if you want to or stay up if you want to. On a bus, if one guy's up, you all stay up, or else everybody's sitting on your bunk drinking.'

Sleep patterns notwithstanding, it was chiefly the lure of the dollar that prompted Bon Jovi – and so many other acts – to drive direct to sheltered corners of airfields and climb aboard planes that bore their own logos, not those of giant multi-national operators. Making money on tour is hard enough for a rock band, with profits almost always directly accounted for by merchandise sales, so a plane allows them to play at the largest practical venues with the minimum amount of time 'wasted' on non-earning days off.

Bon Jovi's manager Doc McGhee, dealing with agents and promoters all over the world, had this thought uppermost in his mind as he booked the shows. He was more than fortunate to have such energetic and dedicated charges, although ultimately their energy – if not their dedication – would begin to fall dangerously low.

At that point, countless bands had turned to drugs, whether for recreational purposes, to maintain excitement levels or simply exploit an opportunity put before them – or for the more practical, genuinely pharmaceutical purpose of boosting endurance. While Jon has hinted that others in the band may have indulged, at the time he himself always claimed to be uninterested. While admitting experiments as a teenager, in July 1987, while still on tour, he dismissed the idea of relying on anything other than his own stamina.

'Many a night people have looked at me and said, "Man, you're stoned", and I'm not . . .' Significantly, Jon later recalled that he was existing on cocktails of 'steroids and anything else' his doctor could give him just to keep him functioning. In 1987, however he would only admit to fear. 'Fear is the greatest thing to keep you going – nervous adrenaline.'

Fear of failure, of disappointing an audience, is what Jon would have been referring to. Such a possibility was, in reality, only weeks away. During the eighties, a number of rock singers – including Meat Loaf, Ian Gillan and David Coverdale – had all taken enforced lay-offs, after being diagnosed with nodes on their vocal chords. Throat specialists all blamed overwork and prescribed complete rest. The fear of 'nodes' became a shadow hanging over many singers who would otherwise have thought themselves merely run down. Already Jon had insisted that McGhee added no more tour dates due to his general exhaustion, afraid this would impair his ability to play to Bon

Jovi's usual standard. And yet always, somehow, he seemed to find the energy to carry on.

'I get up to the back of the stage minutes before we go on and I might still be moping. But the minute I hear that crowd I just get up there and go nuts. I'm Sugar Ray Leonard, Jagger, Bruce, Eddie Murphy . . . I'm fucking Superman.'

And he had the tattoo to prove it. More seriously, while he was always able to motivate himself, then McGhee could continue to book more dates. That 'Callaghan, H.' joke must have worn thin as the skyrocketing sales of *Slippery* . . . prompted the tour to be stretched way beyond anything the band had experienced with either of their first two albums. The tour became almost a licence to print money, with venues selling out as quickly as manager McGhee and the band's agents could book them.

But whatever their sudden out-of-the-box success meant in terms of kudos, Bon Jovi were still like kids let loose in a candy shop. Toothache, however, would be the last of their worries. 'I remember when we initially became huge it was such a shock that we didn't listen to each other,' says Jon.

In fact, they hardly listened to anyone except McGhee who kept on talking numbers and persuading them to make those numbers bigger. Jon himself, though, must shoulder much of the blame for the way the tour turned into a treadmill. McGhee may have told him to take the prize while it was there in front of him, but as the man in ultimate charge it was also his ultimate responsibility to say enough was enough.

Passing through Vancouver, they at least took a break from sports stadia to play a more intimate club. The change was as good as a rest. There, Bon Jovi's path crossed with Def Leppard's, then riding high on their *Hysteria* tour, and their lead singer Joe Elliott invited Jon out for a night on the town. Joe was a couple of years older than Jon and had almost burnt himself out with some severe alcohol abuse. At this point in the tour, however, he was teetotal and probably in the better shape of the two. Jon, who preferred a beer or two to help him relax, at first made his excuses. But Joe persisted, and Jon agreed on the understanding that Joe would break his vow of temperance for the evening. It was an oddly unreasonable request from Jon, given that had he insisted the same of, say Aerosmith's newly 'de-toxed' Steven Tyler, he might have sent the singer on a downward spiral to his grave . . .

Happily, Joe's problems were more in control – even if by the end of the night, he and Jon weren't. Their evening ended with the pair of them, plus Dan Reed (lead singer of Bon Jovi's opening act, the Dan Reed Network) and Darby Mills from Canadian band Headpins being escorted from a nightclub stage after a particularly woeful rendition of Led Zeppelin's 'Rock And Roll'.

The North American tour schedule stretched ahead of them like some never-ending carpet. When it rolled into Washington DC in July, the band once again invited *Kerrang!*'s Sylvie Simmons along to prepare a story for their issue that would coincide with Bon Jovi's headlining appearance at August's Monsters Of Rock Festival at Castle Donington. After watching the band woo the crowd of 18,000, Simmons went backstage to meet them – and was instantly shocked by what she saw. Jon sat crumpled in the corner of the dressing room showing fatigue far beyond the normal post-show exhaustion. His features drained and his voice a monotone whisper he explained his predicament.

'It's been a long tour. It's been over a year already. I'm tired, real tired, and if you ask me now, all I want to do is go home, watch some TV, sleep . . .' The writer recalls that Jon attempted a smile, and to summon some positive thoughts before he continued. 'But this is what I always wanted, isn't it? And we worked our asses off for it. Really, it's great fun.'

The fun he had on stage was obvious. At one point, an

hour or so earlier, he had leapt from the stage into the crowd –
all part of the show – surprise his only defence against physical
harm. That night's damage report amounted to one lost shirt,
a badly bruised shoulder and several finger nail scratches – all
accepted as part of the territory in order to give the best show
possible. Some would call it naive, others foolhardy, but Jon
would merely explain it away in the name of entertainment.

'I got my ass kicked out there tonight, I'm falling apart,
look at me . . . But it's fun, I like that, that's why I do it, and it
makes the kids happier. I always wished the guys did that when
I was at those shows, you know, touched you kind of, said hi,
gave you the microphone . . .'

Another part of the show on the *Slippery* . . . tour was the
'rope trick' during which he was suspended by a pair of
pantomime wires and swung out over the crowd like a long-
haired hybrid of Errol Flynn and Peter Pan. Stunts like that
guaranteed good reviews, good ticket sales and helped the
album become one of the staples of record collections all over
the world. At that point in the States alone the album had sold
8.3 million copies – a figure which Jon could quote as immediately as his own birthdate. Yet no matter how clued into that
statistic, Jon could always deflect any thoughts of him being a
man with one eye on the balance sheet by recalling, with sincere
enthusiasm, what it felt like to be in the position he was
enjoying.

'It's a great feeling, that emotion you feel from everybody.
That's why we still do it. It's emotional when the kids sing –
when they sing "Wanted . . .", that's what it's all about. When
they do that you don't care that you've been on the road for
fifteen months and your throat is a piece of hamburger and all
you want to do is go home – because it's worth it.'

Towards the end of the US leg of the tour, Bon Jovi were
on a commercial – never mind emotional – roll. They played
three nights at New York's massive Madison Square Garden.

They did three nights at Meadowlands. And three more at the Nassau Coliseum. All nine gigs within the New York City catchment area to a total audience reassuringly over the six figure mark.

At one of the Madison Square Garden shows, Jon met and was photographed with, Little Steven. When he was later shown the photo, his pale complexion, drawn cheeks below eyes sunk into big black circles made graphically apparent to him the full physical price the tour was extracting.

'I looked fuckin' dead. I can't believe how bad I looked. It was a picture I was going to hang in my house, an' I looked at it and thought, "Jesus Christ!" Man we had worked hard. 'I can't believe what it took out of me. I knew I was tired but I didn't realize how my body was really wrecked.'

McGhee could see this, too, but did little to stop it. Perhaps because his balance sheets showed that in America in 1987, for example, the band had played 130 dates and grossed over $28 million in ticket revenue. The income didn't stop there either, with the merchandise sales sometimes matching ticket grosses dollar-for-dollar and the tour's consequent knock-on effect on sales of *Slippery* . . . and other items in their back catalogue. For once, though, the band weren't expecting to make any profit from the Donington show, the costs of flying crew and equipment in from the States for a one-off show, no matter how large, making less than economic sense.

Unsurprisingly, the Bon Jovi that flew in by helicopter to the Castle Donington site in August 1987 – as headliners of the seventh (then) annual Monsters Of Rock festival – were a shadow of both the band that had started the *Slippery* . . . tour and the one that had bounded energetically onto the same stage two years earlier. As Jon shimmied down a rope at the start of the set, the spotlight that missed most of the stunt wasn't the only thing not operating at the peak of its capabilities. He'd grown a beard to hide the worst of the ravages that photo had shown him, but although few among the 66,000 crowd complained, he'd had enough of touring.

Nonetheless, the show remains a landmark in Bon Jovi's history, proving them to be a major force in world music and certainly the dominant one in the world that year – as was any band who headlined Donington. For encores, they were joined by Bruce Dickinson, then Iron Maiden's singer, and the Twisted Sister frontman Dee Snider. Together they rattled off covers of 'Grand Funk Railroad's 1973 anthem, 'We're An American Band', and Creedence Clearwater Revival's hit, 'Travelin' Band', a song which first saw the light of day in 1970 when Jon was only eight years old.

It could have been quite a party up there as Jon later revealed. Second-on-the-bill Ronnie James Dio had declined his invitation to jam and all Jon's attempts to contact Brian Robertson, the former Thin Lizzy guitarist – who he wanted to lead them through 'The Boys Are Back In Town' – were also to no avail. Third-on-the-bill Metallica were invited along, too, but declined because they were annoyed that Bon Jovi's helicopters had flown around the arena during their set.

'Metallica were in the middle of their set and we were in the helicopters going, "Holy fuck, what a cool day!" You're headlining your biggest show, you've got Gene [Simmons] and Paul [Stanley of Kiss] in these two helicopters that say Bon Jovi on the side of them – and you're basically whacking off in this plane! I certainly didn't know it was ruining Metallica's show . . .'

When the encores were over the whole band returned, dazed but delighted, to their Portacabin dressing room. The gig should have been a fitting climax to the tour, their 226th show of the tour. Except that the band had another two months' touring commitments to fulfil in Australia and Japan before they finally wrapped up in Hawaii on 17 October 1987 and almost literally collapsed with exhaustion. One by one they flew home, with Richie staying for nearly a month, unable to even face anything but total rest and relaxation.

But even in the Donington Portacabin, Jon knew that he for one had already reached the end of the road. 'I was ready to die. We shouldn't have been there. I was really too physically ill . . . I couldn't sing and we looked like death. That was a shame because I don't look back on that Donington fondly and I should do.'

It would take a few more years before Jon would admit what he had allowed to happen to the band and himself: 'I had a beard, sunglasses, my voice was completely shot, they're shooting me up with steroids, but no, you had to go to work. We trudge on, glad to be there, not realizing we were burned. You'd think that someone around us would have mentioned it . . .'

Or even done something about it.

'The powers that be should have said, 'Fuck it! Go home, sleep for six months.' [But] at that point the machine took over . . . the leeches latched onto us. Accountants were tellin' us to have a good time and managers and agents were having a pay day and making sure we were booked solid. We took advantage at the time, because you never know if it'll all be over tomorrow . . .'

Quotes gratefully taken from:

Malcolm Dome, *Kerrang!* 127, 21 August–3 September 1986; Malcolm Dome, *Kerrang!* 128, 4–17 September 1986; Carol Clerk, *Melody Maker*, 12 September 1986; Howard Johnson, *Kerrang!* 132, 30 October–12 November 1986; Sylvie Simmons, *Kerrang!* 153, 10 August–2 September 1987; Adrian Deevoy, *Q* 14, November 1987; Alison Joy, *Kerrang!* 204/205, 10–17 September 1988; Paul Suter, *Raw* 4, 12–25 October 1988; Mick Wall, *Kerrang!* 301, 4 August 1990; Adrian Deevoy, *Q* 52, January 1991; Paul Rees, *Raw* 107, 30 September–13 October 1992; Dave Reynolds, *Kerrang!* 412, 3 October 1992; Joe Mackett, *Riff Raff*, interview 16 October 1992; Johnny Walker, Radio 1, November 1992; Chris Welch,

## BON JOVI

*Rock World*, January 1993; Sylvie Simmons, *Kerrang!* 500, 25 June 1994; Steffan Chirazi, *Kerrang!* 513, 24 September 1994; Andrew Collins, *Q* 98, November 1994; Sylvie Simmons, *Mojo*, April 1995; *The Music Biz*, BBC2, 15 May 1995.

CHAPTER FOUR

# The Jersey Syndicate

*'I really wanted to do it again, not for monetary reasons –*
*I have plenty of money – but it was such an amazing feeling*
*to have done what we've done.'*
Jon Bon Jovi looks to follow-up *Slippery When Wet*, 1988

*'I stuck by him throughout the whole thing but it was nothing*
*to do with me.'*
Jon Bon Jovi washes his hands of Doc McGhee's drug smuggling
conviction, 1989

*'I became this money-making babysitter, worrying about everybody's*
*everything, both in and outside the band, what with management,*
*lawyers, agents blah-blah-blah . . .'*
Jon Bon Jovi sees the dream go sour, 1989

TOURING WITH *Slippery* . . . had meant watching album sales
figures go through the roof all over the world, reaching
something in the region of 13 million by the time the fourth
album, *New Jersey*, was ready for release. It was a monstrous
figure that no one would seriously expect Bon Jovi to emulate,
but – as much as the band might have tried to dismiss the
thought from their minds – one which many around them
might secretly wish for. As unreasonable as that pressure was,

89

worse was the idea that they were almost doomed to fail, in relative terms at least, with the follow-up record.

After demoing seventeen songs Jon was aware that not one of them was a hit. 'I panicked, to be honest. I really wanted to do it again, not for monetary reasons – I have plenty of money – but it was such an amazing feeling to have done what we've done. There was this real fear of not being able to write "You Give Love A Bad Name" again. We sat in the house and wrote this song called "Love Is War" and it sounded great but I wanted to write another ". . . Bad Name" so much that it came out with exactly the same chord progression. Richie was saying, "Don't worry about it, we'll get back in the groove . . ."'

Eventually, they did. But it took a while. *New Jersey* was recorded 1 May–31 July 1988 at Little Mountain Sound studios in Vancouver and produced, like its predecessor, by Bruce Fairbairn. The rigours of touring with *Slippery* . . . had at least seen the band grow closer together as a unit of friends. They had also become older and wiser and the songs on *New Jersey* reflected a certain increased maturity, as much by design as accident.

'The basis of the whole record was to bring people closer to what we are,' said Richie. 'Everything that's written on that record, all the emotions on it, are things that we feel. They're from life experience. We can't be fake, we can't be actors about it.'

But the over-riding emotion that permeated the creation of *New Jersey* was fear, as Jon later reflected: 'I was scared to death, man. I'm not gonna bullshit you. To be honest, I'd give all the money back for the opportunity to headline Donington again, or to play all the nights at Madison Square Garden that we did. I'd give all the money back just for the success again, 'cause there's no higher high in the world than to know you can play anywhere in the world and know you can sell out.

That's pretty amazing. You can't get that high doing drugs or drinking. It's a great feeling and that's all I want.'

And the fear of losing that feeling was playing havoc with his sleep patterns. 'The thing that was driving me crazy before we sat down to write new songs was thinking, "How do you follow something like that?" Michael Jackson didn't do it. Billy Idol didn't do it. Billy Joel didn't do it. Springsteen, Madonna, Prince . . . How the hell are we gonna do it if these guys didn't? I was driving myself crazy . . .'

An obvious way was to try and deliver more of the same and – however much Jon would later deny it – repeat the formula. *New Jersey* was recorded in the same studio with the same producer and the same engineer. And once again, they used song doctors: Holly Knight helped on 'Stick To Your Guns', Diane Warren on 'Wild Is The Wind' and Desmond Child gets a co-writing credit on four numbers – 'Wild Is The Wind' plus 'Bad Medicine', 'Born To Be My Baby' and 'Blood On Blood'.

Desmond Child's continued association with Bon Jovi brought repeated criticism from the music press. The suggestion was obvious: Bon Jovi weren't good enough and needed a crutch. The suggestion was probably missing the point. Bon Jovi *were* good enough but were looking for an edge, something to make them rise above the competition and were merely making use of something that made them stronger, just as Bob Dylan had done when he controversially employed Ailee Willis in the sixties. To Bon Jovi the choice was clear cut – Desmond Child could tip the balance between making the record a success and making it a major success. That was not an opportunity Jon dared forego.

Significantly, the first US number one hits either Jon, Richie or Child had enjoyed were the songs they had written together: 'Livin' On A Prayer' and 'You Give Love A Bad Name'. Now,

*New Jersey*'s 'Bad Medicine' was set to become the third. The album's 'Born To Be My Baby' might even have joined them, reckoned Child, but he thinks Bruce Fairbairn and the band spoilt it with the production.

'They imposed a "Livin' On A Prayer" production on a song that was just an acoustic guitar chugging anthem. But the song went to number three ... Maybe it would've gone to number one. I thought it was going to be the song of the year the way it sounded when I wrote it.'

But with or without a second number one, Jon was busting a gut to ensure Bon Jovi could live up to at least some of the precedents set by *Slippery* ...

After an early plan to release it under the name 'Sons Of Beaches' in a kind of *Sgt. Pepper's Lonely Hearts Club Band* collage-type affair, the band followed the pattern of *Slippery* ..., and the record came out in a very simple sleeve which suggested nothing of the contents to its purchaser, save perhaps that all-important sense of brotherhood hinted at by placing the logo and title in banners vaguely reminiscent of the Hell's Angels motorcycle club emblems (mirroring the design on the back of a number of Jon's coats and jackets).

In those days, when vinyl was still prevalent and forty minutes was a common running time for an album, the band amassed enough material to make the record a double album – but PolyGram said no. Jon admitted: 'They fought me tooth and nail from the minute I said it ... There wasn't much I could do about it.'

Making *New Jersey* a double would have saddled Poly-Gram with extra costs for materials, production, packaging, etc. – and sales would inevitably suffer, they argued. The relatively new CD format could contain any album up to seventy-five minutes in length but even in 1987, CD sales represented only around a third of the total in the US, much less abroad. Vinyl, especially in Europe, was still a major factor and the album was eventually trimmed to twelve tracks clocking in at a little over fifty-seven minutes, with the band having to ditch some of the lesser songs. Those, they claimed, were the ones which most closely resembled the material on *Slippery . . .*, with the final list chosen in a manner similar to that album's direct market research policy, as Jon recalled.

'It started with Bruce Fairbairn's babysitters and they were allowed to bring in as many friends as they could round up. Then there were a few kids hanging around the studio and a couple of kids from Japan who just happened to be walking by, and we dragged them in. Some loved us, some hated us, some didn't give a shit either way. We just played them the songs and let them pick . . .'

It's a quaint image but one which begs the question: were Bon Jovi merely trying to continue to give the people what they wanted or were they genuinely afraid of making the wrong choices? Whether doing so out of curiosity or indecision, Jon was afterwards man enough to act on the responses.

'They picked two songs that I was absolutely adamant about not putting on the record. One was "Stick To Your Guns" and the other one was "Wild Is The Wind". I, under no circumstances, wanted that on the record. The record company and everyone else told me about it but I said, "No! Tough shit!" Then I played it for the kids and they said, "This is what we like, this is what we hate . . ." and I did it because they are the ones that buy the records.'

Historically, the evidence against double-albums was on PolyGram's side. Elton John's 1973 release *Goodbye Yellow Brick Road* had topped the 5 million mark and Led Zeppelin's *Physical Graffiti* (1975) sold 4 million initially but even critically acclaimed doubles such as Bruce Springsteen's *The River* (1980) went only triple platinum and there had been no double album in the *Billboard* Top 10 since *Slippery . . .* was released.

The decision upset Jon, who at that stage in his career believed he had come far enough to receive a bit more respect and creative freedom. The reality was less glamorous. He might now have been a multi-platinum selling international superstar, but up against a multinational conglomerate he was still a David to their Goliath.

Checking the album's credits, however, it seems surprising that the argument ever arose. A&R men commonly whittle down a band's wish list of songs and now, in addition to the input of Bon Jovi's original A&R person Derek Shulman, there was also thanks given to John David Kalodner. The man's name had already graced the sleeves of some of the decade's most successful albums, notably those released in 1987 by Aerosmith and Whitesnake whose rebirth he had been a driving force behind. Jon knew this and hoped some of the man's magic might rub off on *New Jersey* also.

Kalodner possessed an uncanny knack of hearing a song at its demo stage and instinctively knowing how to work it into a hit – he was also blunt enough to tell a band which songs to drop. His input might mean that one song would be developed at extreme length, but such attention to detail was almost a guarantee of platinum-selling status. On *New Jersey*, however, his influence would appear to have been restricted because at the time he was supposed to be working only for acts signed to Geffen Records. Having established the link, however, Jon would employ him more than once in the years to come.

Constraints on the record's length, however, were trivial compared to its recording schedule – the blame for which must be laid partly at McGhee's door. Inspired by the huge sales of *Slippery . . .* and the unprecedented success of the tour, the lure of the dollar proved too strong for the band's manager and he leant on Jon and the band to complete the album as soon as possible. Figuring three months had been long enough to make its predecessor, the band were allotted a similar period to record *New Jersey*. Doc McGhee and the band's agents plotted the concert tour long before the album was mixed and when they started the sessions, Bon Jovi did so knowing full well that it would need to be finished in time to start touring in August.

At this point it is hard to imagine why Jon, ever keen to establish Bon Jovi as a credible musical force, was unprepared to tell his manager to hold off until the band were content that the album was as good as they could make it. Suggestions have been put forward that after *Slippery* . . . Jon was made all too aware that he had become the head of a massive organization which only he could support – with his songwriting, promotional activities and performances. Such a notion may have appealed to his inbuilt and ever-burgeoning sense of family and brotherhood but with it came a responsibility that no twenty-six year old should be asked to carry.

Just five years earlier that responsibility meant little more than paying the wages of his band, management staff and tour support – still relatively small concerns. But since *Slippery* . . . had catapulted Bon Jovi into the big league, everything had expanded and Jon's every move sent ripples through an organization much larger than was ever expected. In allowing himself to become so concerned about the financial welfare of so many others, he compromised the well-being of himself and many of the very people he sought to protect. McGhee promised him it would be different this time out, told him that it would be easier because they had all learned lessons, but the main lesson learned seemed always to be how to make money.

The worryingly fresh memories of touring with *Slippery* . . . reminded the band that they had a duty of care to themselves to make the album one that would stand up to the demands of extended and repeated live performances. As Richie observed: 'If you're gonna be on the road for sixteen months and stand up there and sing those songs very day, it'd best not be bullshit.'

Four years on Richie would admit: 'I thought that *New*

*Jersey* was similar to *Slippery When Wet* in a lot of ways because we didn't have the time or the life experience to make a different record.' Perhaps all they really had was the bond of the band forged by the touring. 'We got to be a better band, and we got to be closer as people. No matter how close five guys could be, we got closer.'

It was just as well because in that August, as the band rehearsed for the tour, Bob Rock was mixing the album in their absence. In limiting the recording time for *New Jersey* Bon Jovi seemed to be ignoring a vital lesson almost immediately. None of this was admitted at the time, of course, as publicly Bon Jovi looked to accentuate the positives.

The title, Jon explained, was chosen as a simple acknowledgement of the attitude, or collective state of mind, of his home state. Though he had spent so little time there in the last couple of years that the title was perhaps born more out of homesickness than memory. It was, he claimed, a personal statement for the whole of the band, reflecting their own similar work ethic and brotherhood. The track 'Blood On Blood' spelled it out a little further . . .

'The characters Bobby and Danny are two guys I know who used to live in Jersey. We used to hang out . . . When we were about thirteen, we swore we would be friends for ever. And although I haven't seen these guys for years and years, I still remember when I was thirteen and so I started writing. I hope it's one of the best we've done,' Jon said at the time.

Some of the band's critics saw it differently, forcing Jon to defend himself: 'I've read it a hundred times over the years. I pick up a magazine and someone is saying we write clichéd adolescent lyrics about friendship. And I think, shit, friendship's always been pretty important to me, maybe even more important in a kid's life.'

But not many critics buy albums and what they were missing, reckoned Jon, was that for every sixteen or seventeen-year old who was interested in world politics and could be bothered to study the words on a U2 lyric sheet, there were five or six whose biggest worry was not which party would win the next election, but the events closer to home like getting a car, getting a job or simply getting laid. 'That's what I write about in songs because that's what I've experienced. I've never run for president.'

Or, to put it another way, he cared about the bigger picture but didn't want to get involved. Like he told Paul Elliott: 'I don't want to think about the bad shit that's happening [but] I'd be the first guy to donate money to a cause . . . but I'm not gonna reflect that in my songwriting right now. I feel too good about life.'

Perhaps he was too busy plotting the tour. As suggested earlier, Jon and McGhee were under no illusions about the possibility of *New Jersey* repeating *Slippery . . .*'s sales, but they were aware that they might be able to match its tour revenue. *New Jersey*, they figured, was at least as good so people would come to hear it played live, and all those who had bought *Slippery . . .* might well come again. But this time, they should be able to earn much the same by doing fewer shows – as long as they were in bigger arenas.

The logic appealed to Jon, as long as bigger venues did not mean that the band lost contact with their audience. And so giant aluminium runways were designed that would extend over the heads of the crowd to reach further back than the Peter Pan flying apparatus used on the last trek. The sense of intimacy would be further increased by ever more lights aimed at the crowd – plus Jon would still run into the audience when security permitted it. Each night the show would begin with the intro to 'Lay Your Hands On Me' and an almost empty, sloping metal stage with only the drum kit and keyboards on view. Then, as the intro reached a crescendo, Jon, Richie and Alec would all appear simultaneously with a loud bang in a cloud of pyro smoke, catapulted hydraulically to stage level through trapdoors. A very neat trick by any standards . . .

When it came to shooting a video clip for 'Bad Medicine', Bon Jovi once again invited the input of their audience – lining up 150 cameras for use by members of the audience at their first show of the year to be intercut with professional performance footage. This kind of audience involvement had always been central to the band's live shows and Jon refused to do away with it, however big those audiences got.

The choice of *New Jersey* as the album's title also suggested the band's growing self-confidence and Jon's desire to broaden their appeal. When the band first did press in 1984, Jon was reluctant to reveal his New Jersey origins because he was afraid of the Bruce Springsteen comparisons. In 1988, he would take them as a compliment, but two albums earlier and an aspiring heavy metal band would have been laughed out of court if they'd attempted to defend their love of Springsteen. The genre and its devotees just weren't broad-minded enough. So Jon spent much of the time trying to hide the very roots which made the band so special.

'If I mentioned some of the Jersey influences like Bruce, Little Steven or the Asbury Jukes, would that invite too many direct comparisons? For a while it was a whole fucked thing. Like, who are we? Are we doing the right thing?'

Come the recording of *New Jersey*, though, the band had toured enough and grown enough – and their audience had apparently broadened enough – for Jon to be less afraid to wear his musical heart a little closer to his sleeve, and he went to interviews prepared to field the questions about Bruce.

Ironically, he quickly got tired of it, as people rounded on him for (as most of them saw it) trying to rip-off Bruce's style. Bruce, Jon would repeatedly explain, had got it from Bob

Dylan. Dylan had got it from Arlo Guthrie. Elsewhere Little Steven had got it from Keith Richards who owed much to Chuck Berry. In the end, the comparisons exhausted his patience.

'The biggest mistake I ever made in my career was calling an album *New Jersey*,' he sighed to *Q* magazine in 1991. 'Suddenly everyone's comparing me to [Bruce Springsteen]. Making out that we're drinking buddies or something. We're not! I get fucking sick of this Bruce thing. I've only ever met Bruce about twice in my whole life . . .'

Occasionally, Jon could joke about wanting to be Bruce Springsteen. He wanted much more than that, of course, but it was a much better ambition than wanting to be Poison – and there were plenty of takers for that particular crown. Not Jon though. In 1988 it was, as he put it, time to 'strip away all the bullshit and just be ourselves'.

Inwardly, however, he was in conflict. Promoting the album by talking about it only reminded him that soon he would have to promote it by touring. He spoke about how, musically, the band were going back to the place they knew best, the place they called home – but that place wasn't New Jersey anymore, it was 'the road'. Image-wise they were still a long way from looking like men who could walk down the Jersey shoreline and not get arrested or beaten up. True, although the hair was still long, it wasn't quite so teased, but while off stage Jon was close to the truth when he claimed he had 'gotten back to a pair of jeans and a T-shirt again', on stage it was a very different story. Long patchwork coats, tasselled and epauletted jackets, flash shirts, sunglasses and extravagantly tight coloured trousers being very much the order of the day – predictably almost exactly the same as they had looked when the *Slippery . . .* tour ended just months earlier. And there was the rub. The band hadn't had time to draw breath, never mind rest up.

*Kerrang!*'s Alison Joy recalled interviewing Jon in

McGhee's office in New York. 'Jon looked tired and jaded even before the tour had started. He kept tracing patterns on the table-top with his fingernail and avoiding eye-contact. He would even talk about himself in the third person.'

Later he would admit just how much the thought of the forthcoming tour bothered him, but at the time he was keeping his reservations to himself, withdrawing . . . The best clue, he said in 1992, was the shot on the inner sleeve of *New Jersey*. 'The last thing I wanted to do was be me. I have my back to the camera, a long coat down to my ankles hiding as much of my body as I can. My hair's as long as it can possibly be . . .'

Hindsight, as they say, is always 20:20.

Back in September 1988, when *New Jersey* was released, sales were immediately impressive. Although it would never match its predecessor, the record sold well and quickly, shifting an impressive 3 million copies in its first three months. In the States it would go on to double that figure, outselling by two to one that year's releases by U2 (*Rattle And Hum*), Metallica (*. . . And Justice For All*) and Guns N' Roses (the *Lies* mini album). In 1988's rock field, only Poison's *Open Up And Say . . . Ahh* – 5 million US sales thanks largely to its 'Every Rose Has Its Thorn' hit single – came close.

*Q* magazine, not known for its support of hirsute rock bands, made quite a splash of *New Jersey* in its reviews section (accompanied, deliberately, by a dumb shot of Jon posing for the camera wearing only a pair of shorts). Awarding it an impressive four stars, it proclaimed the record a calculatedly commercial but 'crassly enjoyable collection of bubblegum buddy-buddy anthems'.

*Kerrang!* were slightly less impressed, rating it behind *Slippery* . . . and accusing the band of 'sticking to formula'. At least the magazine allowed that 'Bon Jovi's best is probably yet to come'.

With the 'Bad Medicine' single at number one in the *Billboard* chart, the album still at number five and a string of arena dates already sold out, the temptation to add more was impossible to resist. The band began to kick around ideas for a big package tour that could fit in some outdoor stadium tours in the summer of 1989. Initial suggestions were for the bill to be made up of three McGhee stable mates: Bon Jovi, Mötley Crüe and Skid Row. Ironic, considering that all through the making of *New Jersey*, with memories of the post-*Slippery* . . . fatigue still in his mind, Jon was telling 'everyone and anyone' that he had no intention of touring again. The day after the album was finished, however, he recognized that the tour was inevitable, although claiming that financially he didn't have to do anything he didn't want to. 'We've made a couple of bucks,' reckoned Jon with deliberate understatement, maintaining that any doubts he still harboured were those brought about by the uncomfortable memories of a voice, his own, that wasn't able to do what he asked of it at the end of the last tour. That possibility bothered him as much as anything.

'I wanna be great. What I don't wanna do is go out there and be shitty, I don't wanna cheat anybody. That's what bothers me, that's what bums me out – when I can't hit the high notes. It's not the problem of being away from home – I've got a great job, I'm able to see the world and that's a wonderful thing – but if I can't sing I'm fucked and I hate it.

'Every night before the lights went out there was the huge roar from the kids and I waited for my chance to go on stage and honestly, I said to myself a hundred times, "I'll take a day off my life if I can sing good today".'

But equally as important as Jon's own personal performance targets was the idea that once you had played, say, three nights at Madison Square Garden, you didn't go back next tour and play only two. Jon could respond to that kind of pressure by turning it into ambition – and so inspire himself and the band to go out again to convince everyone, not least themselves, that they were still getting better. It was to become a challenge that would push them, once again, far beyond the point of exhaustion.

Sixteen months was the early estimate of how long the tour would last. But with the advance sales for the opening dates in Europe selling so well, the plan for sixteen months was being extended even before the first show had been played . . .

When it came to the first night in Dublin in December 1988, all Jon's earlier reluctance about touring went out of the window on a tidal wave of adrenaline. Speaking to a crew from MTV Europe shortly after arriving at the RDS arena, he completely forgot on-air protocol and offered American viewers the message, 'Get ready motherfuckers! I'm back!!!' He was, too, but he had to find a more polite way of expressing the message for broadcast.

His hand-picked opening act, the former Runaways starlet Lita Ford, was on stage as he arrived in the building and he recalled: 'I was just so nuts I wanted to run up there with her and grab the microphone . . . I was on fucking fire.'

Jon's friend Joe Elliott, the Def Leppard singer and then a Dublin-based tax exile, was backstage to wish the band well, but was careful not to say anything to put Jon under any more stress than he was already feeling. It was crazy, really, a result of pure nerves and adrenaline because Jon was in better shape than he had been for any previous tour, having been preparing for weeks physically and mentally – jogging, taking guitar, harmonica and even singing lessons. 'I was thinking, "You do this for a living, you can't get sloppy about it",' he said at the time.

The band had even undertaken a short, back to-the-roots tour to prepare, where they all piled into a van and played clubs on the US East Coast, largely unannounced, as Jon told Adrian Deevoy. 'We met up with The Stray Cats and said, "We'll open for you!" and they said, "No, no, no, we'll open for you!" In the end, we played together until four in the morning. Then the cops turned up ... and started drinking with us. Tico took one of them out till dawn and the cop gave him his leather motorcycle jacket ... [The tour] was a neat exercise but at the end of it the band were saying, "We've had enough being humble, let's get back to reality again!"'

After Dublin, and with the 'Bad Medicine' single selling rapidly, Bon Jovi moved on to mainland UK for dates at just three cities. But that geographical sparsity belied a more impressive statistic, that on the *New Jersey* tour Bon Jovi were moving up a league as planned. On tour posters bearing the Harp Beat 88 banner of their lager-brewing sponsor, were three of the country's biggest indoor venues: the SE&CC in Glasgow (9,000 seats), the NEC Arena in Birmingham (up to 12,300) and London's Wembley Arena (around 9,500). Nine dates in venues of this size meant that Bon Jovi could play to around 90,000 people in under two weeks. Ticket prices at the time were £11.50 and £12.50 which meant that the promoters could expect gross takings of around £1 million. Even if the shows didn't completely sell out, takings of £100,000 per night were not beyond the realms of reasonable expectation – and this figure could be doubled when additional income from T-shirts and other tour merchandise was added.

The booking of second shows in Glasgow and Birmingham due to public demand, and a total of four at Wembley Arena, put Bon Jovi most definitely among rock's élite in the UK and paralleled their standing over much of the world. Iron Maiden had also added a second NEC date on their tour, and one at Wembley, too, but the latter brought their total there to just a pair. Former Van Halen frontman David Lee Roth, then at the pinnacle of his solo career, was playing only three one night stands in these kind of venues – and then, like Maiden, charging a maximum of £10 for a ticket.

In at least one new territory, however, the band over-stretched themselves. In keeping with McGhee's global approach, this time he would dispatch the band into New Zealand, as well as all the territories where Bon Jovi had visited before. In New Zealand, in particular, this policy backfired and at the Western Springs stadium in Auckland, Bon Jovi drew 'one of the smallest crowds in years'. The reason, according to the local press, was obvious – they had set ticket prices way too high. McGhee would have argued that the fee was merely to cover the costs of shipping their production to the island, but Bon Jovi paid the price by playing to only a quarter-full house.

In Europe, however, the shows were generally very well received. *The Times* called Bon Jovi 'The Beatles of the eighties', although the *Sun* took a different tack, lambasting them as 'cleanshaven tripe'. At one of the Wembley shows, Bon Jovi were joined on stage during their encore by Elton John, Brian May of Queen and Def Leppard drummer Rick Allen.

After the show, as Jon made his way to the shower, May stepped forward to whisper some words of advice. 'You're doing the same thing we did,' said the curly-haired guitarist. 'All I thought about was the next album, the next stadium – bigger, bigger, bigger. You've got to learn to enjoy where you are.'

It was sound advice from a man who was a member of a band who had sold around 100 million records worldwide (around three times Bon Jovi's total at the time). The well-intentioned words struck a chord with Jon who, even through his fierce ambition, could see much truth in them. And with just one glance at May's incredibly mellow and relaxed disposition, he could also see the benefits of following his advice. Brian May had been to the top of the mountain and was still there looking down.

But Jon was excitable and still fired-up after his show. It was in his nature to live for tomorrow and it would be a few more years before he would really learn to take things at a steadier pace. So at the time he took the advice politely – and failed to act upon it. But the memory of May's advice would remain with Jon and years later he would recall that it had come to make more and more sense to him, and would change the way he viewed his professional life.

But back in 1989, his mind was still on an almost schoolboy-like overdrive. It was displaying an almost schoolboy-like attitude to the band's opening act, Lita Ford, too. Regularly invited up on stage to play along with Bon Jovi's encores, Jon wasn't averse to watching her from the side of the stage, too.

'I enjoyed watching her play every night. If she told me to jump off a bridge I'd have done it for her . . .' Jon remarked of the girl known as much for her skin tight leather pants and her black bra tops as her actual music. Fortunately for him, by this time Dorothea had clearly come to recognize the difference between his fantasies and his indiscretions. When Ford played her own headline show at London's tiny Marquee Club, Jon, Richie and Dave Bryan went along to show their support, wedging themselves into the surprised balcony crowd before Jon moved downstairs again to join her on stage for a run through the Bon Jovi encore standard, Grand Funk's 'We're An American Band'.

After the UK, Bon Jovi moved on to dates in Europe and, in March, to the States with Jon and Richie's protégés Skid Row as the opening act. Business there was good, too. Reviewing a show at the Omni Theater in Atlanta, Georgia, Elianne

Halbersberg was astute enough to notice that, despite the much larger venues the band was now playing, Jon was still going 'out of his way to clasp as many grappling, sweaty palms as possible'. It was his way of maintaining the intimacy the band had always prided themselves on. It's no mean feat, and something many bands fail to retain as they move up a peg or two.

Perceptively, Halbersberg also observed how it had become fashionable among heavy metal fans to dislike the band, criticizing them for their 'commercial radio pop' whilst all around her was a broader than ever cross section of fans. 'Look around the sold-out house: that's your little sister down front, and your mum in the upper seat level. And they're both enjoying the hell out of the show.' If this tour was proving anything, it was that with the more mature Springsteen-influenced songwriting on *New Jersey*, Bon Jovi had broadened their fanbase way beyond their original heavy metal and hard rock roots.

Away from the stage, in between shows, the band were trying to improve themselves too. Whilst in Minnesota they had gone out to Prince's Paisley Park headquarters. He and Jon had met one night at Tramps in New York and had got drunk together over a bottle of wine – and so when Bon Jovi played Minnesota, he came to the show then invited them back to Paisley Park. Originally, Prince had agreed to get up and play with Bon Jovi but at the eleventh hour changed his mind. 'We had rehearsed a version of "All Along The Watchtower" at the soundcheck,' said Jon, 'but he backed out. We were ready to do it but between the encores he said he didn't want to . . .'

Later at Paisley Park, however, Prince was happy to play all night and an after-hours jam session ensued between himself, and members of Bon Jovi and the all-black American rock band Living Colour. Spreading their musical wings like that was a gradual process but indicative of Jon's desire to move forward. He was aware he would need to adapt in order to survive and was keen to explore all possible avenues. Before the tour had begun, he and Richie had relocated briefly to Los Angeles, ostensibly for press duties but also to make themselves available as songwriting partners to all comers. Cher was one of the first takers, with Alice Cooper and Fire (an LA outfit who subsequently failed to get a deal), not far behind. Billy Squier, Jennifer Rush, Loverboy and Ted Nugent were all keen to make use of their talents also. After their recent 'adoption' of Skid Row, this could be seen as another step forward for Jon and Richie.

Yet although everything was going so well, looming over the whole *New Jersey* tour was the spectre of manager Doc McGhee's murky past. In 1982, apparently before he had signed Bon Jovi to McGhee Entertainment, the manager had been arrested by officers from the US Drug Enforcement Agency for his part in a drug smuggling operation. The arrest was kept out of the public eye until April 1988 when the case came to court in North Carolina.

The trial revealed that he had been arrested after the seizure of a shipment of 40,000 pounds (over eighteen tonnes) of marijuana confiscated by US Customs en route from Columbia to North Carolina. Perhaps fearful of the term of imprisonment that helping to fund a multi-million dollar operation to smuggle marijuana into the US could bring, McGhee entered a plea of guilty and threw himself on the mercy of the court.

The court did indeed show mercy. McGhee avoided a custodial sentence and was instead ordered to pay a $15,000 fine and serve a seven-year suspended sentence. In addition, McGhee was bound to undertake 3,000 hours of community service and spend 150 days in a rehabilitation centre.

Initial reports suggested that the lion's share of his

community service would comprise the setting up of an anti-drugs, alcohol and substance abuse centre in North Carolina (at an estimated cost of $250,000). This plan received no further publicity, however, and was subsequently over-shadowed by his Make A Difference Foundation, under whose banner he offered to raise funds to assist those suffering from drug and alcohol abuse.

McGhee's admission of guilt reflected very badly on Bon Jovi, even though they were in no way implicated in his crime, having had no connection with him at the time. Nevertheless, the band, and in particular Jon, became involved in the attendant publicity and also worked hard for McGhee's Make A Difference Foundation. The foundation's major fund-raising event was announced a year after the verdict, in May 1989 – an ambitious plan for the first ever Western-style rock festival in the fast-disintegrating Soviet Union. Publicists latched onto the idea that the festival coincided with the twentieth anniversary of the original Woodstock Festival but the Moscow Music Peace Festival, as it was christened, was certainly no hippie love-in.

It was, first and foremost, to be a charity event with all proceeds over and above 'production costs' earmarked for the foundation. A proportion of these funds were to be spent on various rehabilitation centres and programmes in the Soviet Union, with others presumably going to similar coffers in the States. With McGhee and Jon instrumental in assembling the bill, it unsurprisingly leant very heavily on the McGhee Entertainment roster: booked to play were Bon Jovi, Mötley Crüe and The Scorpions (who signed to the stable around this time), with further support coming from Skid Row and Jon's buddies Cinderella. The one major artist not linked to McGhee was Ozzy Osbourne – at the time perhaps the biggest Western star behind the Iron Curtain. The rest of the festival's line-up was completed by a token handful of Russian bands: Nuance,

Brigada S and Gorky Park. McGhee subsequently came to represent the latter act, also, reinforcing the impression that over and above his charitable intentions, McGhee was not averse to making a few business inroads at the same time. Most obvious among these was his coup in securing a release for Bon Jovi's *New Jersey* on the state-owned Melodiya label, joining a roster that hitherto featured only back-catalogue collections from the approved likes of The Beatles, Paul McCartney and Elton John. *New Jersey* would be the first contemporary Western rock album to be granted such a privilege. The Soviet economy at the time was a very weak one and it is unlikely that McGhee or the band earned any significant profits from such a release but, in a country where Western vinyl was a very rare but much taped and bootlegged commodity, McGhee's negotiations meant that should the Soviet Union open up further to Western music, his biggest act was already represented in a potentially huge market.

Away from the realms of the possible, and into the land of the improbable, was the Moscow Music Peace Festival itself. The show was to take place over two days, 12–13 August, at the Lenin Stadium, the same bill being repeated at each show. The venue was the same one used for the 1980 Olympic Games, a massive arena capable of holding 140,000 – way in excess of any other rock venue in either North America or Europe.

Announced at the same time as the Moscow show was the plan to release an album recorded by the main acts appearing at the festival, each covering a song made famous by an artist whose career had been ended by death following drug or alcohol abuse. When it was released in December 1989, bands represented by McGhee Entertainment Inc. once again featured strongly. In fact, the main acts from the Moscow show each spent a day or two in various studios recording their chosen cover version. The tracks had all been completed before the festival, and added to these was the live recording of the 'jam' which closed the show. Bon Jovi elected to donate their cover of Thin Lizzy's 'The Boys Are Back In Town' (recorded back in July 1988), a song they frequently performed live on the *Slippery* . . . tour, as a tribute to Phil Lynott who had died on 4 January 1986. It was an affectionate if strangely lacklustre salute.

But although the foundation seemed to be a fine and worthy cause, the Moscow festival and the *Stairway To Heaven: Highway To Hell* album have proved to be its only public activities and the foundation has long since disappeared from the limelight. Less than five years later, Jon himself was quite unaware of what it had done since the album.

'I certainly supported it and [Doc] to the hilt. I thought going to Russia was a great thing. I was also making speeches in high schools in North Carolina, so I felt like being part of the Make A Difference Foundation was a real positive cause that related to our audience . . .'

Like a Get Out Of Jail card in a game of Monopoly, the Make A Difference Foundation appeared to offer a short term solution to an immediate personal problem and has certainly never achieved anything like the status of, for example, the Nordoff-Robbins Music Therapy charity which Bon Jovi have also supported. Jon has maintained this tight-lipped silence on the matter whenever it has been raised, deflecting interviewers' interest with remarks like: 'You'll have to ask [Doc] about that. I stuck by him throughout the whole thing but it was nothing to do with me. Talk to him.'

Yet McGhee has chosen not to comment about it either.

When it kicked off in December 1988, the *New Jersey* tour represented business-as-usual with McGhee's guilty plea apparently casting no shadow over proceedings. Indeed, the band appeared to find the idea of their manager as a quasi-underworld character – highly amusing – as evinced by some apparently tongue-in-cheek tour paraphernalia. Draped over the PA at the largest shows were sepia-tinged paintings of gangsters (similar artwork to that used by Alice Cooper for the cover of his 1974 *Greatest Hits* collection) portraying lots of cigar-chewing mobster types. With New Jersey band Skid Row in support, the trek was dubbed 'The Jersey Syndicate' tour, with fans at the US leg choosing from merchandise labelled as the 'Saints And Sinners' dates. This gallows humour even extended to the adhesive passes given out to guests and working personnel featuring the caricatured image of McGhee, black shirt, white tie and tommy-gun in hand – printed overleaf, on the tear-off backing paper, was the legend 'Say No To Drugs'.

In early July 1989, a month ahead of the Moscow show and in the wake of (unfounded) rumours of a similar UK event at Wembley Stadium, Bon Jovi announced an open air headline show at the Milton Keynes Bowl. Inspired by the impressive ticket sales of their UK tour six months earlier, they were convinced that selling out the venue's 55,000 capacity would be well within their capabilities. It was a great piece of opportunism for two reasons: one, the band would already be in Europe for the Moscow Music Peace Festival; and two, there was to be no 1989 Monsters Of Rock show at Castle Donington. This was because of licensing difficulties following the deaths of two fans at the 1988 event. UK rock fans, by then used to Donington being an annual event, could take solace in a similar show at a site relatively new to them. Although only three bands were subsequently added to the bill below Bon Jovi – Skid Row, Vixen and special guests Europe – the Milton Keynes bill nonetheless looked a reasonably attractive option.

The hunch shared by Bon Jovi and their joint promoters, ITB and MCP (the latter normally behind Donington) proved correct. Within a day the band had sold 12,000 tickets and six weeks after the first announcement, the Bowl was sold-out. This was good news for Bon Jovi who, although comfortably selling out arena shows, had struggled rather at a few of the bigger outdoor arenas they had slotted in during the summer.

In the States that summer, a touring Monsters Of Rock bill had consistently failed to live up to ticket sales expectations, confirming the industry's worst fears of a recession. Jon would later claim to have sold twice as many tickets for his outdoor shows as the Monsters bill (featuring Van Halen, The Scorpions and Kingdom Come) but still lamented the fact that they could, for example, only pull 26,000 to the 40,000-capacity Akron Rubber Bowl (exchanging Skid Row for support from Cinderella, Winger and The BulletBoys) the week before they flew to Moscow.

Whilst in Akron, *Kerrang!* journalist Alison Joy was disturbed to see bassist Alec John Such and manager McGhee clowning around in the dressing room with handguns: *real* hand guns. Jon seemed barely phased but played along by taking the precaution of ducking as his interviewer froze in fear. If nothing else, this extraordinary, if harmless, incident served as an indication of the fantasy world in which McGhee and the band were living. Being protected by professional security men was one thing, carrying your own firearms was another. Jon admitted, seven years later and somewhat uncomfortably, to having a gun of his own but explained that it was a gift and that he would 'probably shoot himself in the foot' if he ever opted to use it. The weapon would appear to be more of a rich man's toy than an item retained out of fear or paranoia.

Across the Atlantic for the next leg of the tour, the ticket sales outlook was altogether rosier. The first of the pair of shows in the then unknown territory of Russia had sold all its 140,000 tickets and the second night was into six figures also.

In the event, Bon Jovi became major players in what turned

into a multi-media circus. The idea of such a gig in Moscow was sufficiently novel to attract full live TV coverage on MTV and gain the attention of the more serious elements of the media. The Soviet authorities, at the time learning day-by-day the virtues of President Gorbachev's new Glasnost policy, were clearly keen to make the most of the publicity. Seizing on the drug and alcohol rehabilitation ideals of the Make A Difference Foundation, the USSR took the unprecedented step of owning up to their own problems, especially among their youth, as Jon explained.

'The Russians have a problem with alcohol and [the Make A Difference Foundation] was a way the Russians could sanction the show, actually let it happen. Even though Billy Joel went in there, Elton John and a few other bands, no one's ever done it on this scale, so the government have to have a reason to endorse it.'

But turning an endorsement into a real show was not without its problems. It had taken McGhee five visits and countless telephone calls and faxes to find a way through the bureaucracy as well as take care of the usual hassles. Not least among the problems was the fact that nowhere in the Soviet Union was there the kind of equipment needed to stage such a show to Western standards.

'In a nutshell,' explained Jon, 'we're taking the whole thing over there. A Live Aid type [revolving] stage for ten bands – all the gear, everything.' 'The Russians have never done this before so they said, "It'll be nice, we'll have a great time", and we go, "Okay, we'll do it every year". Then they say, "You're gonna leave all your gear here, we can keep it?" They think it's a gift, you know. So it's like, "No, no, no! Let's sit down and talk". We've got people trying to work this stuff out daily, it's getting crazy . . .'

But there was, supposedly, a far more serious issue to be addressed, namely: just how appropriate was it for a bunch of decadent rock'n'rollers to be acting as cultural ambassadors, above all in the name of an anti-drug, alcohol and substance abuse charity? Looking at the bill, it was easy to be sceptical. Skid Row and Mötley Crüe in particular were notorious party animals, living life to the full and then some, frequently making thinly veiled and even blatant references to drug usage (Crüe's then singer Vince Neil published songs under the banner of Krell Music, krell being LA slang for cocaine). The Scorpions were known to enjoy the odd lager, and whilst Cinderella and Bon Jovi might have kept their after hours drinking a little more discreet, the loveable Ozzy Osbourne was the grand daddy of all addicts. A former cocaine freak who had written a song called 'Snowblind' while thanking for inspiration 'the great COKE-Cola Company of Los Angeles', he was now a man fighting very desperately, very publicly and occasionally very unsuccessfully to overcome his alcoholism. But despite his manager's criminal record and the evidence all around him, Jon felt his conscience was clear.

'I think all that's a thing of the past to tell you the truth, it's made to look much less glamorous. There's none of this, "Wow man, I'm in a state". Now you see Stevie Tyler [Aerosmith's detoxed heroin and alcohol addict singer] running five miles a day and telling you, "I don't remember 1977 and I don't ever want that to happen again". That would scare me, so I never did drugs since I was a little kid.'

Nevertheless, many remained sceptical and said so.

'People are always ready to question why a bunch of rock stars would want to get together and do something like this. Sure, you get a clash of egos occasionally . . . But at the end of the day I look at it like this, I wouldn't have known about Nelson Mandela's situation like I do now had I not been drawn to it because of the artists [supporting] Amnesty International. Or I don't think I would have ever known about Ethiopia the way I do now if it wasn't for Bob Geldof . . .'

Reinforcing his conviction, he recorded a short 'ident' for Sky TV to underline the message. It came across with a good deal more credibility than those by some of the other bands on the bill.

Despite the intention of celebrating the Woodstock anniversary, any thoughts of peace, love and goodwill evaporated not long after the bands touched down in Moscow.

In those early days of Glasnost, the festival was far from the world unifying event it was billed as. In 1989, Moscow was very much a city in need of a boost. After years of pointing a brave, if not deceitful, face of prosperity toward the West, visitors were finding the reality – of food shortages, empty shops, an impoverished people struggling against a black market economy and endless queues – far less welcoming. After a few hours, Ozzy Osbourne had seen enough to observe: 'If I was living here full time, I'd probably be dead of alcoholism, or sniffing car tyres – anything to get out of it.' It was patently obvious why so many youths had an alcohol problem: there was nothing else to do.

And so the authorities found themselves welcoming the cream of the Western world's rock'n'roll circus. All the bands and about 100 members of the world's media flew into Moscow's Cheremetyov airport on the same plane. In sunglasses and fringed suede jacket, Jon led the posse down the rollaway steps and onto the tarmac while all around him cameras hummed and clicked. The events were being recorded by TV crews from international news network CNN as well as Sky, MTV, the BBC and ITV. All the bands posed for a massed team photo on a terminal balcony and then moved into a fleet of Zil limousines for the ride to their common city centre destination, The Ukraine Hotel.

However worthy the cause, it was almost inevitable that the foundation's pro-responsibility message took second place to the novelty value of the show itself. Perestroika and power-chords were two words never used in the same sentence before, as Jon was forced to admit.

'At this stage of the game,' he said to Mick Wall, covering the event for Sky TV, 'you ask yourself, "What can we do that The Stones and The Beatles didn't already do?" And being here is it.' But thoughts of international human rights and politics would, for the time being, have to take something of a backseat to the ego clashes Jon hinted at. Charity or not, McGhee had seen to it that Jon's was the name at the top of this particular tree: in the West he was the biggest star about to take the stage, and it was he who fielded most of the dumb questions at the international press conference. But there were those who had just flown in on the same plane that didn't like it at all.

Digging a little deeper, as Doc McGhee had done with a unique 'market survey', it was fairly obvious that back in the USSR, Ozzy Osbourne was the hero. The albums by his previous band Black Sabbath had spent almost two decades filtering their way into youth consciousness. The Scorpions, meanwhile, were running a pretty close second, having played ten nights in Leningrad, on their own, seventeen months earlier. And so the spectre of inter-band rivalry raised its head and cast a shadow over the apparent spirit of goodwill. The running order showed Bon Jovi would close the show following sets by Ozzy and then The Scorpions. At the eleventh hour, Ozzy's formidable wife and manager Sharon threatened to pull her husband client from the bill when McGhee suggested one of his acts, Mötley Crüe, replace him in his third on the bill spot. McGhee relented and so Sharon, Ozzy and band did indeed board the plane – only for McGhee to suggest again, the night before the first of the two shows, that Ozzy played before Crüe.

But like all the best scripted soap operas, the conflicts and feuding didn't end there. In fact, for Mötley Crüe, they were only just beginning. With the kind of collective egomania that most psychiatrists could make a career out of analysing, they refused to take their apparent pegging at fourth on the bill lying down. Although ostensibly under the same management as Bon Jovi – McGhee Entertainment Inc. – their day-to-day affairs were taken care of by one of McGhee's partners, Doug Thaler. It was a situation that would change within hours of the Moscow show.

'The way it was set up wasn't that cool,' moaned singer Vince Neil, a man clearly familiar with the taste of sour grapes and who Jon would later delightfully describe as 'the Rolex Axl Rose'. 'It turned out to be a fucking Bon Jovi show, which it wasn't supposed to be. It looked like it was done to push Bon Jovi's album in Russia. If it was known that it was gonna be a Bon Jovi show, you wouldn't have got us or The Scorpions or Ozzy to play on the bill.'

Crüe's bassist and leader Nikki Sixx added: '[Bon Jovi] are like a bunch of babies. It was meant to be equal billing over there. No one was meant to be headlining. Bon Jovi ended up trying to undermine things with pyrotechnics. We were very disheartened that there was not, like, this "brotherly" thing . . .' he added, sounding more like a child disappointed that there was not this everybody can play with the same toys thing.

And yet he may have had a point. McGhee's 'market research' ought to have suggested that either Ozzy or The Scorpions close the show. Mötley Crüe clearly thought so and weren't afraid to *say* so. The rock world's media loved them for this kind of outspoken bravado and delighted in the chance to reproduce Crüe's attempts to score points at Bon Jovi's expense. Sixx and the band (including the drummer Tommy Lee, who would marry Pamela Anderson after a whirlwind romance in 1995) were so unhappy with their treatment at the hands of Doc McGhee that they immediately severed connections with him and McGhee Entertainment and signed over to Doug Thaler alone and independently. They even flew home on a different plane. Petulantly, the band, who hadn't played a live show for twelve months previous to the first night's show, claimed their performance had been sabotaged by 'second rate treatment' from Doc McGhee.

Crüe really shouldn't have worried. With armed soldiers from the Red Army in attendance as security, and tickets priced too high to allow most of the regular Russian rock fans the chance of seeing their heroes, the atmosphere was relatively stifled. The damage to their reputation in the eyes of the 140,000 who attended each night would have been minimal and the millions more witnessing the event on the live world-wide telecast (via Europe's then fledgling Sky satellite network) surely noticed no problems either.

Jon sat back and heard all the tales before finally giving his version, with uncharacteristic bitterness, to Australian journalist Steve Mascord. 'Bon Jovi's was the first and only name on the bill for this Russian show. As we promoted it since last summer, we were going to be the spokespersons for the show. Mötley didn't do anything for it [but] when we were deemed the headliners on what was supposed to be an equal billing, they were upset. Well, it truly was an equal billing but we were closing the show. Everyone got the same sized billing on the posters, everyone got everything the same, but we were going to close . . .'

Jon also threw more light on the quarrel between Ozzy Osbourne and Mötley Crüe, maintaining that he personally settled the argument between the two parties when he happened to walk by them as late as one-thirty in the first afternoon, with Skid Row already on stage. 'I said, "Well, I've put this thing together for a year, with my name on it, doing all the fucking press work while all you fuckers were everywhere. I'll tell you what, Oz, you close the show because I think you're the best known guy here anyhow. I'll go on fourth, I don't give a fuck. I don't care if it's The Beatles out there, I'm going out to kick your ass."'

If Jon was bluffing, Ozzy and Nikki Sixx never called him on it and the first show went ahead with the 'agreed' running order: Skid Row, Nuance, Brigada S, Gorky Park, Cinderella, Mötley Crüe, The Scorpions, Bon Jovi followed by an all-star jam to close. By all accounts, the first night was good but not great for everyone except The Scorpions.

On the second night, events took a turn for the comical. The do-or-die Osbournes got the last laugh and just reward for sticking to their guns with an audience reaction that beat all others hands down. But Jon would admit to a piece of oneupmanship as a last minute trump card. For the second show, which was the one being broadcast live, he hit upon an idea that was pure theatre – he approached the stage from the front, wearing a Red Army cap and greatcoat. The TV cameras picked him out, sneaking through the ranks of the Russian army there as security, flanked by bodyguards like a prize-fighter entering the ring for a title bout.

'The great thing about being on a festival where all bands are equal is that everything is fair game,' Jon later grinned in explanation. Everyone was impressed, some more than others, while Mötley Crüe viewed the trick with stony faces. But for Crüe, things were about to get worse as a fireworks display accompanied the climax of Bon Jovi's set. It was so perfect, Bon Jovi should have planned it. Except they didn't. In fact, nobody did . . . the way it eventually happened.

'The Russian army, right after the show was done, were putting on a fireworks show,' explained Jon. '[But] this Russian soldier hit one button on one twirly thing – not even on a downbeat – in the middle of one of our songs. We never even knew it happened, but the Mötleys were out in the crowd and they saw it happen and they went nuts . . .'

More fireworks followed, on the side of the stage, where Crüe raced to find McGhee. Someone in their party registered their complaint in the form of a punch and that was pretty much how McGhee found himself fired. Mötley Crüe, who at that point had followed Bon Jovi's example by recording at Little Mountain Sound studio in Vancouver with producer Bob Rock, began to lose ground on the band they had enjoyed a head start on back in 1984. Crüe changed their image, lead singer and style but never made the move into the nineties with anything like the grace that Bon Jovi would manage, and are currently hovering perilously close to the file marked Where Are They Now?

Fresh from all the Moscow shenanigans, Bon Jovi took the Milton Keynes stage one week later, bristling with confidence. The crowd, warmed by the uncharacteristically sunny English summer's day, were quickly impressed. They were watching a Bon Jovi who had been on the road for nine months, having played a little over 130 shows, but (at least on stage) showing no signs of fatigue. Moreover, Jon, in particular, was convinced that after the heartaches of the *Slippery When Wet* marathon, they had cracked the nut. Physically Jon was in control and mentally he had found a new way of coping with the schedule.

'We're about 130 shows in and – knock on wood – I haven't lost my voice once . . . We always have these things to look forward to. Like two weeks ago it was playing the Giants Stadium [in New York] . . . So it's always like, "Only four weeks to go till this" and it keeps you moving. We've been out nine months and I'm still having fun. What's the point in doing it if you don't enjoy it, if it's not what you live for?'

Also helping to make the day-to-day pill of travelling a little easier to swallow were the album sales figures. As of July 1989 *New Jersey* had sold around 8 million copies worldwide, predictably some way short of *Slippery When Wet's* then current standing of 14 million but very close to the mark *Slippery* . . . had reached after an almost identical ten months' road work. Over the remainder of the tour, sales of *New Jersey* would begin to slow down, but still remain a long way ahead of what could be described as a disappointment.

Four days before the Bowl, at London's Hippodrome rock night, Jon limbered up alongside Richie, Motörhead's Lemmy plus Snake, Sebastian Bach and Rob Affuso from Skid Row for an impromptu and, as any who witnessed it may recall, hugely unimpressive jam. The Milton Keynes show, too, although sold-out and fondly recalled by the band, was thought by many to be merely perfunctory, with the band doing just enough but seemingly lacking the energy to give the extra something they usually saved for the big event. Returning for their encores, the band slipped in a version of Thin Lizzy's 'The Boys Are Back In Town' before Jon also announced a couple of 'surprise guests' in the form of Aerosmith's Steve Tyler and Joe Perry as Bon Jovi tripped their way through that band's 'Walk This Way'. Jon's comments about Tyler running five miles a day must have come back to haunt him as the guest upstaged the host, leaving Jon trailing in his wake on a series of athletic runs and only gawping in amazement as Tyler performed three running backflips. Bon Jovi were already clearly much more exhausted than they were prepared to admit.

But ahead of them lay a wintertime trek around the concert halls of continental Europe and Scandinavia, and then a third *New Jersey* tour visit to the UK for two more dates at the Birmingham NEC after Christmas then another four at Wembley Arena and a couple in Ireland – all in the first week of 1990. Europe was proving to be a stronger market than usual for them but by coming back so often in such a relatively short period of time meant that McGhee's plans were starting to suffer from the law of diminishing returns. Certainly, the tour revenue was coming in very nicely, but they had apparently already persuaded just about everyone in Europe with even a passing interest in Bon Jovi to buy *New Jersey* and so the band began to look like dogs chasing their own tails. Yet still the tour continued . . .

In support on the 1990 dates, at Jon's personal request, was Dan Reed Network, the multi-racial Portland, Oregon, band whose music had been described at times as a hybrid of Prince and Bon Jovi. Led by the handsomely enigmatic Dan Reed, the band shared mutual friends with Jon in the form of Little Steven and the producer of their first album, Bruce Fairbairn – not to mention one Barry Bongiovi, studio manager at the Power Station where some of their second and then current album, *Slam*, was recorded.

From the moment the association was announced, the media began to build a concept around it. Dan Reed was either the natural successor to, or soul brother of, Jon Bon Jovi. Certainly, Reed's band shared much with the Bon Jovi of five years earlier, a clean-cut image, cutesy pin-up looks and a natural flair for a great song and an irresistible hookline. Jon must have seen a lot of his more youthful self in Reed and, given his love of Prince's music, was also enraptured by Dan Reed Network's funky approach to rock. (*Slam*, although heavily laden with rock guitars, had been co-produced by Nile Rodgers, the driving force behind Chic.) To coincide with the UK dates, *Kerrang!* took the unusual step of running a joint story on both bands, getting the two frontmen together for a photo session and cover shot. Howard Johnson went to Copenhagen to interview the pair and found Jon in very good spirits, brandishing a bottle of wine and spilling much in the way of confidence and pride as he looked back over his career.

'To steal a phrase from Eddie Murphy, when the first album came out I was like an eighteen-year-old fucking. It was all very quick, with no technique and no rhythm. There I was thinking I was a star – and nobody knew me . . . The second album came along and I began to understand how to work the live thing. I started to learn the moves. [But] it was really only by the time we headlined Castle Donington in '87, when *Slippery*... had done its thing, that I felt totally in control. That day I went on knowing that stage was mine.

'Now here we are with *New Jersey* and a year after the album was released we're still selling out shows and breaking merchandising records and it makes me feel like we really did something. It's pretty hip.'

Jon was right in many ways, even the more sceptical corners of the media were admitting, however begrudgingly, that with *New Jersey* the band had improved musically on the hugely successful *Slippery*... Anyone attending the shows couldn't help but be impressed, as they scanned the vast arenas looking in vain for an empty seat, at the level of professionalism and showmanship the band had attained. Moreover, however he was feeling the second before he took the stage, whatever else may have been on his mind, when Jon ran to stage centre – and indeed anywhere else for the duration of the show – he managed to maintain an apparent level of sincerity that would charm all but the most stubborn of doubting Thomases. As a new decade dawned, Jon could be forgiven for basking in the glory.

'We've reached a certain level and we've learned to do whatever it takes to make each show as good as we possibly can. Today was number 206 on this tour and while I wasn't as good as yesterday – I was good yesterday – it still reached a certain standard.'

Jon Bon Jovi was very obviously a man high on life, keeping track of the tour date by date and somehow monitoring his own performances for personal goals even Dorothea – who he had married six months earlier – was at a loss to fully understand. In his Danish hotel room that night he admitted she had questioned his intention to play so many shows in support of *New Jersey*. 'Why so much? How much money do you have to make?' she had asked incredulously, perhaps mindful of what the last tour had done to his physical and mental well-being. Jon claimed he had told her, as he would countless journalists since, that financial reward was one of the last things on his mind. Instead, he cited the spirit of competition between his band and their earlier opening act Skid Row.

'I've decided that I'm gonna put a credit on the next album to the Skids which will read: "Thanks for keeping me hungry". That's what has been inspiring me. Sebastian [Bach] is just so into what's happening to him, "Hey, I'm in the UK! Hey, I'm getting my own apartment!" He used to come into our dressing room when they toured with us telling me he was gonna kick my ass. That made me work real hard when I got out there and it made me feel good when he came to the side of the stage and threw his hands up in a gesture that said I hadn't failed. I knew I had to get the kid in the hundredth row up out of his seat so I moved and I sweated. That had nothing to do with business, that's personal.'

Considering Jon was speaking just a couple of months after he and Sebastian Bach had come to blows backstage, Jon was very obviously a man not interested in harbouring grudges. Skid Row never did get the credit Jon spoke of, perhaps because he forgot, more probably because Bach would later chose to 'kick Jon's ass' in a bitter war of words over money (see *The Godfather Part II*, next). Right there in Copenhagen, however, Jon was going to enormous lengths to convince his interrogator that money was of little interest to him.

'I wouldn't pretend that things are the same as when we started. It's much different. We fly around in jets, we sell out shows – we have single rooms with running water! I appreciate those days, I'm glad we had to fight our way to the top from a position when five years ago people were saying, "Fuck you!" all the time. But I'm not sorry to see those days gone. I didn't want to play [little clubs] for the next ten years. Now I can do it because I want to and not because I have to. And I don't miss busses – I don't miss them at all.

'Money is nice. I like the money. But I'm wearing the jeans that I stole from my little brother, I got these sneakers for free and this T-shirt is five years old. Sure it would be scary to think that I'd lose all these financial rewards, that I could do this many shows and not make any cash. It's scary as fuck to think of my wife having to work and my parents having to scrape a living, but all this that I have wasn't a gift, we had to fight for it . . .'

But come Christmas 1989 the fight was taking on foolish proportions and the probability of repeating all the mistakes of the *Slippery* . . . tour was staring Jon in the face. After a show in Germany on 23 December, the band spent Christmas in a hotel in London – seemingly unable to find room in their schedule to spend the holiday at home with their friends and families, as Jon later reflected.

'How rotten, when your managers, your agents and your lawyers are at home – and you're in a hotel room. We got hammered on our plane over London, and I remember going to the hotel thinking, "This is great, man. This is so rock! This is all I ever wanted . . ."'

He was wrong, of course, but the lesson would only be learned later.

As the memory of their lost Christmas faded and Bon Jovi came to the end of the European leg of the *New Jersey* tour, they found themselves sharing a stage with former Led Zeppelin guitarist Jimmy Page. The occasion was a charity show at London's Hammersmith Odeon – by that stage quite an intimate venue for Bon Jovi to play in – to raise funds for the Nordoff-Robbins Music Therapy, on 10 January, 1990. The show was a sell-out with over 3,500 punters paying up to £50 for a balcony seat and an invite to an after-show reception.

Bon Jovi took the opportunity to play a different kind of set, beginning with just Jon and Richie (in seventh heaven at the opportunity to work with his hero Page) in front of the curtains, perched on stools with acoustic guitars running through versions of 'Wanted Dead Or Alive', 'Livin' On A Prayer' and Bad Company's 'Shooting Star'. After forty-five minutes, the curtains drew back to reveal the rest of the band and a bar-room stage set. It looked like a neat homage to Jon's earliest gigs and was intended as such – but had in fact been borrowed from English band The Quireboys, who had used it on their recent tour. Bon Jovi customized the set by hanging a poster of their own logo over The Quireboys' and adding a pool table and a jukebox. (Jon then took the whole set-up back to New Jersey for the band's Christmas show and later resurrected the idea on the 1995 world tour.)

The rest of their set followed the pattern of the most recent Wembley shows but added the band's own versions of Little Richard's 'Good Golly Miss Molly', Creedence Clearwater Revival's 'Travelin' Band', a medley of 'It's My Life' and 'We've Got To Get Out Of This Place' from The Animals' back catalogue, 'We All Sleep Alone' – the song Jon and Richie had written for Cher's last album, and brand new number 'Cadillac Man', written for the soundtrack of the forthcoming Robin Williams movie. The evening ended with Page joining the band for their reworking of 'The Train Kept A-Rollin'' – the song he made famous with his pre-Zeppelin band The Yardbirds – and Lennon and McCartney's 'With A Little Help From My Friends'.

Although by not attending the after-show party Bon Jovi upset a few of those who had paid £50 expecting to meet them, they were clearly winning more and more friends should they ever need their help. Working alongside the reclusive Page was testament to their stature at a time when his public appearances were about as frequent as Earth-threatening comets.

The band had now completed all but the final month's worth of Central and South American dates and could afford to relax a little as they watched 'Living In Sin', their thirteenth single, become the tenth to reach the American *Billboard* top ten. Which meant that although *New Jersey* hadn't sold as well, it had at least produced one more hit single than *Slippery . . .* – five to its four. Before the release of 'Living In Sin', they were also apparently feeling confident enough to rebel against all they had achieved in terms of their almost untarnished image. Perhaps inspired by the success of Guns N' Roses with the uncompromising anti-authoritarian stance of their debut album *Appetite For Destruction* – but more likely feeling just a little bored and trying something different for a giggle – Bon Jovi had made a video that proved too controversial for MTV to broadcast in its original format. Having to spend more time and money re-editing the clip wasn't anything that his accountant would recommend but at least Jon could laugh at the outcome.

'Enough of the nice guy for a while. The best bit is where the girl is getting communion and the shot fades to her sucking her boyfriend's fingers . . . Isn't sucking fingers the nastiest thing you can do?! Hey, it's in me. I can make a girl do things,' he joked, uncharacteristically. 'I decided, "Let's get fucking nasty" and no one could accept it . . .'

The idea had, he said, actually come from Dorothea while he suggested the location, a motel he used to go to. Whether it was his present wife he took there, he declined to say. No matter, the single sold anyway and the success brought him a great deal of personal satisfaction as it was the first Bon Jovi hit he had penned without a co-writer like Richie or Desmond Child. It represented another personal target achieved, another first for the twenty-seven-year-old who was going to have to set himself some new goals.

But first he would have to face up to the fact that his goals and ambitions were creating real stress within Bon Jovi itself. On the whole, the shows were still going well enough, but the members of the band who sat wearily in hotel foyers awaiting the drive to the night's venue or slumped afterwards in the dressing rooms were having less and less of a good time.

Richie summed up his version of the way the tour ended: 'In terms of my validity as a musician, I lost my way on tour somewhere. It was just another day, another dollar, another stage,' he said, before clarifying. 'We weren't doing it for the money, the glory or the satisfaction. We were just doing it to get it done.'

Perhaps inspired by McGhee, perhaps by his own demons, Jon had been so keen to keep the 'Jersey Syndicate' touring ball rolling that he had pushed the other members of the band beyond their limits, expecting each to have reserves of stamina to match his. The statistics, at least, were impressive. When it finished, the tour had visited twenty-three countries and included 232 shows in front of over 3 million people. The band had played fewer shows and to less people than they did with *Slippery* . . . but had cut their costs by playing generally bigger venues and selling more merchandise. Most significantly, however, they had stayed out on the road just as long. It was the result, as Jon would eventually concede, of McGhee's pushing and his own almost blind ambition.

They were big earners. No question. Aside from the money brought in by ticket sales, there was a roughly equal amount from merchandise (of which, according to the territory, they could expect to keep 30 to 45 per cent of the gross) and of course, the income from record sales: even after the *New Jersey* tour had ended, sales of a further 4 million records from the rest of their catalogue followed. Predictably, interviewers equated Bon Jovi's persistent touring with income maximization. Jon found himself having to deny this was the case again and again. 'Money has never been my concern – though I guess it's easier to say that when you got it, because you *can* pay the rent.'

Besides, however big the pay cheque, there were only so many hours overtime anyone can do. More important, he argued, was the strength of the band unit, the family ties.

'It's down to wanting people to share it with. There's nothing like the feeling of having a record go to number one and you call each other up to pat each other on the back. Being in a rock band is like being in a gang. It's much better to be up there on stage and look across and see people you've grown up with and who believed in you ten years ago, rather than just session musicians. Even if their places were taken by, say, Jeff Beck or Eric Clapton, then the only thing you have in common is the moment, rather than the trials and tribulations you've endured together.'

Yet much later he would admit that by getting away from the thing he loved most – the music – he did become disillusioned. 'I felt I became this money-making babysitter, worrying about everybody's everything, both in and outside the band what with management, lawyers, agents blah-blah-blah . . .'

Those words say much about the conflicts underlying Jon Bon Jovi's deepest personal motivations. Motivations that he had lost all sight of in February 1990. At first the tour had been fun, but eventually it went on way too long, ending, with fitting irony, with two shows in one day in Mexico. But long before that day, Jon's precious 'Jersey Syndicate' family ties were stretched to breaking point. The results would plunge himself and the future of Bon Jovi into eighteen months of doubt and confusion.

Quotes gratefully taken from:

Alison Joy, *Kerrang!* 204/205, 10/17 September 1988; Paul Henderson, *Kerrang!* 206, 24 September 1988; Pippa Lang, *Metal Hammer*, December

1988; Mick Wall, *Kerrang!* 217, 10 December 1988; Sylvie Simmons, *Raw* 4, 12–25 October 1988; Mark Cooper, *Q* 26, November 1988; Adrian Deevoy, *Q* 28, January 1989; Elianne Halbersberg, *Kerrang!* 232, 1 April 1989; Alison Joy, *Kerrang!* 252, 19 August 1989; Mick Wall, *Kerrang!* 254/255, 9/16 September 1989; Paul Elliott, *Sounds*, 10/17 September 1988; Steve Mascord, *Kerrang!* 264, 11 November 1989; Howard Johnson, *Kerrang!* 271, 6 January 1990; Mick Wall, *Kerrang!* 301, 4 August 1990; Adrian Deevoy, *Q* 52, January 1991; Ray Zell, *Kerrang!* 349, 13 July 1991; Paul Rees, *Raw* 107, 30 September–13 October 1992; Joe Mackett, *Riff Raff*, interview, 16 October 1992; Dave Reynolds, *Kerrang!* 426, 16 January 1993; Andrew Collins, *Q* 98, November 1994; David Cavanagh, *Q* 101, February 1995.

# The Godfather Part II

*'I'm not doing it for any financial reward nor am I insisting on any co-writing credits. I just wanna help a struggling group whom I think are good, along what is a very difficult and treacherous path.'*
Jon Bon Jovi, 1989

*'As a headliner now, I look down on my opening bands as part of my organization,'* Jon Bon Jovi explains a ground rule to Skid Row, 1988

WITH TWO MASSIVELY successful albums and their respective tours almost running into one another, Jon was afforded only a minimum of time to return or distribute favours as Don Corleone's son Michael might have done in Francis Ford Coppola's 1974 sequel to *The Godfather* . . . Indeed, the back-to-back tours and the recording of *Slippery When Wet* and *New Jersey* meant that Jon had very little time even for his immediate family between the summer of 1986 and the spring of 1990. He had, remember, not even gone home for Christmas 1989.

So 1990, then, was a low point for the extended Bon Jovi family, the 'Jersey Syndicate' as it had come to be known, with splits in the ranks, arguments and bad feelings surrounding much of what Jon did. Following McGhee's conviction for drug smuggling, the good name of the family had been

**131**

tarnished and although the solution was at hand, Jon – with typical loyalty to his manager and friend – would take another year to realize it. But he could at least cast his eye back over the happier times that had begun after his first taste of big business with *Slippery When Wet* . . .

With Cinderella's *Long Cold Winter* in the process of turning platinum, Jon was already looking around for new acts to nurture and – even during the recording of *New Jersey* – was not too busy to offer help to musicians who were already signed. Jon went to an AC/DC gig at which White Lion were the opening act. Before the show he was in White Lion's dressing room when their singer, the Danish-born Mike Tramp (now fronting Freak Of Nature) came in. 'He could hardly speak and I got shivers down my spine. All I could think of was the pain that guy was going through . . .'

Jon took him to one side and, as a man who had only come through the last tour through the use of steroid injections, offered Tramp a sympathetic ear and the benefit of his own painful experiences. When reminded of this story, Jon modestly shrugged off the idea that it was anything heroic, although he would admit it was, sadly, an uncommon gesture.

'I guess it is, but I just don't get it. When I was in a young band all I wanted was for The Scorpions – or whoever we were playing with – to say, "I dug this band". No one ever said that. As a headliner now, I look on my opening bands as part of my organization. With Cinderella, every night we would bring them out on stage with us – every night. What's great is that Cinderella are now doing that with their support bands [Winger and The BulletBoys]. Every night they do a jam. I had something to do with that. Tommy [Keifer] is a great guy, he has no ego.'

This kind of comment was perhaps a true indication of

what Jon Bon Jovi was about in 1988. A young man keen to be a father figure but equally, away from all the business that his success had inevitably generated, he was at heart still a young man inspired by a genuine love of music.

But inevitably, that love of music and business got irretrievably entangled as when, just prior to the release of *New Jersey*, he and Richie began touting for business as songwriters. Here a distinction should be drawn between this and extra-curricular work like his encouragement of Cinderella and even his advice to Mike Tramp. One of the first to call was Billy Squier – a man who Jon had previously acknowledged as being the first professional musician to offer to produce one of his early demos. Surrounded by evidence of what good songwriting could lead to, and almost certainly encouraged by his manager McGhee, here was Jon not returning or offering favours, merely looking to expand his business interests and develop his dream of the 'Jersey Syndicate'.

Flashing back in sepia tones ... to 1987, however, Jon was inspired by the success of his discovery of Tom Keifer and Cinderella, and keen to embark upon a similar quest to help his old schoolfriend Dave 'Snake' Sabo. Sabo had lived close to Jon in Sayreville and, in 1977 when they were both just thirteen, had dragged Jon and a bottle of wine along to see his favourite band Kiss. Jon forgave him but never forgot him. As they each drifted in and out of bands they made a pact, that the first one to make it would come back and help the other. The pair played together occasionally, but when Jon signed to PolyGram he hired Richie instead and not Sabo, certain that Sabo's guitar playing was far too Kiss-influenced to ever suit his vision of Bon Jovi.

Perhaps the memory of passing on his friend had nagged at Jon ever since, perhaps he genuinely felt bound by the pact, but certainly he was there to help Sabo when the time, in Jon's eyes, was right. That time proved to be when Sabo sent his latest demo of his latest band to Jon, as friends do, for an honest appraisal. For once, as honest friends often don't, Jon came back and said this is the one.

'I'd been in loads of bands that weren't worth a shit and Jon just watched and let me do my thing,' remembered Snake. 'He didn't lift a finger until he saw something that was worthwhile . . .'

The band, based conveniently in New Jersey, had been put together by Sabo with a bassist called Rachel Bolan and was called Skid Row. Jon wasted little time in using some of his royalties from *Slippery When Wet* to finance a more pro-fessional demo. From there he helped hook the band up with McGhee Entertainment, and started spreading the word that here was a band some label really ought to sign. This time, Derek Shulman passed but Doc McGhee, sharing management of the band with his brother Scott, oversaw their signing to Atlantic. First, however, Jon and Richie volunteered to help Skid Row with their song arrangements and work alongside them in pre-production.

At the time of hooking up with Sabo and Skid Row, Jon spoke of it in terms of a favour to an old friend. 'I'm not doing it for any financial reward nor am I insisting on any co-writing credits. I just wanna help a struggling group, whom I think are good, along what is a very difficult and treacherous path. I got stung by so many people when I was trying to get my first break that anything I can do to help others will give me great pleasure.'

But in reality, the favour was on more of a business footing. In exchange for their foregoing any co-writing credits, McGhee signed the band to Jon and Richie's newly established New Jersey Underground Music company. The Underground was set up in 1987 to handle the publishing royalties of some of

Jon's own writing collaborations. Skid Row's Underground contract called for Skid Row to waive their rights to publishing royalties and that these be paid to Jon and Richie, through the Underground. Jon and Richie were not going to be credited for their input to the band's songs, but they would certainly be paid for them.

Whether Skid Row signed the deal out of naiveté or because they believed they genuinely stood a better chance of making it with Bon Jovi's support rather than their own money is still open to speculation. What is almost beyond question is that as manager of both bands, McGhee Entertainment's position was unusual to say the least when it sanctioned a deal that was in fact taking income from one of its acts to support another.

Unquestionably, the deal served Skid Row well enough to begin with, but ultimately proved so loaded in Jon and Richie's favour that it became the source of an uncomfortable public humiliation for Jon and led to much friction between himself, Richie and manager McGhee. In doing so, it all but destroyed the image of Jon as a benevolent Godfather.

That was all a long way off, however, as Jon and Richie got on with the nuts and bolts of getting Skid Row started. Their input was also financial, as Skid Row's profusely profanatory singer Sebastian Bach explained: 'I had to pay a former manager $20,000 when I joined Skid Row – just to be in this fuckin' band. I didn't have that kind of money. I'd never sold any records. But Jon gave me that money to pay this guy off, or I couldn't have been in this band.'

Months later, with Skid Row's songs knocked into shape and their eponymous debut album recorded, Atlantic geared up to promote it. Jon and Richie were also on hand to plug their protégés in interviews and Jon had posed for photos alongside Sabo. More significantly, even before Skid Row's album had hit the shops, Jon announced them as the opening act on Bon Jovi's *New Jersey* tour.

Skid Row were pitched into the fray in front of the *New Jersey* arena tour's first night sell-out crowd in Dallas, Texas. As the tour progressed, they learnt fast and their seemingly limitless energy impressed Bon Jovi's audiences. The tour went well for both bands, with Skid Row getting the kind of exposure most bands could only dream of – playing to around 16,000 fans each night while gaining confidence and a fanbase.

'Watching Bon Jovi is a great learning experience,' said Sabo. 'It's great seeing the way they relate to the crowd and try to touch every person. The biggest shock so far is definitely how well we've been treated – it's almost ludicrous. The entire Bon Jovi tour is a case of one big family. That's why they call it 'The Jersey Syndicate' tour . . . We've been treated so well by Bon Jovi and their crew. They wear our T-shirts, sing our songs. It's rare to find such camaraderie.'

After eight months touring as Bon Jovi's special guests, Skid Row were a band of no small promise. Immediately following the US trek, they were able to fly to their own debut headline tour of Japan where their profile there was so high they had sold out seven shows. But the link with Bon Jovi didn't end there. The band were booked as the support on the 1989 European tour and when McGhee set up the Moscow Music Peace Festival for August 1989, Skid Row opened the shows.

Thus far, the band had no reason to complain or regret their deal with the Underground. Soon they were able to reflect on 1.3 million albums sold worldwide, whereupon Sabo spoke of his gratitude to Jon ('We certainly have had a lot of help from him, and believe me we're really grateful for it . . .') while politely suggesting that 'at the end of the day people still have to like the music.'

But as a result of the deal the band had signed, Skid Row were not reaping the fullest monetary rewards from their platinum-plus debut as Sabo, who had co-written nine of the *Skid Row* album's eleven songs explained: 'I'm still a poor boy.

I haven't seen shit yet as far as money's concerned, but whether people believe it or not, I'm really not that bothered. The most important thing for me, for us as a band, is just that we're out there doing it . . .'

One of the band, however, the Canadian born singer Bach, *was* bothered. For him, things soon reached the point where being poor but 'doing it' wasn't enough. He wanted to be paid for it, too. The underground deal had not been formally publicized at this point, but rumours abounded. The link was plain to see, in any case as the Underground logo (a variation on London Transport's famous bar and circle design) which had appeared for the first time on the *New Jersey* album when it was released in September 1988, was there on the back of *Skid Row* also. The following year, Jon finally explained why: 'The Underground is a production company that supported Skid Row for two years. It's mine and Richie's company. For about a year and a half of that we were writing songs with them, re-writing songs, paying for studio time, paying their rent and every single thing that came with them. I hooked them up with agents, managers, gave them gear . . .'

With the benefit of hindsight, Skid Row had all this and more to be grateful for. But eventually, gratitude turned to bitterness in one of the sourest and most controversial episodes of the whole Bon Jovi story. Controversy and Bon Jovi are not words normally associated. Jon is too smart to do anything that would upset anyone or the proverbial applecart. So in October 1989, as the band's American tour began to approach its later stages, it was bad news when friction between Bon Jovi and Skid Row began to develop. Families weren't supposed to work that way and Jon wasn't amused.

The first rumblings of discontent started, not with Jon or Sabo, but with Bach. He had been the final recruit and the missing part in Sabo's Skid Row jigsaw, a terrific no-holds-barred livewire frontman who was and is a good deal smarter than some of his between-song raps suggest, but his damn-the-torpedoes insistence on speaking his mind without a care for the long term consequences has always been at odds with Jon's measured and, Bach would argue, calculated and therefore un-rock'n'roll style. This never bothered either party when the Underground deal was signed, but Jon was less than amused when Bach began flying in the face of touring protocol by shooting his mouth off on stage.

Making unflattering remarks about the headliners, to an audience that had mostly paid to see just the headliners, was the height of ingratitude in Jon's opinion. Any band who did that could expect to be thrown off the tour just as soon as a replacement could be found. And – as Bach well knew – the queue of bands offering to step into such a breach on a Bon Jovi tour would stretch as long as any ticket line.

When asked about it months later, Jon was predictably diplomatic. 'It's tough for him to grow out of my shadow. I mean, every fucking interview [the media] were saying, "Jon did this for you, Jon did that". I'm sure he got sick of it, like, "Fuck Jon!" I understand that.'

Closer to the event, however, Jon was anything but sympathetic. Bon Jovi were selling tickets on the strength of *New Jersey* and its singles, and not their adopted support band. Having volunteered to give that band the chance of a lifetime, he clearly didn't expect them to turn round and bite the hand that fed them.

'I don't give a shit about the ego involved,' he complained. 'All I expect is, if this is my house then treat it nicely. Don't spit in the house, you know? That's all I would ask of anyone. If you don't like us then fine, go about your business, but don't ever slag it because that's why you're here.'

Bach didn't agree, and although the rest of a grateful Skid Row got along just fine with Jon and the band, he didn't. He didn't like their music and, although Bach wasn't admitting it yet, he no longer liked the Underground set up. Instead, in interviews he belittled the idea of Bon Jovi as anything other than a corporate rock'n'roll machine.

Bach argued that when Skid Row started touring with Bon Jovi he spoke to Jon and said: 'Listen, I have total respect for you. This is your stage and I want to know what I can and can't do on your stage because you're the headliners.' Jon, in return told him something along the lines of: 'Do whatever you want, man, this is freedom, this is rock'n'roll.' Gradually, though, said Bach, Jon began to change his way of thinking. At a venue in Johnstown, Pennsylvania, Bach had punched an out-of-uniform policeman who had pushed him around after mistaking his cup of water for vodka (alcohol is banned at many American venues). A meeting was called just before Skid Row took the stage at which Jon told Bach not to say anything about the incident or the police, and also asked him not to swear quite so much.

This kind of appeal was like pouring gasoline on a fire as far as Bach was concerned (BBC Radio 1, when broadcasting the Skid Row set live from the stage at Castle Donington in 1992, would count over 70 f-words in the band's set, roughly one a minute and around 70 more than they had been expecting to air). Moreover, seeing the cop's confrontation as just another example of authority against the nation's free-thinking long-haired youth, Bach went out and declared: 'I just wanna tell you people that you elected a real load of fuckheads in this city, and you've got guys out there who shoot stun guns at you just for drinking water . . .'

When Skid Row came off stage, Jon was there waiting and yelled at Bach: 'You fucking stupid idiot, you don't understand what rock'n'roll's all about. You don't understand the big picture.' Bach replied that, no, he didn't, because as far as he could see, the crowd went wild when he made those remarks. Bach said Jon told him that each city they played in was worth around $100,000 to the band. And if you made remarks like Bach just had, and upset the promoters enough to not have you back on the next tour, then that was as good as taking $100,000 out of your pocket in the future. The Skid Row singer replied that he would have paid $100,000 to have been able to say what he had just said, to which Jon laughed at his naiveté and suggested that one day, getting that sort of crowd reaction would become boring.

It's not a remark that Jon has ever admitted to, and certainly he's often been quoted as saying that, the only thing not boring about being in a rock'n'roll band is the two hours of the twenty-four he spends on stage. But Bach, although prone to exaggeration when excited, has stuck by his claim and went on to say that he told Skid Row guitarist Sabo: 'If you ever hear me say anything like that in my whole life I want you to fucking take a knife and cut off my nuts . . .'

Sabo was well used to Bach's outbursts and chalked it down as another one for the scrapbook. There was, however, more to come. At the penultimate gig on the tour, the word went around the bands' road crews that tonight was to be 'gag night'. The first gag was played on Skid Row. As the house-lights went out and their intro tape rolled, the band waited in the darkness. Bach, in particular, was in for a shock, as he explained: 'I was grabbed just as I was going on stage. Somebody poured a gallon of freezing cold ice-milk over me. But the intro tape was rolling and I just had to go on there covered in all this shit . . . So I go out there – big gag – and when I get to the mike I go into this rant against Jon: "Come on up here, pussy, and get a piece of me, motherfucker!"'

Bach insists his remarks were intended as a joke, but later admitted, having watched a video of the episode, that to 20,000 people who weren't in on the gag it 'came over really fucking harsh. It was like a riot was gonna start'. It was, after all, his first tour and he didn't know all the rules yet, he offered

Bon Jovi (Dave Bryan, Tico Torres, Jon Bon Jovi, Alec Jon Such, Richie Sambora) as the world first knew them: 'You look back and cringe a bit.' (Ebet Roberts/Redferns)

*Above*: Jon in concert: constant touring during the 1980s turned the road into 'a treadmill'. (Mike Cameron/Redferns)

*Right*: 1986's *Slippery When Wet* album made Jon a star: 'It was like a comic book phenomenon: KAPOW!' (Ebet Roberts/Redferns)

The band 'rested' in 1990 and Jon's foil and guitarist Richie Sambora worked as a solo artist. (Mick Hutson/Redferns)

When the band re-emerged with
*Keep The Faith* in 1992, Jon sported
a radical new image: 'It's only a
haircut.' (Mick Hutson/Redferns)

Above: Promoting and touring with *Keep The Faith*, the band were anxious to quell rumours of disquiet in their ranks. (Mick Hutson/Redferns)

*Right*: In 1994, a little late in his career, Jon took to busking – as a promotional tool. (Mick Hutson/Redferns)

Come the mid 1990s Bon Jovi were regulars on the big music awards circuit, such as the 1995 MTV Music Awards, *right*, and The 1996 Brit Awards, *main picture*. (Mick Hutson/Redferns and Kieran Doherty/Redferns)

*Opposite page*: These days, Bon Jovi can sell as many tickets as the Rolling Stones and regularly play the largest outdoor venues: 'Stadiums are a real blast.' (Michel Linssen/Redferns)

Jon as the house-painter in *Moonlight and Valentino*, 1995: his first real movie role. (courtesy of Pictorial Press/PolyGram Filmed Entertainment)

Jon with Elizabeth Perkins, one of his *Moonlight and Valentino* co-stars: 'A girlie movie, like *Steel Magnolias*.' (courtesy of Pictorial Press/PolyGram Filmed Entertainment)

sheepishly. After he came off stage, Jon was waiting to explain some of the rules to him and as Bach himself admitted: 'It turned out that Jon didn't know anything about what his road crew had done to me . . . He got pissed off and we got into a fight.'

All of this petty squabbling went largely unreported by the media and remained so until Jon was asked by *Kerrang!* journalist Mick Wall, fully nine months later, about Bach's widely reported ingratitude. In a rare gung-ho moment Jon let his guard slip and ended his reply with the remark: 'I can punch the bastard in the face and be very happy I did it . . .'

A one-off altercation, that should have been long forgotten, was about to come back to haunt Jon Bon Jovi and get blown out of all proportion.

To Bach, that kind of remark was an affront to his ego and wild man of rock sensibilities, and like a red rag to a bull. It seemed to take the bull three months to reach full stampeding gallop but he finally did so in October 1990, when a phone rang in the *Kerrang!* office at 9.45 one morning and a bitter-sounding voice announced itself as Sebastian Bach wanting to get something about Bon Jovi off his chest. Alison Joy took the call and hastily gathered together her tape recorder and a couple of spare tapes, and headed off into a quiet corner, not so much to talk, but to listen, only to interrupt occasionally as Bach not so much spilled the beans, as fired them at her from a machine gun.

Bach was anxious to give his side of the events that Jon had described to Wall regarding their contretemps at the end of the US tour. He claimed this was the main reason he was calling.

'First of all,' he began, 'I'd like to say that this new tactic of getting press by putting someone down is stupid and very sad. Rock'n'roll should be about all the bands being together against everyone else who doesn't like it. [Skid Row] are good buds with every other guy in Bon Jovi, but now there's one guy who thinks Axl Rose is the hippest thing around. Axl Rose likes to fight, so I guess it's time to be a bad boy of rock, because that's what's in right now . . .'

Bach was referring to a much publicized story from April of that year concerning the Guns N' Roses singer's desire for a meet-and-beat with Mötley Crüe singer Vince Neil. 'Vince Neil's gonna get a good ass whippin', and I'm the boy to give it to him . . . I wanna see that plastic face of his cave in when I hit him,' boasted Axl, promising revenge for a scuffle that took place in America at the MTV Music Awards when Neil and GN'R guitarist Izzy Stradlin' had briefly exchanged blows. It all amounted to little more than a handbags-at-ten-paces scrap, but Bach was right, it had amused magazines, readers and other bands enough for that kind of press to become prevalent. It was with no apparent sense of irony, then, that he proceeded to give a lengthy account of the punch Jon had briefly hinted at.

'Why does he have to lie straight-faced to all the people who listen to his music, saying he beat me up when this is 100 per cent false? He's just saying this 'cause he's trying to make himself look tough, when in actual fact he's a 32-year-old [sic] Bruce Springsteen fan and I'm a fucking 22-year-old Motörhead freak on speed. So, y'know, I'm not really too scared of him retaliating against me talking like this, because it's just a big bunch of bullshit.'

Bach's latest version of events differed little from the account he had given in November 1989, but the story got even more salacious as he offered a few extra details. Bach told how, as he walked away after the show with his tour manager, he was approached by Jon, Jon's brother, father and – at Bach's estimate – four bodyguard/security types. The Skid Row singer was still annoyed and swore at Jon. To which Jon replied and threw a punch. A haymaker, according to Bach, 'like he couldn't hit the side of a barn door', which he merely ducked and returned with a blow to Jon's chin. Instantly, Bach found himself pinned to the wall by the bodyguards. In the war of words that followed, Bach offered to take Jon on one-to-one, chastising him for needing the backing of paid staff and his family: 'Dude, the day you gotta get your dad in to fight your battles for you is the day to hang up the gloves . . .'

The bitterness in Bach's voice that October 1990 morning – approaching 5 a.m. in New Jersey when he called – was impossible to miss. He was one very upset young man. Completely overlooking the fact that he and Jon might just be two very different personalities and that Jon had no problem with the rest of Skid Row (later that year he spent a week's vacation with Snake and Rachel Bolan) Bach continued while Joy's tape machine rolled, complaining that although they lived four miles apart they hadn't seen each other socially in 'about a year'.

Gradually, however, Joy could notice the angle of Bach's rant changing. It was not about his perceived horrors of supporting Bon Jovi, of having listening to their music, or even the fact that Jon had claimed to have punched him on the nose. Not at all. Bach was calling to bitch about money, and more specifically, his lack of it despite having had his band's debut album sell hundreds of thousands in America and despite having had a promo video, for '18 And Life', be number one on MTV . . . Jon, said Bach, explained 'the big picture' to him in a way that made him lose all respect for Jon.

Then, finally, he got to what surely must have been uppermost in his mind: the publishing deal Skid Row had signed with Bon Jovi's company, New Jersey Underground Music, Inc.

'I stuck up for Jon Bon Jovi all fucking year while he took 100 per cent of our publishing, telling people to shut the fuck up when they cut him up. Then he treats me like this . . . We are getting out of that deal with Jon now because Doc [McGhee] understands that I'm not the naive nineteen year old I was three years ago . . .'

'Snake grew up with Jon. Snake writes "I Remember You", "18 And Life" and "Youth Gone Wild" and Jon Bon Jovi takes all the money. Oh yeah, that's fair,' said Bach sarcastically. 'Hasn't he fucking got enough? Does he really need our two million dollars so he can have seventy-one million dollars instead of sixty-nine? How much fucking money does somebody need? I'm living in a condo right now, with a used car, and I've sold 5 million records worldwide.'

Amongst all the vitriol, Bach unwittingly offered a truth that may explain why Jon never took the issue any further in public: 'Jon definitely deserves something on the first record for helping us out, but not on any other records . . .'

Bach, clearly, was on a roll.

'I'm not in this business to buy Bon Jovi's brother a Christmas present instead of my fucking brother, y'know what I'm saying? . . . Richie gave the money back. He was too embarrassed about people like Slash coming up to him and going, "You know what, man? It's a really shitty thing you did to the kids." He fuckin' gave it all back. So you can see what kind of person [Richie] is – rock solid.'

Today, when interviewers persistently try to needle Bach by raising the subject of Bon Jovi, the otherwise verbose singer remains tight-lipped. In 1995 he finally admitted: 'I'm not allowed to talk about that, because Bon Jovi made me sign a legal document saying that we couldn't talk about each other in the press . . .'

The topic is continually raised with Jon, too, who normally opts to deflect the question. In July 1995, however, he, too, gave as succinct an answer as anyone could ever need.

'I took a gamble. It's like we said years ago: if it works, it works. If it had failed, I'd have been out [of pocket] and Skid Row would have said thank-you and that's that. Fortunately, it worked . . . I *know* I didn't give them a bad deal. I don't want to get into the business of it, but I invested almost a million dollars into that band to make sure it happened. And I barely got my money back . . .'

But once the story had been made public, no amount of money could repair Jon's ideal of an extended 'Jersey Syndicate' family . . .

(To be continued . . .)

# CHAPTER FIVE

# The Break-up

*'I don't want anyone thinking this is a solo thing. I have to restate it
time and time again. This is a soundtrack.'*
Jon Bon Jovi says what nobody believes about *Blaze Of Glory*, 1990

*'I hope that I can keep it together, but I'll only keep it together if it's
fun. I can't do it for the money and I can't do it to keep the record
company happy. I can't do it unless it's going to be a good time.'*
Jon Bon Jovi says what everybody believes about Bon Jovi, 1990

*'I said, "Look man, I pretty much gave my life to this band for
ten years. I'm trying as hard as I can . . . It's gonna be done
when it gets done and that's it."'*
Richie Sambora on being asked to hurry back to Bon Jovi, 1991

ORIGINALLY, WHEN the band ended the *New Jersey* tour, the
plan was pretty clear cut: stop work now, or stop work for
good. That choice was presented to Jon as little short of an
ultimatum by the rest of his band. Although he still had reserves
of strength and ambition left, he had pushed the other four to
and beyond their personal limits.

Despite all the lessons they thought they had learned
touring with *Slippery When Wet*, the band had fallen into a lot
of the same traps and no one in the set-up was feeling

particularly pleased. What should have been a case of once bitten, twice shy had instead left the band, even before the end of the tour, feeling fatigued and antagonized, needing time away from the road and – for the first time – each other.

Jon felt let down. Bon Jovi had always played together and stayed together. He felt he'd looked after them well. On the last tour, compared to most other bands, they had lived in comparative luxury on private jets and the world's finest hotels ... Jon was the last one to appreciate that the band had been on the album-tour treadmill for way too long. And while he claimed he was happy to continue, the others were gradually closing ranks against him.

'If you looked in the dictionary under "burned out", you'll find our pictures,' joked Bryan yet again. Alec Jon Such, too, told Jon that he was so burned out he hardly knew what he was doing, that he only kept going because Jon wanted him to. In the end, Richie just had to spell it out to him: 'We were a little tired, burnt out. Constantly travelling for sixteen months, you kinda like lose yourself. I left the Richie Sambora I knew back in a hotel room in month eight. You just end up becoming a walking rock'n'roll zombie, a robot . . .'

So as Bon Jovi came to England in January 1990, a month before the tour would end in Mexico, the band sat down together and came up with a plan to take a year out. Actually, Jon somehow found himself volunteering to continue to work, albeit in an entirely different vein, sifting through tapes made of shows on the tour and mixing them for a proposed live album. Richie and Dave Bryan were also planning busman's holidays: the guitarist plotting to do his own thing and record a 'Richie Sambora And Friends' album, a mixture of cover versions, some new solo tunes and perhaps a reworking of a Bon Jovi tune or two; while, according to Jon, Dave Bryan planned to make a New Age instrumental album (it surfaced as a suitably morbid score for the soundtrack of a movie called

*The Netherworld*). Tico Torres was seemingly the only one smart enough to take a proper break, ultimately spending his time working towards a pilot's licence and uncovering his latent talent as an artist.

But just a month later, as the tour actually ended, the plans changed. Maybe Jon was thinking that a few months holed up in the studio listening to tapes of himself didn't sound too much like a vacation after all. He took a little time out to jam at a charity show in Asbury Park with members of Springsteen's E Street Band and steadily came to realize that, with this amount of time set aside, it was as good a chance as he'd had since he started the band to just please himself. And so it was that he found himself not concerned with Bon Jovi live albums, but with *Young Guns II*, out in New Mexico with Emilio Estevez, watching the movie being shot and thinking about writing more songs to complete the soundtrack album.

The way Jon tells it, it happened that simply. It didn't happen because of internal strife or Bon Jovi all going their separate ways. It was the result of coincidences and his own spur of the moment decision. That his decision would ultimately act like a wedge driven into the future of the band was something he could not have known when he took it.

Nevertheless, when in August 1990 Vertigo released the single 'Blaze Of Glory' it was quite a step forward for Jon Bon Jovi – not least because it made it all the way to the top of the *Billboard* charts. It was the first time since the coming together of his band that he'd gone out alone. The record was a song inspired by the title of the movie, *Young Guns II – Blaze Of Glory*, a sequel to the youth-oriented brat-pack *Young Guns* Western released two years earlier and also starring Emilio Estevez as Billy The Kid.

The release of the single occurred at a time when many people assumed that it confirmed what rumours had been maintaining for months – that Bon Jovi as a band were no more, ostensibly because since the last tour, Jon and Richie Sambora were no longer on speaking terms. So with the single getting loads of airplay and climbing somewhere near the top ten of America's *Billboard* chart, it seemed fair to assume that here was Jon proving that he could do it on his own. That the band was then and he was now. Fair, but wrong.

'I don't want anyone thinking this is a solo thing. I have to restate it time and time again. This is a soundtrack. It's for a movie. And that's all it's supposed to be,' he told Mick Wall. 'I had to write it to fit a certain parameter [and] the parameters I had to write to were so limiting . . .'

His reluctance to have it seen as a solo album made on his own terms, whatever the future of Bon Jovi, probably also stemmed from a never spoken admission that he would have been expected – and wanted – to do a lot better if this were really the record to launch his solo career.

When Jon Bon Jovi makes seemingly off-the-cuff remarks like 'I set out to write ten songs, hope you like them, end of story' and then refers to the record as 'this soundtrack I just spat out', it's fairly obvious that it's not up to the standards he has publicly or privately set himself.

In the interviews to promote it he would say he was excited by the idea of it, but never came right out and said how he ranked it alongside what he was capable of with the band. In truth, *Blaze Of Glory* contained a couple of good songs but was a far from classic album, and a much lesser work than, for instance, *New Jersey*. For a frame of reference he used the songs of one of his heroes, the late Phil Lynott, self-styled outlaw leader of Thin Lizzy, but Jon felt himself creatively limited.

'I could only write songs for particular scenes that some other guy came up with,' he continued, almost apologetically.

'I have to keep restating that 'cause I don't want anyone reviewing the album as if this is a solo album and I can only write about this . . .' 'This' being cowboys. Over the years, he'd taken a lot of flack, most of it good-natured, but all of it ultimately tiresome, suggesting that he was obsessed with the days of the Wild West and could only write songs about it. A wholly exaggerated notion but one that was fuelled by the constant success of 'Wanted Dead Or Alive' and its unforgettable line about a cowboy riding a steel horse. Which was, of course, exactly what attracted the movie's producers to him in the first place. Originally, they wanted to use that track in the sequel, even going as far as to claim that it had played a big part in the genesis of the first *Young Guns*, a movie they wrote with 'Wanted Dead Or Alive' very much in mind – especially given its target audience of MTV watchers who (unlike Jon) may never have seem a John Ford Western or even heard of John Wayne or Gary Cooper.

'I was really flattered. I like the first *Young Guns* movie a lot. And I always said that if I'd ever acted in a movie, it would have been in *Young Guns* . . .

'Lyrically, though, ['Wanted Dead Or Alive'] wouldn't have worked . . . So I said, "If you want, I'll write something in that vein to fit this part of the movie." I knew where it was going, they told me what it was about. [So then] I went there with a song in hand, which was 'Blaze Of Glory'. They liked it. And then I came home and wrote three more. So now I'd got four songs, all based upon what they told me about the movie, so they said, "Great! Let's do an album".'


The album featured guest appearances by three very big stars, namely: Elton John, Little Richard and Jeff Beck. At one time

Jon considered approaching Keith Richards, too, although this notion remained only the stuff of fantasy.

Formerly of The Yardbirds, and the Jeff Beck Group and lately solo star, Jeff Beck is the guitarist's guitarist, respected the world over for his unique approach to the Fender Stratocaster: a mind-boggling mixture of gentle touch and violent string bending. He was an old friend of Jon's, having watched the band play in London on many occasions. Beck was the first person Jon contacted and he agreed so quickly – recommending their respective managers talk immediately – that Jon believed he was merely trying to get him off the phone. But Beck was as good as his word and arrived at the studios in Los Angeles a day earlier than Jon.

Legendary rock'n'roller Little Richard had also been to a Bon Jovi gig before, even playing with them on the previous tour, and so had no hesitation in accepting Jon's invitation to come down to the studio. When he arrived, the man most anxious to meet him was not Jon, but Jeff Beck. 'Jeff was so excited and nervous,' laughed Jon later. 'When Richard walked into the control room [Jeff's] fingers started playing "Lucille". Richard put his hand out to me and Jeff jumps out of his seat and gives him his hand and says, "It's so nice to meet you. You're the reason I got into this business." Then asks him for his autograph . . .'

Ironically, Beck never got to record alongside Little Richard, whose contributions to 'You Really Got Me Now' didn't need the embellishment of a guitar solo. But in return for the introduction, Beck later introduced Jon to one of his old heroes, Rod Stewart, who had so inspired Jon when he sang in the Jeff Beck Group.

Jon's childhood idol, Elton John, was yet another of the Bon Jovi backstage alumni. After going to one of their shows he had later invited Jon to play with him at Madison Square

Garden in New York. An honour Jon was delighted to accept. 'There's a guy that's a songwriter, consummate songwriter and performer, and a great guy as well . . . a real sweetheart who just loves playing piano. [When] I played with him at Madison Square Garden . . . I felt I had a friend in Elton.'

Strange to think, then, that Jon was afraid to ask him to do any more than play piano once he arrived at the sessions. 'One song in particular that I wrote on the piano really lent itself to Elton – "Dyin' Ain't Much Of A Livin'" '. To me, it sounds like an Elton John song. To me, it was like he's the only guy who can play this song. Then in the control room he started to sing the harmony. All along I was dying to get him to sing the harmony and he started doing it, so there was my in. I went, "Hey! Why don't you sing it?" So we did it live and the vocal was right there . . .'

Bruce Springsteen's piano player, Roy Bittan, had once been booked for the session but Bruce vetoed the plan as he wanted Bittan to concentrate all his energies on the tracks he was co-producing at the time – Bruce's *Human Touch* sessions, which eventually saw the light of day in 1992.

Others in the *Blaze Of Glory* studio included Jon's old friend Aldo Nova and co-producer Danny Kortchmar – but none who would have been involved were it a Bon Jovi band album. To Jon, this was to be a studio-only project and he gave no thought to touring in support of the album. Still, though, he tried to avoid giving the impression that he was ditching the band and going it alone.

'I honest to God had no intention of doing a solo venture because to me, Bon Jovi albums are my solo albums. There's not any songs, really, that I adamantly didn't want on any of the Bon Jovi records. If I didn't want something, it wasn't there.'

But as of August, when *Blaze Of Glory* was released, he really was out on his own. From that perspective he was able to consider what kind of person he had become since he first broke onto the international scene.

'I'm a little more cynical and sceptical. I hope I am nicer [but] other people would have to tell me whether I am or not. I still have a lot of energy and I am excited. That's probably another reason why the band are going their own ways. We are supposed to, like human beings do, take some time off.

'I gotta settle down. The way I figure it is, if I was to sit with Freud or one of those guys, he'd tell me it was because I hate my wife or mother or something. Because all I like to do is go and work. I dig making records . . .'

It's unlikely that Freud – or any of those guys – would have told him anything of the sort. Although they'd doubtless be curious about why he himself would suggest it. Instead, any cod philosopher could read between his lines and see that in reality Jon was merely a workaholic, a little selfish maybe, a little insecure perhaps, and seemingly driven by the fear of losing the limelight and all the respect that came with it. Continuing on his own while Bon Jovi took a break was merely his way of gaining self-assurance. He actually continued to work until March 1991, thirteen months after the *New Jersey* tour ended.

'I think it was like withdrawal, in retrospect. I did the *Youngs Guns II* thing which was never planned but when that was done I was like, "Oh god, what now?" You can't go on the road with a soundtrack thing so I kinda reached around, went out, did a short tour with Southside Johnny And The Asbury Jukes, my heroes, I went on the road just playing guitars with Johnny, from there I withdrew into producing Stevie Nicks, Hall & Oates and Aldo Nova, that kind of stuff, again kinda further removing myself – because had I stopped [I would have gone] cold turkey, gone into convulsions. I had to detox slowly.'

The work with the former Fleetwood Mac songstress and

lovably infamous airhead Stevie Nicks arose off the back of the *Blaze Of Glory* sessions in Los Angeles' A&M Studios. Together they recorded one track 'Sometimes It's A Bitch', later used on her forthcoming Best Of album. When it was released, she said of her sessions with Jon: 'When I first heard this song, I really did not quite understand what Jon was trying to say . . . but over the two weeks that we sang it together [at my mike], I started to realize that Jon, without knowing it, had sort of taken a time machine back eighteen years and watched my life . . . He dreamed about what the notorious Stevie Nicks had been like.' Quite.

The opportunity of writing and producing a single with rock/soul partnership Hall & Oates (the long established act he had once supported years back) again arose through his work on the soundtrack. 'I'm real excited by [that] avenue,' he said. 'I'm blown away that Daryll Hall and John Oates have asked me to work with them. I was even happier afterwards when they would tell people, "He's a real producer". I guess coming from them, that's a compliment.'

Working with his friend Aldo Nova, Jon wrote fifteen songs, then produced and released the album *Blood On The Bricks* on his own Jambco label.

As well as avoiding going cold turkey, all that activity was a kind of insurance against what so many were predicting. When asked if there would ever be another Bon Jovi band album, it was clear that thoughts of making the split permanent had obviously entered his mind, however reluctantly. He was forced to admit that the answer was only a tentative 'I hope so [but] I don't know so . . . I'm as confused as anyone. I want it to stay together because it's been so good but I don't want it if it is no longer good. Unless I want to have a beer with those guys every night like we always have, then . . .'

\*

The doubts had begun, he explained to Mick Wall, when *Kerrang!* magazine had printed a short news story that read: 'Don't be surprised if and when Bon Jovi record again, it's with a different line-up. Drummer Tico Torres is rumoured to be leaving ... The band have a live record in the pipeline, but plan an extended break so that Jon and the others can pursue different activities. Richie Sambora, of course, is to make a solo LP and show us that he is, as many have already observed, the best singer in the band.'

The item, written by Los Angeles-based stringer Brian Brandes Brinkerhoff, was based on grapevine gossip and, with hindsight, rather bizarrely buried on page six of the issue after a clip that announced Yes were about to appoint former World Trade vocalist Billy Sherwood as the permanent replacement for founder member Jon Anderson. This, like the Tico Torres rumour, never turned to fact but whereas Yes barely blinked an eyelid, Bon Jovi suffered a major trauma.

'We were in Mexico, at the end of the tour, with nothing but wonderful things happening,' said Jon. 'We were finishing the tour doing stadiums, which is just how we wanted to end, and we were feeling real good.

'Suddenly, we got drummer tapes and pictures and everything coming in. It was like, "Hey Tico, are you quitting the band?" He was like, "First I've heard of it man!"' (Tico subsequently worked alongside Jon on the Stevie Nicks sessions.)

*Kerrang!* is a UK magazine that has only ever sold abroad in limited numbers, usually less than 3,000 overseas, but that story was seen by enough people in the business, including drummers hoping for a better gig, to turn the smoking ember of a rumour into a raging inferno of a crisis. Jon claims to have thrown his copy out of the window, upset because he knew the story was untrue, but the idea wouldn't go away. Meanwhile, the magazine fielded calls from ambitious drummers, and, convinced it had the inside track on the hottest gossip, ran a follow-up story a couple of months later. 'Bon Jovi Split!' blazed a coverline, while its lead news story was tagged 'Bye-bye Jonny . . .' This time, the magazine quoted rumours, believed to have stemmed from members of the roadcrew, that pointed to a row between Jon and Richie in Mexico after the final show, and even went as far as to suggest that the bone of contention between the pair was the guitarist's cut of the purse. Doc McGhee, meanwhile, had allegedly taken Richie's side in the disagreement.

The guitarist later denied this rumour saying dismissively: 'We fought before – but it wasn't at the end of the tour. We've certainly duked it out a few times, but there's definitely no problem with that. Listen, man, in New Jersey where we come from, if we can't kick the shit out of each other, who *can* we kick the shit out of?

'You've got to be man enough to be able to get mad at each other. You can't be sissy. You have to be grown up enough to have differences of opinions sometimes. You can't be afraid to air that. It's just getting used to growing up . . .'

But growing pains or not, the story also referred to another source of friction between the pair, suggesting that Richie was growing tired of second billing in the partnership and of having to stand by while Jon spoke to audiences about the band in the first person, and the records as 'my albums'. Also highly significant, but at that time not widely known, were Jon and Richie's disagreements over the Skid Row/Underground deal.

Unaware of this darker side to the story, the UK's best-selling daily tabloid the *Sun* picked up on the conflict between Jon and Richie and ran its version under the predictably flamboyant heading 'All Ovi For Bon Jovi'. Intrigued by the *Kerrang!* story, the *Sun* had apparently done some digging of its own and suggested that Richie was leaving the band to work with Cher, whom he was dating at the time. Jon had always known the value of the UK media as a supportive tool, now he was discovering that it could be an equally potent destructive force.

'That's the English press,' he later told Q, 'and, man, the English press is powerful because that shit goes world-fucking-wide. Once it gets in the English gossip rags it goes across the board and to tell the truth, it caused a lot of tension in the band, an incredible lot of tension . . .'

Official sources would comment only that a double live album, compiled from recordings made throughout the tour, was due later in 1990 (it never materialized) and as far as they and the band were concerned, the issue was closed, with Jon and Richie looking forward to their respective solo albums and the rest of Bon Jovi apparently about to take a long overdue rest.

Meanwhile, in New Jersey, a bemused Jon Bon Jovi was standing by his fax machine, watching the white paper curling out and getting more and more upset. After four months of fielding calls from guitarists volunteering their services, Jon could no longer laugh it off.

'It's got to this point,' he said at the time, 'because the five of us haven't been in the same room together since before the last show and it's added fuel to the fire. So now all of us are believing there are problems. I can't tell you what the problems are about, but we think we've got problems . . . Right now, in July 1990 . . . things are not happy in the Bon Jovi camp, that's for sure. They're not happy at all.'

Part of the problem was undoubtedly with Richie and all the positive attention the media had granted him lately. In a totally candid moment Jon admitted: 'Everyone gives Rich a lot of attention – and well deserved it is, he's a fine musician and a fine singer – but I don't think it's fair to harp on about him all the time because it was us and the *band*. For the first two albums, he never wrote any of the singles. Dave Bryan co-wrote the singles. It was Dave and I who did it. Richie came in on the third album when he had begun to understand the way I like to write. It wasn't until the third album so it's not fair for everyone to pick on him.'

If he was aware that he was coming over like a spoilt schoolboy, Jon wasn't about to bite his tongue. But pick that quote apart and it doesn't take a genius to see that, as *Slippery When Wet* was the third album, Richie was clearly instrumental in catapulting Bon Jovi to the position they now enjoyed. Who could blame the press if, after watching Richie shine so spectacularly singing 'Blood On Blood' on the previous tour, they chose to focus attention on the hitherto largely overlooked sideman. Perhaps, after seven years of reviewing the band, many had merely run out of new things to say about the frontman and were casting their net wider in search of good copy. Given that premise, it wouldn't take the eyes and ears long to focus on Richie Sambora.

Jon could surely see that but was nonetheless upset by it. Publicly, he was looking around for reasons why the band weren't communicating and the future was so vague. If things in the Bon Jovi camp weren't as they had been, he could only look to the past and hypothesize why. First and foremost in his mind was the seen-it-all, done-it-all factor. After all their years together, each member had seen just about every personal and professional ambition fulfilled. They'd gone from an opening act to a headliner, from a moderate seller to a band with platinum discs, after relative flops they'd had number one singles.

After the early successes, much of what the band were doing in 1990 was retracing their steps, confirming their status, broadening their demographics in an effort to consolidate their markets. There were no real challenges anymore and life on the road had become more of a job than a thrill-a-minute roller-coaster ride into the unknown. But Jon was still perplexed –

how could something that had gone so right, have suddenly turned so wrong. It left a sour taste in his mouth and no predisposition, it seemed, to pick up the phone and call the band together for a clear-the-air meeting. Jon could merely reflect that the band might be at the same crossroads so many other bands had reached.

'We always grew up hearing , "Boy, Van Halen were dumb to split [with singer Dave Lee Roth] . . ." But none of us in the general public know what the real problem was. Same with Journey, same with Aerosmith.'

Drugs and alcohol abuse had played a major part in the problems of Van Halen and Aerosmith. With San Francisco band Journey, the issues were more about ego clashes when their hugely talented singer, Steve Perry, walked out in 1985, leaving behind a string of multi-platinum successes in North America that made a mockery of their stature in Europe. Five years later, when Perry was struggling to get a solo career back into gear, he and Jon met. 'Steve said to me, "You're right where I was when I left Journey . . ." You go like, "Wow, I don't know if I should walk away from it."'

It was a sobering thought but one Jon could counter with reason. 'I know that I'll still make records and I'll still be able to tour but who cares about the money? That's not why I'm doing it. It's only if it's going to be fun that I'll continue with those four guys . . .' Somehow, the very crux of Bon Jovi, that one-for-all all-for-one camaraderie had been forgotten. All the talk about brotherhood and 'till kingdom come' in 'Blood On Blood' on *New Jersey* was developing a noticeably hollow ring. 'That period in our career was definitely a dark time. We were mentally and physically exhausted,' Jon later reflected.

'Regardless of money and stadiums, or who I played with, if [the *Blaze Of Glory* musicians] were the band tomorrow and Elton was my new keyboard player, it would never be the same. All of that would be lost and I don't want that to happen. I definitely don't want that to happen. I want to keep it together 'cause these are the guys who [were here] seven years ago ... when we didn't have enough money for a pretzel across the street and no one knew whether Bon Jovi was jeans or what the fuck it was.

'We had to fight for everything we got and we had to fight even on the *New Jersey* album to prove we were gonna be around. It's a rewarding feeling to know that the band as a unit did this. I could play with better musicians, and they could play with a better songwriter and singer, but it wouldn't be the same, ever.'

For a while in 1990, it looked as if all parties might get the chance to find out what life would be like without each other when Sebastian Bach of Skid Row let the cat out of the bag about his band's conflict with Jon over the Underground deal – and how Richie had already returned his share of the monies earned. It was a huge story that others all over the world picked up on, but Jon maintained a silence. The next week his second solo single 'Miracle' was released but he still never offered a comment on the matter.

The silence was all the more intriguing because of the recent history of disquiet in the Bon Jovi camp. Now that evidence of another friction between Jon and Richie had been made public, one of them might reasonably have been expected to come forward with an explanation, an olive branch even. That neither of them did only seemed to underline the fast-spreading belief that the band would never work together again.

Richie, in particular, was keeping his cards very close to his chest as he set about securing a deal for his own forthcoming solo record. Only Jon was contracted directly to PolyGram and some reports suggested that another major had bid $5 million for the guitarist's signature. Whether that was true or not, it certainly wouldn't have done Richie's case any harm when he and Doc McGhee came to negotiate and settle with PolyGram's Mercury imprint.

Whatever battles he was fighting in private, Richie later claimed to have been certain of the outcome. The guitarist finally broke his silence on the matter in March 1991 when, already hard at work on his own solo album, he spoke of Bon Jovi having enjoyed a 'healthy break' and a 'period of adjustment'. More importantly for his and Jon's personal and business relationship, the matter of Skid Row's publishing royalties had, he said, been settled to his satisfaction. He would, however, offer no details and refused to be drawn when asked if Jon had followed his reported lead and returned to Skid Row his share of the monies earned through the Underground contract, merely adding obliquely that, 'the situation is changing'.

It must have been a welcome respite for Jon then, to sit tuxedoed and groomed at the Golden Globes awards ceremony where he had been nominated for 'Blaze Of Glory'. He went along with Dorothea just to see what it was like, genuinely expecting nothing more. 'When I won the Golden Globe, I had no idea who was even up for it, I didn't know. We went, Dorothea and I, and Meryl Streep was singing a song from whatever movie that she was in so we both said, well, she's gonna win it. So when they called my name we were just shocked. We had no idea. The people we went with said, "Listen, right after your award, when you lose, we'll just slip out this door . . ." But when we won it was just, "Shit! I don't believe it."' A month or so later they were in LA again, this time at the Academy Awards.

'But we knew we weren't gonna win the Oscar because it

was Sondheim, it was that kind of deal, Stephen Sondheim [up for his *Dick Tracey* soundtrack]. Especially at the time I did it, rock songs and rock artists weren't going to beat *Sondheim* . . .'

But even though to be nominated was no mean feat, Jon was not a happy camper. In fact, in terms of his contentment with the Bon Jovi situation, he had reached the lowest point and even as the Golden Globe offered him a chink of light, proof that there was another way out, still the idea that he was losing his band infuriated him.

'All the innocence was being sucked out. What I wanted to do as a kid had all gotten taken away. And it took a while to come to terms with that. I thought about not doing it any more or doing it by myself. Because *Blaze Of Glory* was successful, I certainly didn't need the guys in the band. I had a number one record. I was sitting at the Oscars, which was pretty good.

'But I didn't want that. I wasn't mad at the band. It was just that we didn't know what was the matter . . .'

At the peak of his career in terms of personal public recognition, Jon reached the very lowest ebb of personal and private esteem. For the first time in his life he admitted his depression to the extent of accepting a friend's advice to visit a psychiatrist, not a profession he has ever held in very high esteem. With a one hour appointment made, he drove to the address he had been given – and promptly got lost. Having arrived three-quarters of an hour late and apologized, his counsellor called time as the minute hand reached the hour, after just fifteen minutes, and Jon left a psychiatrist's office for the last time.

'I was on . . . fuckin' . . . the bottom. Where you looked out the window and thought, Jesus, well, that's not the answer. But I looked, you know? And I thought, "You scumbag . . ."' And from there Jon found his own inner strength and devised his own solutions.

In 1995, speaking to Jeffrey Hudson, Richie admitted that

his and Jon's problem was very much of their own creation, born of stubbornness.

'It's just that we were together – literally – for the eight years preceding that time. We were the kind of band that holidayed together – we were disgusting. We were in each other's faces all the time for eight years, and when you're that successful that you do two sixteen-month tours back to back, you find yourself desperate for your own space.

'We just weren't really communicating at that point. He was doing his solo album, I was doing mine and we never seemed to tie up. [But] I don't think there was ever any real danger of us splitting, it was just a question of when we'd get together again. In my heart I always knew the band would survive, because no one ever said, "Fuck you, the band stinks, and I'm out of here".'

Ironically, it wasn't until around the time that Richie himself was working on a solo album that Jon actually took a break from recording and producing. Even then he couldn't let work – or Bon Jovi – go completely. 'I took a full year to do nothing but concentrate on writing for us and living my life. Really not doing interviews, not doing photo sessions, not recording, not going near a studio. And it was a wonderful time.'

Most significant amongst that time, were the weeks he spent riding across America on a motorbike. 'To me that was my solace. I found a place where I could go and be absolutely by myself. And then stop and be with my friends again – there were five bikes in all (five guys, four girls, five bikes). In essence I was just rediscovering America, finding out who I was, where I fitted, how I felt about things. I came to a lot of realizations doing that.'

He spent three weeks out on the road, regularly rising at seven in the morning and riding until seven at night. 'Whenever it got dark, that's when we would sleep. We stayed wherever we stopped, motels . . . Anything more than twenty-five bucks a night was too good for us. Instead of seeing Mount Rushmore out the window of your own private plane and telling the pilot to circle it again, I could really see it the right way.'

For most of the time he could genuinely turn his back on his public persona and be just another biker, given anonymity by his helmet 99 per cent of the time. 'The odd time when I did get into a situation it was more like in a tourist town on a weekend, like when we were in Carlsbad [New Mexico]. Carlsbad Canyons are there, the word got out. It became a situation where it was, "Oh right, I've got to be *him* again." But I forgot what all that was about for quite a long time.'

The trip was a wholly rejuvenating experience for Jon, allowing him to discover new truths not only about himself but also his country as he travelled through towns that Bon Jovi had never played in. 'It was my Jack Kerouac "On The Road" experience,' he quipped, 'and it changed my life.'

It may even have changed Jon to the point where he was prepared to cement his relationship with Dorothea and become a father (although that wouldn't happen for a couple more years) and more trivial things would filter through first. Things like a new grasp of native geography.

'It was a wonderful re-discovering of America. I found a lot of great culture there. I've always thought there is no culture in America – you want culture? Go to Europe. You want tra-dition? Go to Asia. I always said, America's too young, too varied in its populace. But it's not the case . . .'

The real reason Bon Jovi survived, however, was not the refreshment offered by all this extra-curricular activity, but Jon's dawning realization of what he stood to lose by going it alone.

'It built my own confidence to know I could write number one songs by myself, and play with guys like Beck and Elton. It was a big coming of age period for me. But what was missing was the camaraderie. It was pretty lonely. Because [Bon Jovi] really did hang out together, those stories weren't bullshit . . .'

Measuring the quality of the stars he had worked with as a solo artist against what he had been missing, he concluded: 'Great musicians don't necessarily make great bands. There are 50,000 better singers than me and at least that many better songwriters than me, but when the five of us are together, it's magic because it's fun . . .'

Jon finally made the decision to get the band together to talk once more when they were offered the chance to play a short tour of Japan at the end of 1990 – a show in Tokyo on New Year's Eve followed by a short Japanese tour in early January 1991. It was clear to all concerned that this would be a 'make or break' outing. Jon was reported as saying that if the dates proved fun to play, the band would regroup in the spring – if not he would continue to work solo.

According to Richie: 'I remember getting a call and him saying, "Hey, look, they're booking this gig in Tokyo . . ." At the time, I was in the middle of my record. So I basically put my record on hold for three weeks while Bon Jovi rehearsed and then played. But we just said if we went out there and had fun together, then we would continue. We did. It was blast . . . I think it was more [important] to Jon than the rest of us because he was having success with his solo record at the time – his record sold 2 million copies – and he certainly didn't need to come back to the band if he didn't want to.'

And so the five agreed to give it another shot. They organized a charity concert at the Count Basie Theatre in Red Bank, New Jersey on 23 December then after Christmas flew to Japan. Tellingly, they chose as support acts Cinderella and, to open the show, Skid Row. Whatever Jon may have thought about Sebastian Bach, and whatever the irony, he clearly wasn't going to let it affect his relationship with and support for his good friend Snake or, of course, Richie. On the back of the news of these dates, in December 1990 the band made a very public display of unity by assembling for a press conference to announce the release of nothing more than a video – *Access All Areas: A Rock 'N' Roll Odyssey*. It was a calculated step to pour a little oil on the troubled waters. The plan worked. Public perception of Bon Jovi began to revert to that of a band who were a living breathing unit, not one on the verge of a split.

Even more successful, however, were the Japanese shows. 'Japan proved to us just how good it could be,' said Richie. 'When the five of us get together it can be magical.'

Despite all the evidence to the contrary, Jon has always adamantly denied that the band had ever actually broken up repeating over and over that 'we had to take time off. That's all part of what kept us together,' and adding with a degree of finality: 'The family should keep things to itself . . .'

Ironically, though, before the family could truly get together again, it would have to cut one of its members – Richie Sambora – the necessary slack to do his own 'solo thing' . . .

While history suggests that those Christmas 1990 Japanese gigs tipped the scales in the favour of old friendships, Richie's solo album, *Stranger In This Town*, was already in hand and so took precedence over Jon's hints that he planned to get the band back together once more. Nevertheless the guitarist, too, was quick to squash rumours of a permanent split. He had little choice, it was inevitably the first question he had to face as he sat down to begin a bit of advance promotional work for his album.

'Bon Jovi are a family and families fight. Yes, me and Jon had our differences but the family is back together again. Bon Jovi are full-on again.'

At that point (in 1991) this was pretty far from the truth. It was damn close to bravado but it wasn't a line that would get him through a lie detector test. For despite the relief of Japan, Jon was then writing songs that might just as easily become contenders for a second solo album as the next Bon Jovi group record. And lurking in the background, like an angry cloud, was Jon and Richie's differences over the Underground deal with Skid Row. An uneasy peace had been reached, although initially Richie wouldn't be drawn far on the nature of Jon's settlement.

'I didn't want to be a record company executive, I wanted to be an artist, so I decided to bow out. Jon dissolved The Underground and he has his own company [Jambco]. He decided to continue but I really had no interest in it . . .'

Richie, instead, was trying to put the messy business with Skid Row far behind him by looking for positives. 'I think the time Jon spent on his record has afforded the rest of the band a period of adjustment. As a band we just didn't give the public a break. For almost three-and-a-half years we were constantly in people's faces. Bon Jovi were ever present. It had to come to the point where we all needed space and time to breathe again.'

More importantly, after three-and-a-half years, it was the band who were enjoying a break from being in each other's faces. 'I actually took my free time right at the end of the tour,' said Richie. 'I was dead. I fell off the cliff. I was living with Cher at the time so I went to stay at her house. I took about three months off before I even started to write.'

Richie's romance with Cher earned many inches in tabloid gossip columns around the world. They had met in 1987, a busy year for her which saw the release of three movies – *The Witches Of Eastwick*, *Moonstruck* and *Suspect*. The same year, Richie and Jon worked with her on 'a Led Zeppelin-esque reworking' of her 1966 second solo hit 'Bang Bang (My Baby Shot Me Down)' and also co-wrote her 'We All Sleep Alone' hit with Desmond Child.

As a teenager working at the Power Station, Jon had met and lusted after her, but by this time he was content with Dorothea and it was Richie she was attracted to. Jon later claimed he found the turnaround highly amusing. 'I thought it was the greatest thing ever! I always thought she was a very sexy woman [and] here we are working with her, and before you know it Richie's *really* working her. I used to get a kick out of it – I'd ask him for gory details . . .'

Richie rarely spoke of her in interviews and whether he ever passed anything on to Jon seems unlikely. In any case, she used to hang around the band often enough for Jon's curiosity to (presumably) pass. 'Whenever she was with us,' said the singer, 'she acted like one of the guys in the band. She never had any star trips. She's a classy chick. Boy, she could deal with the president tonight and the road crew in the morning. Hey, I meant that in a *social* manner . . .'

Away from the band, she helped Richie come down from the rigours of touring with *New Jersey*.

'That was the detox period,' he recalls. 'When you get out of that rhythm of just getting on a plane every day and going to a different city, a different hotel room, going to the gig, doing the gig, getting the adoration of 20,000 – although we were doing stadiums at the end so it was more like 80,000 people per day – it was kinda like a fix so I detoxed from that. I wrote my record. And then I went to the studio.'

Richie Sambora is the only part of the Bon Jovi set-up apart from Jon himself that could truly be described as irreplaceable. In the early years of the band he was just another haircut alongside the pretty face in the picture, but as the albums and tours rolled by his stature within the band – and in the eyes of the fans – had grown to the point where he was very nearly a star in his own right.

Playing no small part in this has been Richie's penchant for dating beautiful and high profile women, with names like Cher, singer Bekka Bramlett (later of Fleetwood Mac), actress Ally Sheedy all going into his address book before he more recently met and then married actress Heather Locklear.

During that time, his personal and professional relationships with Jon blossomed and advanced as they became two often very different sides of the same rich coin. 'With us it's like thunder and lightning,' Richie once said. 'It's basically a healthy debate, but we do stand there and yell at each other. To outsiders it can be alarming [but] we don't fall out often at all.'

A lot of that is based on the conflict between Jon's workaholic persona and Richie's more chilled-out and laid-back style, but that is the very thing that makes their partnership strong – and precisely the reason why Richie warrants a chapter of his own in any Jon Bon Jovi story.

He went out on his own with a mixture of relief and concern. He really had no wish to leave Bon Jovi. 'It's a privilege to be in a big band like Bon Jovi and also have the artistic ability to vent your creative juices in a solo project,' he argued. 'I'm a very lucky guy to be able to do that.' But the truth was that however often he said that – and it would be very often, in interviews all around the world – the decision was not really in his hands.

As the name behind it and the singer at the front of Bon Jovi, Jon called the shots. And if Jon wanted to continue solo without Richie, or even reform the band without Richie, he could. All such decisions would ultimately be made by Jon and when Richie later ventured, 'I always thought there would be a band [again]. I didn't know when, exactly, but . . .' he was doing so with a mixture of gratitude and relief. For a while, a worrying thought had occurred to him: 'I think with the success of Jon's solo record he had a little thing in his mind that maybe he didn't want to go back to being in a band any more.'

These kind of thoughts, as much as any artistic ambition, were at the back of Richie's mind as he began to write material for his album. Only later, in the autumn of 1991 when *Stranger In This Town* was completed and ready for release, would hindsight allow him to paint over the cracks of his earlier nervousness with a few well chosen quotes.

'It was a dream of mine. It was inevitable that I was gonna do this record at some period of my life, I just didn't know when the right time was gonna be . . .' It might be inglorious to suggest it, but the right time was clearly whenever Jon decided, even if Richie maintained: 'I dedicated ten years of my life and cleared everything out, basically everything I had for Bon Jovi. Then it was like some little switch in my bio-circuitry went off and said, "This is your time right now. Your destiny is to pursue this."'

All those years sitting alongside Jon in interviews had clearly taught him a lot. Any conflict could be explained away with a liberal dose of rose-tinted hindsight or a humbling admission of frailty: 'It was something that I had wanted to do, something that I had always dreamed about doing. I guess that every artist wants to see if he can paint the picture by himself sometimes, too. It was a lot of fun. It was also very challenging, to become a frontman all of a sudden was a very frightening and challenging thing to do. I really enjoyed making the record.'

Yet to Richie's eternal credit, the record he made was an honest endeavour. He could have taken the easy route of updating or revising a dozen Bon Jovi hooks and harmonies. Instead, with one exception, he did it his way and proved that he was no sleeping partner in the J. Bon Jovi/R. Sambora partnership. Much has been made of the nature of the professional relationship between Jon and Richie, with comparisons even being drawn with the likes of Lennon/McCartney or Jagger/Richards, but Jon has always dismissed such conjecture as just milking a cliché. There is, of course, no reason why any of these pairings should function in the same ways. The only real similarity between the Bon Jovi/Sambora pairing and any of the others one might care to name, compare and contrast is that it doesn't *always* work. When it does, it works very well indeed, but like most things it scored best when one or both of them was particularly inspired.

Although the two shared much in common besides their professional relationship, they were both gifted individuals and the time spent apart allowed both of them to prove that. While Jon was off riding his motorcycle, Richie chose to kick back and enjoy being his own boss for a change. As Jon cruised the backroads of New Jersey, Richie was holed up in A&M Studios in Los Angeles recording his solo album with co-producer Neil Dorfsman. Alongside Richie were David Bryan and Tico Torres from Bon Jovi, sometime Peter Gabriel and King Crimson bassist Tony Levin and – on the track 'Mr. Bluesman' – a solo by Eric Clapton. Bryan co-wrote a couple of the songs but, with the exception of one other track, 'Rosie', Richie was clearly determined to break the Bon Jovi mould. ('Rosie', in fact, was a Bon Jovi leftover written by the guitarist with Jon, Desmond Child and Diane Warren.) But Richie was not making this record to produce more of the same. Indeed, as he admitted: 'The pressure was to stay away from anything like Bon Jovi.'

And although Jon's name appeared in the record's thanks list, as if to underline the tension between the two, it was not one of those that appeared in bold type. But enough, already . . .

In the writing and recording of the album, Richie had the chance to do more than score such points Although things were looking happier upon its release, when he started work on it his future was far from clear. He knew then that the record might need to be used as a possible launching pad for a future solo career. He went out of his way to make an album that proved he could stand on his own two feet, and as fine as the guitar work is, he devoted noticeably greater energy to his vocals while aiming for an altogether more adult-oriented sound.

As had Jon, Richie also took time out to turn his talents to help others. He worked with Cher and also recorded a cover of Jimi Hendrix's 'Wind Cries Mary' for the *Ford Fairlane* movie soundtrack.

When Richie came to speak in depth about making his own album, he inevitably talked too about the conflicts that had contributed to the band's current state of confusion.

'I wrote *Slippery When Wet* with Jon, recorded it, then toured it for sixteen-and-a-half months. Then we wrote *New Jersey*, recorded it, toured it for sixteen-and-a-half months. So for a four-and-a-half year period of time, I played just fifteen songs . . .

'It really bummed me out. I really wanted to go home. I asked Jon: "*Please* man!" It ain't worth the money, to me. I was losing my soul and I was losing myself . . . I wasn't getting anywhere with my personal relationships, because I was dedicating my life to just being in the band.

'In the time I took to make this record it seemed like all I was doing was slowing down life long enough so that I could get to be *better*. So that I could expand myself as a musician. So that I could become a better guitarist, a better singer, writer, producer . . . It was important to me because I felt very sterile towards the end of the last Bon Jovi tour – like I wasn't doing anything special.'

Richie cut no corners in the making of *Stranger In This Town*. The studios, the technicians and not least the musicians were all top-drawer high-earners. He took his time in making the record and was proud to say it had been completed without any 'financial ceiling' and exactly as he wanted it.

Much of his motivation was to re-inject a bit of humanism in an age when, as he saw it, MTV was laden with videos of bands who only knew how to look good but not necessarily how to play or write. (A situation, many have suggested, that Bon Jovi themselves had, albeit unwittingly, played no small part in creating.) Then, climbing down off his high horse, he would smile and admit:

'I'm a bit of an old hippie. That's the time period I come from. When I was a kid I used to rehearse down in my mother's basement with my "garage bands". I'd light candles and incense, drink beer and do psychedelic music . . . When we did pre-production for this record we used Tico's basement and did the same thing. We re-created that kind of innocence where it was great to play again . . .'

He created a similar kind of mood-lighting scenario in A&M studios. 'Instead of the studio being a way to do business, it became my laboratory. I had this wonderful, huge studio. I had everybody's equipment all set up, stage lighting, candles, millions of dollars worth of recording equipment – I didn't ever want to go home. At the end of the sessions, everyone else would but I'd stick around. I'd slip the engineer fifty bucks and say, "Hang with me, man. Roll the tape!"'

So pleased with this atmosphere was he, that Richie took the concept one step further by insisting the album artwork bore the following 'listening instructions': 'Turn down the lights, light a candle . . . welcome . . .'

Yet even while he was in the studio, he was still being plagued with 'a lot of legal things and business shit' – the dissolution of The Underground, Jon arranging new management and representation. Richie hinted at this aggravation but tactfully declined to name names and point fingers.

'There was a time frame in which people wanted me to get it done so that I could get back to the band. That was pretty much of a pressure – which I fucking ignored, basically. I said, "Look man, I pretty much gave my life to this band for ten years. I'm trying as hard as I can. I'm not bustin' anybody's balls ... It's gonna be done when it gets done and that's it."'

The record was released in August 1991, a couple of months later than originally planned but no one seemed to be counting. Its contents were true to Richie's simple promise of 'rock with an edge of blues and soul'. It also fulfilled his personal ambition to showcase his prowess on the guitar, something he thought had been stifled of late in Bon Jovi. 'There was more guitar playing on the first track than on the last two Bon Jovi albums' he later quipped.

The album was well received by the British press. Much better, in fact, than Jon's *Blaze Of Glory* album had been. But then, much of the media had become incredibly bored by the whole on-off Bon Jovi saga and instead were hoping that Richie's album would fare better than his (possibly former) employer's. Whether he'd been in the shadow or under the thumb of Jon Bon Jovi he wasn't saying, but here was his chance to hog the limelight.

'I think people might be surprised by the depth of this record,' Richie suggested. 'It's definitely not a Bon Jovi record, it's more spontaneous. It's something intimate. My heart and soul are all over this record.'

Later he would reflect: 'It was kinda about finding myself. After the huge success we'd had, it was a real whirlwind of constant recording and touring. I had to stick my head out of the water to breathe in and be able to see where the hell I was and who I was. And I needed to do it to find out if I was a valid musician.'

That's as may be, but he wrote 'River Of Love' not as a paean to some romantic waterway where he exchanged sweet nothings with a sweet someone, but as a celebration of cunnilingus . . .

Richie took to the road in the States in November 1991. By the time the tour was booked, it was already obvious that *Stranger In This Town* was unlikely to be vying for wall-space with Bon Jovi's platinum disc awards. Its sales, although far from the bottomless pit marked 'flop', were well below hopes. The tour itinerary kept him on the road for a couple of months, spilling over into 1992, playing theatres of – broadly speaking – around the 2,000 capacity mark. He took with him the same core band he had used on the album – Levin, Bryan and Torres – plus a second guitarist named Dave Amato and backing singer Crystal Tellava.

Many watching him believed he really was carrying on alone after Bon Jovi. Although the bulk of the show comprised material from *Stranger In This Town*, three BJ songs graced the set – 'Bad Medicine', 'I'll Be There For You' and 'Wanted Dead Or Alive' – and he admitted that without the familiar presence of Bryan and Torres in the band he would have struggled amidst all the other neuroses he was suffering from by working as a frontman. The sets also added 'We All Sleep Alone', the song Richie and Jon had written for Cher and covers of Greg Allman's 'Midnight Rider' and Lennon/McCartney's 'With A Little Help From My Friends' (as an encore).

Dates in Europe and the Far East, however, were never played because, as Richie put it, 'the money ran out'. 'The economy of the [US] went to pot. There were really bad problems with the record company – there was an interchange period of different people coming in and out – and it just kinda went south . . .'

Richie would come to be less circumspect about the record label support, describing it variously as 'sad' and 'a total disgrace'. In the end, the new staff just weren't prepared to stump up the cost of even a handful of dates overseas, considering them unlikely to recoup their investment in terms of record sales generated. (In the end, sales of *Stranger In This Town* fell just short of the platinum mark, peaking at 800,000 shortly after the tour had ended.) Richie ended up spending 'a lot' of his own money financing the US tour for his staff of twenty-five people, but the eventual lack of further tour support from Mercury meant that the rest of the projected dates were cancelled. He was hurt and disappointed but took solace in his belief that the relative failure had not been the fault of the music.

All the time he toured the States Jon was regularly speaking to him about getting Bon Jovi up and running again. With the US touring obligations fulfilled and no further dates on the horizon, Richie had little choice but to swallow his disappointment and return to the Bon Jovi fold: older, wiser and almost certainly rested and improved.

Quotes gratefully taken from:

Brian Brandes Brinkerhoff, *Kerrang!* 274, 27 January, 1990; Jon Hotten, *Kerrang!*, 283, 31 March 1990; Mick Wall, *Kerrang!* 300, 28 July, 1990; Mick Wall, *Kerrang!* 301, 4 August 1990; Adrian Deevoy, *Q* 52, January 1991; Chris Watts, *Kerrang!* 332, 16 March 1991; Paul Henderson, *Kerrang!* 362, 12 October 1991; Steve Mascord, *Kerrang!* 382, 7 March 1992; Dave Reynolds, *Kerrang!* 412, 3 October, 1992; Joe Mackett, *Riff Raff*, interview 16 October 1992; Johnny Walker, Radio 1, 7 November 1992; Chris Welch, *Rock World*, August 1993; Mick Wall, *Raw* 151, 8–21 June 1994; Dave Ling, *Raw* 151, 8–21 June 1994; Sylvie Simmons, *Kerrang!* 500, 25 June 1994; Steffan Chirazi, *Kerrang!* 513, 24 September 1994; Jeffrey Hudson, *Guitarist*, June 1995; David Hochman, *US*, August 1995.

# CHAPTER SIX

# The Faith

*'When it didn't come in at number one in America people were very quick to say it was over. Was I worried? Probably, yeah. But it was like, if it's done, it's been a pretty good ten years . . .'*
Jon Bon Jovi starts again with *Keep The Faith*, 1992

*'It's only a haircut.'* Jon Bon Jovi, 1992

NOTWITHSTANDING THEIR own recent history of conflict, when Bon Jovi regrouped in 1992 they were almost literally fighting for survival. To reach anything like the level of success and popularity they had enjoyed at the end of the eighties, Bon Jovi were faced with a mountain to climb. A mountain that had built up while the band had been out of the limelight. It wasn't really anything to do with the constant media specu-lation suggesting that they had split up. Or that the tabloids had been full of pictures of Jon, fat and bloated, sitting around a guitar-shaped swimming pool eating cheeseburgers – they hadn't, of course. But since the last note of the final encore of the *New Jersey* tour had echoed away in Mexico, the rock business had undergone the biggest shake-up since a bunch of irreverent oiks led by the carrot-topped Johnny Rotten had driven a tank named punk through the business back in the late '70s.

This time, safety pins and bondage trousers were nowhere in sight and those shaking the tree were wearing Doctor Martens and checked plaid shirts – not as a deliberate fashion statement, more as a subconcious antedote to the pristine and pouting hordes of MTV-tailored rock acts (mostly Bon Jovi clones, ironically) clogging the US rock charts and major label rosters. Alternative music, in a form soon to be universally dubbed Grunge, had exploded out of Seattle and America's North West and Bon Jovi suddenly found themselves a long way from the flag marked 'cool'.

Alongside the Grunge explosion, the months of rumours about unrest and infighting paled into insignificance. With solo albums behind them for better or ill, when the band re-entered the public eye, they knew they had better be in prizefighting shape. Their traditional friends in the American rock radio stations, so supportive of *Slippery*... and *New Jersey* and crucial to 'breaking' any new release, had moved on. The stations had not only shifted their musical stance but in the time Bon Jovi had been away, many had either restructured completely or actually gone off the air – even LA's legendary rock/metal station KNAC was soon to close, turning the LA airwaves into a Bon Jovi-free zone. Few of the band's old allies could be relied upon for support. Any evidence that the band had grown complacent or lethargic would be leapt upon like carrion by the scandal-hungry vultures of the world's media.

This number, Jon understood, was likely to include the rock magazines, those organs which had done so much for Bon Jovi all the way through their career to date. Titles like *Kerrang!*, *Metal Hammer* and *Raw* in Europe and the UK, even *RIP* and *Hit Parader* in the States and maybe even *Burrn* in Japan could no longer be relied upon for an unending reservoir of support. Jon knew these magazines, and many of their staff, very well. He had seen them change editorial direction recently to embrace the likes of Pearl Jam, Nirvana and Soundgarden. And he knew it was going to be tough coming back.

The first time anyone not directly connected with the band knew that Bon Jovi had weathered their personal storms and intended coming back was in August 1992, when word got out that Bon Jovi were back in Little Mountain Sound, with Bob Rock producing, at work on an album to be called *Keep The Faith*. It had been over two years since anyone had seen the band play live and the projected release date would set it almost exactly four years after their previous studio album, *New Jersey*, whose sales figures had then reached around the 9 million mark.

In September, PolyGram announced that the first release from the sessions would be the title track, co-written by Jon, Richie ... and Desmond Child. But if that combination sounded like the band were returning to business as usual, it certainly wasn't how Bon Jovi viewed it. After the lengthy break from the band and each other, they approached this new record with all demons purged, a freshly wiped slate and a plan to do things just a little differently. That had been the plan last time, of course, but the news that a dance mix of the album's title-track was being prepared seemed to confirm that this time a new Bon Jovi was definitely on the cards – although whether ordering such a remix indicated that *Keep The Faith* represented a major rebirth for the band, or, was just a one-off aberration, only time would tell.

There is no doubt, however, that although it probably came closer to the latter, it at least showed that Bon Jovi were determined to be seen to have moved on. It didn't take a genius to suggest that they needed to. Following the months of media speculation about the band's future, fuelled by the solo albums from both Jon and Richie and the less-than-private animosity between the two, 'Keep The Faith' and the album of the same name which it heralded, could not afford to be anything but strong to prove to Jon that Bon Jovi still had a future.

In the weeks leading up to the release of the single and the album, Bon Jovi worked as hard as they'd ever done to pave the way and ensure maximum positive publicity. The master-stroke turned out to be something as simple as Jon cutting his hair. He knew that the band's earlier image was going to drag like an anchor around their collective necks. And so opting to cut one more link with his past, he had gone for it in a big way. If not quite the Haircut From Hell, it at least seemed to have been undertaken in the nearby district of Drastic. After it, he looked as cool and handsome as ever but this time more likely to be mistaken for another of his all-American rocker heroes, John Mellencamp, than Bret Michaels of Poison – who, incidentally, were at the time on the comeback trail themselves with *Flesh And Blood* and much more of the same old same old. When the Jovi clones' *Flesh And Blood* sank without trace, Jon could afford a self-congratulatory smirk as well as a sigh of relief.

Jon's haircut attracted intense interest and wild speculation. The best rumour suggested that he needed the drastic trim after his mane caught fire tending Bob Dylan's barbecue. The haircut debate would ramble on for months (much to Jon's dismay) while he appeared to try to deflect attention from it by offering: 'A young lady asked if she could cut it and I just said, "Yeah!" It was no big deal.' But nobody really believed him. He could take solace in the fact that it had done the trick: people who had previously dismissed Bon Jovi were prepared to take him and the band more seriously now.

'We were definitely the band you'd point at when you thought about the eighties, there's no doubt about that,' he has admitted. The trim was a chance to cut loose some of the baggage that accompanied the band around in that decade.

Initially he pretended not to understand all the interest it had caused, responding to all inquiries with an impatient 'it's only a haircut' but he knew it was more than that. Whatever his personal reasons, professionally the restyling was perfectly timed and he chose to maximize its first exposure by going before the cameras of MTV. The station's European viewers caught their earliest glimpse of 'the new Jon Bon Jovi' on MTV Europe's *Headbangers' Ball* programme in September 1992.

Shortly after, the band prepared for the potentially difficult process of courting their (perhaps) former allies in the rock press. Jon knew these would be looking for the slightest reason to write-off Bon Jovi as relics of another era – or worse, not write about them at all. With great deliberation, he considered how best to make sure he retained their support and settled on enticing them with two particular songs. Cunningly pre-empting the printed media's desire to rubbish Bon Jovi as a lightweight rock band, reworking their old hits for maximum success in a tried and tested formula, he decided to give them the chance to hear a couple of tracks that would do most to destroy such pre-conceptions and suggest that Bon Jovi had made the largest possible creative advances. The two were 'Keep The Faith' and 'Dry County' and it was very deliberately only these that the journalists flown over for interviews in New York were allowed to hear. Both tracks were presented very much as works-in-progress, rough mixes, and both sounded suitably like a big step forward.

*Kerrang!*'s Dave Reynolds well remembers being very impressed: '["Dry County"] was an epic, perhaps the most mature piece of music Bon Jovi had ever performed, but really heavy too.' But Reynolds believes that the band played him a mix they knew he would want to hear and later remixed the track into the more sanitized version that graces the *Keep The Faith* album.

Prior to this, it had been a guitar-fuelled tour de force, a real showcase for Richie, and the guitarist himself had earlier described it as 'Bon Jovi-esque with different twists' and promised it would surprise many people. But 'Dry County' had been penned by Jon alone and perhaps, just perhaps, he had the last word in the watered-down remix.

Jon explained the genesis of the track, written after he and his friends got thirsty and made a stop on their motorcycle tour, to Radio 1's Johnny Walker:

'I pulled into a gas station and asked where the local watering hole was. Where [Richie and I] are from, there was a town that separated the two towns where we lived called South Amboy, New Jersey, and it was in the *Guinness Book Of World Records* for the most bars per square mile, honest to goodness. So to pull into this place where they said, "This is a dry county . . ." The words were so foreign to me that it made a great song title. And [then] I drove across the border where they now have drive-through liquor windows – imagine being able to pull up on a motorcycle, buying a six-pack of beer and being able to drive down the street with a beer in your hand, drinking it, and be totally within the law. It baffled me. But I pulled into this bar, sat down, had a beer, and amongst the people found this same sort of confusion and delusion in their lives that I was having in mine. Although they weren't the same they most definitely paralled. The disappointment in a lot of these guys that were down there, searching for their pot of gold and their dreams in this oil town, [like] I was looking for in my music. The disillusions I was having at that time really paralleled. It hit me so that I wrote a song . . .'

Richie said 'Dry County' was one of the last songs worked up for the album (which again suggests that it was chosen to be previewed because of its nature, not because it was one of a handful finished) and had been worked up as a jam by the band in pre-production and bore little resemblance to the germ of a song brought in by Jon.

And in the studio, the band had approached the recording very differently to before. *Keep The Faith* had taken six months to make – twice as long as any of its predecessors, and in that time the band amassed around thirty songs from which they selected the eventual thirteen. Along with engineer Randy Staub and producer Bob Rock, the band had worked hard at getting new sounds distinct for each song and befitting such diverse material as the R'n'B-flavoured 'Little Bit Of Soul', the epic 'If I Was Your Mother' and the heavy driving feel of 'Fear'. Richie used about thirty-five different guitar and amplifier configurations, again employing care and attention far in excess of anything Bon Jovi had ever shown in the past.

'We were in five studios at one time come the end of the record – and I loved it,' said Jon. 'I was running from studio to studio, everybody doing something different, writing right up to the last minute then finally saying, "We've gotta let it go . . ."'

By modern standards, six months in a recording studio is no marathon, but for Bon Jovi it represented a mark of the seriousness with which they viewed their comeback.

Yet the full-on dance mix of 'Keep The Faith' proved to be something of a red herring. The band weren't really pushing back the parameters quite that far and whilst the track itself was previewed for journalists, the remix wasn't. The band were seemingly happier to talk about it as evidence of their new awareness than actually let anyone hear it. At the time, the announcement of their decision to hand over a tape of the 'Keep The Faith' single to one Mike Edwards, frontman of and driving force behind Britain's electro-pop heroes Jesus Jones, was inspired. And whether designed merely to court controversy and drum up a little extra press, or to win new fans from a genre they had not previously appealed to, Bon Jovi were hugely proud of their decision. In the staid world of hard rock, Edwards was a baffling choice of remix producer and some suspected Bon Jovi were unwittingly about to commit commercial suicide. But, in fact, Jon was once again attempting to distance himself from that world.

Richie, speaking whilst the band approached the end of the album's mixing stage, was toeing the same line and hiding any doubts he had: 'We're doing an acid house mix just to see what happens. It seems to lend itself to that. We didn't want to stay on the level we were on with *New Jersey*. There's no point in regurgitating stuff . . . you just have to move on.'

Richie's solo experience had convinced him that Bon Jovi should no longer be in the business of making 'pop' records but this was something on which he and Jon had widely differing views. To Richie, it meant avoiding the (by then) clichéd choruses of their earlier hits. To Jon, it meant searching for something just as successful that could broaden their appeal. Still popular – but not trite.

Sitting beside him, and echoing sentiments expressed four years earlier when the band were about to follow up *Slippery . . .*, Dave Bryan concurred: 'It would be boring for us and our audience to do *New Jersey II*. It's gotta be a totally new listening experience.'

Jon himself, never afraid to milk a cliché, wandered in later on the same interview and again suggested: 'If people are hoping for a *Slippery When Wet III* they're gonna be disappointed. Lyrically, emotionally and mentally it wouldn't work. That was a fine album for that period of time, but this one truly sums up Bon Jovi going into the 90s . . .'

In the final analysis, though, Bon Jovi got cold feet and opted to put out the original, Bob Rock-produced version as the A-side and save Edwards' 'acid house' remix for a bonus. Jon said later that he was 'not totally convinced' by the remix after all, fearing that its complex layering would be impossible to reproduce on stage without resorting to backing tapes – a compromise he wasn't prepared to make, even in the name of progress.

The single was released on 21 October 1992 – two weeks ahead of the album. On the eve of its release, while Bon Jovi weren't exactly dead in the water they were certainly looking a little green around the gills. It was kept from the top of the rock charts by AC/DC's live version of 'Highway To Hell' but make no mistake, it proved that unlike the antipodean boogie maestros, Bon Jovi were a band not content to trade on past glories. 'Keep The Faith' was a song of the 90s *about* the 90s and laid the foundations for the band's rebirth despite all the inter-band tensions – and Grunge.

Richie was keen to point out that as a former garage band themselves, Bon Jovi had something in common with the new stars rising out of Seattle. 'The corporate machine of the music industry these days puts people together – bands, producers and video directors – to make these monsters. But we're just a bunch of guys that got ourselves together and we're still doing it and we're still successful. That, to me, gives kids and young musicians around the world hope, it shows that they can still do it.'

It was no coincidence that Bon Jovi not only intended to make 'Keep The Faith' the title-track but the first single from their fifth album. Credit to them, too, for having the courage of their convictions and refusing to concede to the record company belief that as a single it wouldn't sell.

It was a song that Richie described as 'getting down to the bare essentials of the human condition. Which is, you have to believe in yourself. It's very positive and it has a real element of faith in it, also. It's a very powerful song.'

The words, however, are conveniently vague, aligning themselves loosely with the less privileged among the world's youth battling discontent and social ills, stressing an individual's power to fight against the masses. But even if the lyrics addressed the real world from only a pop politic point of view, then at least they took a brave step forward from references to adolescent fumblings in the backs of cars. And when Jon sang, his words could just as easily be viewed as a canny rallying call to Bon Jovi fans who might have been losing interest – who might have switched allegiances, for example, to an angst-ridden trio from Aberdeen near Seattle in Washington State . . .

Said trio, Nirvana, fronted by the impossibly gifted yet star-crossed Kurt Cobain, had been at the forefront of bands emerging from the Seattle area and/or signed to the city's SubPop label. After a critically acclaimed debut album, *Bleach*, the band were snapped up by Geffen Records and made for them an album called *Nevermind*. From it they had scored a massive worldwide hit with the single 'Smells Like Teen Spirit' – at almost exactly the same time, September '91, that Sambora's solo album slipped into the racks. MTV ran Sambora's 'Ballad Of Youth' video and they ran ' . . . Teen Spirit'. But whilst the former quickly fell off the playlists, the latter was stamped 'ultra heavy rotation' and any thoughts the guitarist may have dared to harbour of going solo and quitting Bon Jovi for good surely flew out the window. Grunge had arrived. In the autumn of 1992 it was impossible to watch MTV for more than twenty minutes without being force-fed Nirvana.

Collectively, and individually, Bon Jovi had every right to be worried. Other bands were riding along on Nirvana's coat-tails: bands like Soundgarden (who had burst through simul-taneously with their *Badmotorfinger* album on A&M); Alice In Chains (who earlier in '91 had made their Columbia debut with *Facelift*); and Pearl Jam, as 1992 dawned, were watching their *Ten* rewrite debut album sales statistics. The times, as Bob Dylan had first observed and countless others since had nodded sagely in agreement with, were a-changin'.

'These guys truly have something to say,' observed Jon.

'They're not coming out looking like they're wearing their clothes and the rhyme scheme isn't moon, June and spoon. These guys are writing from the gut, this is their life experience . . .'

But it wasn't so much that ' . . . Teen Spirit' et al were directly targeted (or even likely) to appeal to Bon Jovi's core audience, more that they had offered an alternative to those of a more fickle disposition and in doing so undermined the band's bankability. In the 1990s, youth had short attention spans and a myriad of opportunities with which to occupy themselves. Back in 1988, the release of a Bon Jovi album was a big event. But in 1992, so much water had gone under the bridge that only Bon Jovi fans really gave a hoot. The press, the radio and the all-important MTV were far more interested in Nirvana, their contemporaries and with Grunge fashions and 'slacker generation' hype. And fans of those bands, while quite possibly being prepared to give 'Keep The Faith' a cursory listen, were then just as likely to move on and listen to Ice-T or Neil Young. Genre boundaries were coming down and Bon Jovi were facing much broader competition.

But they weren't about to jump onto the Grunge band-wagon, as so many other bands – including the likes of Mötley Crüe, Warrant and Mike Tramp's new band Freak Of Nature – would attempt to do. 'It's not like I'm coming out with hair down to my ass and some shit on my chin an' sounding like Pearl Jam . . .' spat Jon in disgust. He certainly wasn't.

'The last thing I would do is start chasing fads and fashions. You always end up a dollar short and a day late. I didn't have to prove to anybody that I was capable of writing a song . . . So for me to go to Seattle just didn't feel right. I wasn't going to go to the Lollapalooza tour organizers and say, "Let me play on the bill, we're hip". It didn't smell right.'

Whatever, Bon Jovi were coming back with their eyes and minds open to all possibilities. But they were clearly aware that they were treading a tightrope between success and failure, nervous of the fact that they could easily alienate their established fans whilst attempting to cross over and reach new ones. So while Jon seized the chance to make a fresh start image-wise, Messrs Sambora, Bryan, Such and Torres sobered down their clothes a little – but didn't do much except look four years older. One scurrilous rumour suggested that Torres had undergone liposuction in order to get himself in better shape. Worse, it was suggested that Jon had ordered him to do so. The rumour was one of Jon's favourites and he would repeat it himself, laughing each time that the story was given any credibility.

More seriously, Sambora matched every 'bold leap forward' promise with a sympathetic look over his shoulder at the core of 'the 33 million people who've bought our records before – we can't just leave them in the dust, they have a certain expectation'. Thirty-three million might have been a piece of creative accounting that overlooked the possibility of many Bon Jovi fans buying more than one of their records but, hey, he was proud of the milestone reached and you had to sympathize with the guy's dilemma, if not the heartaches that accompanied his bank balance.

While Richie had beavered away on his solo album, Jon had been writing songs alone, all these factors gnawing away at his self confidence. *New Jersey* may have sold 9 million copies worldwide but – just as it had been unlikely to match the sales of *Slippery* . . . – getting close to those kind of figures with the fifth album was not going to be a realistic target. Just as they did in 1988, Bon Jovi were once again going to have to scale down their expectations.

Despite, or perhaps because of such pressures, Jon's writing had gone well enough for six of his solo compositions to be later deemed good enough to appear on the album. Jon had written the odd song unaided before but putting forward so many at this point was a brave step that risked straining his and Richie's relationship further. But Richie, too, was aware that something, indeed many things, needed to change. 'To stagnate would have been a disaster. Since that last album so much has happened in music and in our lives.'

Refreshed, and with their minds open to any new opportunities, he and Jon got together and wrote some more. They were fired up by the young bands from Seattle and regarded their pre-eminence as a challenge to prove that they could compete. Fired up, they worked on and eventually amassed around thirty songs. Somewhere along the line they took that ironic and seemingly retrograde step of going for what they knew: enlisting the services of Desmond Child to smooth off the edges on a couple of the numbers. Once again critics – and even other artists – raised a collective eyebrow and wondered aloud if maybe it wasn't about time Bon Jovi gave up on Child's trademark 'who-oah' choruses, first heard to such great effect on 'Livin' On A Prayer'. Jon, who had never once taken the short cut of recording a cover version, was peeved not only because of the slur on himself but on Child, too.

'I totally respect the guy, because in 1986 he taught me the next level of songwriting, and so I really hate to see people pissing on his Wheaties. He's had hits, but he's not like any of those Tin Pan Alley songwriters who sit in an office writing hits to earn a dollar. He truly tries to give you that heart, soul and emotion . . . Des just ended up getting pissed on 'cause he jumped in the pool and wrote with a lot of other people.'

He certainly did. After *Slippery . . .*, artists old, new and desperate beat a path to his door. First in were Aerosmith whose *Permanent Vacation* (1987) and *Pump* (1989) albums he had a Midas-like hand in, but there were many others. Through his connection with Geffen Records' (and Cher's) A&R guru John Kalodner, Child's career resumé began to look like a who's who of rock, with artists including Joan Jett

(1988), Alice Cooper (1989), Saraya (1989) and the fast-rising Michael Bolton (1989) clamouring for a piece of Bon Jovi's action. Ratt, for example, later gave Child a co-writing credit on every one of the ten songs on their (admittedly best forgotten) 1990 album, *Detonator*.

'The truth is Desmond is a genius,' argued Richie in defence of the band's decision to re-employ Child. 'The guy has written amazing songs and can adapt his style for a lot of different writers. But when he works with Jon and I, we kinda make his style a little bit different. Something happens when the three of us get together – we just write really good material . . .'

In 1990, on a promotional collection of his most successful songs, Child had saluted Jon, Richie and the others he had worked alongside in this rather hideously flowery tribute: 'You have seen the best and worst of me. We have left each other raw and wounded . . . We have laughed and healed. Together, we have travelled to deep, dark, dangerous places and peaked into the abyss of the infinite. We have known each other intimately. Writing a song together, after all . . . is like making love.'

Perhaps it is. Having also tried his hand at production, Child then made a second stab at seeking the limelight in his own name with a solo album called *Discipline* in 1991. Richie was among the first to offer his services. Later both he and Jon would say that *Discipline* suggested Desmond Child the artist couldn't match Desmond Child the songwriter, but it was the latter who concerned them when the threesome started working on the demos that would become 'Keep The Faith' and 'I'll Sleep When I'm Dead'.

Bon Jovi needed a hit, but not at any price. More than anything, they needed a hit which would suggest to the sceptics that they still had something to say in the altogether more serious post-grunge climate.

Had they chosen the party-hearty barrelhouse rocker 'I'll

Sleep When I'm Dead' as that all important first single, the band might well have sunk without trace – although the track did do the business when released as a single a little further down the line. Instead, opting for 'Keep The Faith' proved a masterstroke. A cunning blend of experience and ambition, it exhibited an urgency and a seriousness that had been lacking from most of their earlier work.

Jon Bon Jovi had got married and turned thirty in the six months before the single's release. Here was the perfect song to show how he now intended to act his age. 'America's waking up from twelve years of Reaganomics and believing a dream that was a lot of bullshit. You see LA having a riot, kids in high school with guns and crack, and there's AIDS. I'm not going to write about what a wonderful world it is because it wouldn't make sense. What I can do is write my version of the story . . .'

Yet one of his more lyrical efforts on *Keep The Faith* was the introspective 'Bed Of Roses', written by him, alone, in a Los Angeles hotel room 'at a piano with twenty-nine bucks in my pocket and a bottle of vodka' – as he would sometimes tell audiences when introducing the song live. A piano was an instrument Jon had very rarely used for songwriting, but it was the lyric rather than the method that seemed more significant to him.

Another explanation of the song, given to an MTV *Unplugged* audience in New York was even more candid: 'There's been a long hiatus after the last album . . . We spent way too many years having fun. While I was away I wrote quite a few songs and realized a lot of things about, not only how much I dug playing music, but life in general, I guess. And it's tough sometimes when you have to grow up in public, which is more or less what's happened, this song reads sort of like, I guess, a confessional.'

He would hark back to his lost Catholic heritage and repeat

this idea of the confessional in interviews time and again. 'I feel that the lyrics are the best ever because of the soul cleansing. In the last two and a half years I think I've come to terms with who I am, where I fit in and whether or not I actually please people. The first eight years and those four albums were just a case of us runnin', runnin' and runnin' ... I was loving the high of the roller coaster so much that I didn't want to give it up. It was too much fun.'

His new maturity was another aspect Jon stressed, each time allowing him – however casually – to look to the future and once more distance himself from the band's past. 'I don't think [we ever made a] conscious attempt to ever ... duplicate anything of the past. I think if we had done that we would have given the world *Slippery Part III* which would have been a big mistake. Not only from a commercial or record company standpoint – because that's minor – but for our well being. After having had a couple of years off, with the re-energizing of the batteries, I think we had to come out with something that depicted us *now*. We couldn't come out with 'Livin' On A Prayer' again. That was six years ago. It wouldn't work.'

Publicly, he would maintain this stance whenever the issue was raised, insisting that they thought nothing of these kind of pressures. But whether they worried him or not, Jon certainly knew the realities. When, in September '92, PolyGram began to gear up the publicity machines, they knew they were doing so for a band not only desperate to prove they could still hack it, but also very nervous that they might fail. Jon, therefore, helped plot the promotional activity even more carefully than usual. This time around, Bon Jovi would have to concentrate harder than ever on TV and broaden their appeal by doing interviews for pop and, they hoped, lifestyle publications too.

By 1992, Bon Jovi were not a band who relished the prospect of endless rounds of radio and press interviews, but they were experienced enough to know they were necessary.

The promotional tour which heralded the *Keep The Faith* album was their most extensive ever.

It began in the States in October with a mixture of face-to-face domestic and advance phone interviews to 'prime' the media in the rest of the world, all interspersed with the band's first live dates together since February 1990. These would give Bon Jovi the best possible opportunity to get over the message that they were alive and kicking, as well as acting as public rehearsals to blow away a few of the cobwebs that had gathered since the *New Jersey* tour ended. The band slotted in low-key shows to reintroduce themselves in New Jersey, Phoenix and Los Angeles, then played a prestigious MTV *Unplugged* show at New York's Kaufman Astoria Studios in October (later released on video as *Keep The Faith: An Evening With Bon Jovi*).

In November – as the album was released – the band flew to Europe for a promotional tour that would place them in twenty countries (including some in the Far East) in just five weeks. Encouraged by the experience of the US shows, they played live dates wherever possible to announce the message of their rebirth in the best possible way.

In England they played a 'secret' show at the 1,800 capacity London Astoria. Actually, it was one of the worst kept secrets in recent history and almost didn't happen at all. Press reports that the band were to play to around a quarter of that number at Ronnie Scott's jazz club, as The Black Crowes had done a year earlier, were premature enough to force a rescheduling at the Astoria on 4 November, with the show only officially confirmed on the morning of the gig on Radio 1. Publicity surrounding the Astoria date was typical of the techniques employed at every city they played. Its impact was maximized by offering Radio 1 the rights to tape and broadcast it along with an 'exclusive' interview. This meant that the Radio 1 audience could hear the gig exactly as the band hoped – a major act playing a small venue as a special treat while able to stress that they weren't about to deliver the regular full-scale Bon Jovi show. They had hired sound and lighting equipment and had not brought over a full crew, Jon preferring that the show, as with its predecessors in the States, would be a 'free for all', a euphemism for under-rehearsed with the odd rough edge.

As well as previewing material from the forthcoming album, the band threw in the odd cover version like 'With A Little Help From My Friends', The Animals' 'It's My Life', even Peggy Lee's 'Fever' and an Elvis Presley-styled 'Baby What Do You Want Me To Do?' At the Astoria, haircut notwithstanding, the audience saw a new Jon Bon Jovi. He smashed up a guitar and, during 'Lay Your Hands On Me', even dived into the crowd for a spot of body surfing. He'd clearly been watching a lot of the younger bands on MTV in his time off. Nordoff-Robbins Music Therapy got a treat out of it, too, with the band donating £1,000 to the charity.

During the Radio 1 interview Jon and Richie made light of their troubles, citing their long held intention to take two years off and blaming 'the scandalous press' for making it seem otherwise. The casual listener didn't need to hear about the band's internal politics and the pair weren't about to waste the time they had to promote *Keep The Faith*. As the interview ended, Jon spoke directly to the audience: 'I'm gonna get in the car and turn up my radio.' Then, leaning forward for maximum impact he breathed: 'I suggest you all do the same.' It was a brilliant example of working the medium from a man who sounded perfectly relaxed and in control. At the beginning of a new chapter, the radio audience would be a far more crucial factor to Bon Jovi's success than the readers of the rock magazines. Jon understood that, and had made a pretty good start at winning them over.

Jon had long been a fan of U2 and couldn't help but admire the way they had re-invented themselves, cunningly retaining much of their old fanbase while shifting themsleves a little further to the mainstream and an older, larger audience. As well as U2's music, their image had changed, and they had a new style of presentation thanks in no small part to photographer Anton Corbijn who did a similar job for Depeche Mode. Corbijn, one of the legendarily small number of famous Belgians, was contracted to shoot the cover and promotional shots for *Keep The Faith*. He captured scowling disaffected poses that were a million miles away, for example, from the shots of them soaping up girls and cars on *Slippery* . . . . The main image of the album's cover – the five band members' hands interlocked, looking like some pre-battle talisman – seemed to underline their determination.

But as a reminder that all had not been well, the sleeve notes advertised the band's fan club, revealing that it had been renamed as 'Backstage With *Jon* Bon Jovi'. Richie Sambora noted that the name change was beyond the band's control: 'That was done during the hiatus. Jonny's mommy runs the fan club and when he did *Blaze Of Glory* she decided to change it to the Jon Bon Jovi fan club. We haven't gotten around to sorting that one out yet . . . but we will.'

Actually, they never have . . .

But with Phil Joanu's promo video for the 'Keep The Faith' single echoing the themes of determination and brotherhood, it mattered not. The clip featured lots of moody close-ups, atmospheric monochrome and rapid cuts with a bare minimum of performance footage. And as further evidence of the gale of change flapping the coat-tails of the band, the clip was the first time in a decade Jon had chosen anyone other than Wayne Isham to direct.

Behind the scenes, there was one further change: that of management. After Richie's solo album and before the release of *Keep The Faith*, the band and their original mentor, Doc McGhee, finally went their separate ways.

Replacing McGhee Entertainment Inc. came Bon Jovi

Management (BJM) comprising former tour manager Paul Korzilius (who took prime control of Jon and the band), Jon's brother Anthony (acting as the band's road manager) and, originally, Margi Vangell. It was a small company solely handling the band. BJM was a simple solution to a complex problem: how to scale down the management of a band that had become ever larger. However, who should replace McGhee wasn't immediately obvious.

'I made a shortlist of six managers who I wanted to talk to about looking after the band. In the end I spoke to *twenty*-six managers. I would speak to anyone if I thought they had something to offer – but I couldn't find anyone who suited us . . .' The solution – Korzilius et al – was at first too close to home to be seen. The BJM team was reshuffled in 1994 – with former McGhee employee Margaret Sterlacci and Christine Richman replacing Vangell on record sleeve credits, and again come 1995 with Dave Davis being added to the ranks as tour manager – but still this was a small team with a single purpose. Back in 1991, McGhee Entertainment was anything but. It kept offices in both LA and New York and had a small stable of artists to its name.

When asked directly about the dismissal of McGhee, Jon was reluctant to say much in public, with any possible criticisms being heavily disguised. 'Doc was there from the beginning and he was also a friend. But his interests diversified. He got into other business [and] my seven days a week, twenty-four hours a day attitude finally caught up with him . . . There was nothing wrong with either Doc or our agents, but in order for us not to slip into our old ways again it was better just to turn the page.'

But sometimes, talking about the situation in general, he would say a little more: 'The *Slippery* . . . tour ended in October 1987 and we were back in the studio within four months recording *New Jersey*, before going back out on tour again for a total of 237 shows. In retrospect, we didn't allow ourselves the chance to pull back and take a break. When we finally came up for air, we got to do what we wanted to do . . .'

In short, they knew they had been overworked but were older and wiser. BJM, said Jon, 'only looks after Bon Jovi. That's what it's there for. And if any member of the band wants help on outside projects, then, of course, all the facilities would be at his disposal.' The future looked a far cry from the mess of the past.

'There were holidays spent in hotel rooms instead of at home with families, a lot of abuse, alcohol . . . All I wanted to be was the singer in a rock'n'roll band and I turned into the chairman of the board of a multi-million dollar corporation. We had to dismantle that machine and regain control of our destinies . . .

'That was the reason we fired everyone. We were just this big machine that made a lot of money for a lot of people. There's no harm in the words that I'm saying towards those people. I've only very, very recently become aware and educated of the fact that they were trying to do their job well for us. Your agent, manager and publicist might all come to you with four things each to do, right? Which leaves you with twelve things to do. I'd never say no, and I'd do all twelve . . .

'Everyone was just tryin' to do a good job, so they could say, "*We* did it." Nobody ever stole money; Doc never stole a nickel, and the reality of it is that Bon Jovi was the band he loved . . .'

The change produced more uncomfortable friction between Jon and Richie, as the latter initially opted to remain with McGhee as a solo artist. Eventually, Jon all but ordered Richie to follow his lead and sever professional ties with McGhee Entertainment Inc.

Richie was left with no choice as he admitted: 'That's what had to happen if I was going to be with the band so that's basically what went down. There was much hesitation because we had a successful thing going. Not only was there a strong business relationship but there was a very strong friendship also. But what can you do? Sometimes things happen in this business and you just have to roll with the punches.'

Jon put his decision, perhaps couched as a proposal, to the band at a meeting on the Caribbean island of St Thomas.

'We all stayed together in one house – no wives, no girlfriends, no managers, no agents. I told my family that if I was home before Saturday then it wasn't good. I had a bunch of songs written and we discussed ideas and hung out together. I wanted to see if we were all thinking on the same wavelength.'

Quite obviously, they were and later Richie would, given pause for thought, reflect that: 'The record company was good to us. The record company really wasn't the thing that was ever holding us back. It was more or less the management and the agencies who would have us booked to tour before we had got to make the record, which was not good artistically. There should be no time limit on creativity. We would start an album in June knowing that by the end of August we would be playing dates.

'Maybe they were afraid that we were a flash in the pan. That we weren't good enough and that it was only going to happen once or twice. They wanted us to take all the money so *they* could take our money. They were pushing us into the ground, they really didn't care about what we were like personally.'

In effect, the band now manage themselves, with Korzilius handling the day-to-day business affairs and the band – Jon in particular as the self-styled quarterback of the team – contributing on policy decisions. Under the previous set-up, Jon has admitted that it would very often be he and McGhee working together with the band almost shut out. After the change 'the five of us definitely grew closer together' even if BJM's set-up is, as he has joked, a 'benevolent dictatorship' with him holding the casting vote.

'Everybody's opinions are considered. I think when somebody has a vision of what they want something to be, not everybody can have the same vision – or any vision . . . I don't think Bill Wyman got as involved as Mick or Keith in picking out the singles' bag art . . .'

But the band still waited to learn if any of these changes had worked, to find out if, for example, the press would give *Keep The Faith* the thumbs-up – or condemn the band to obscurity. Broadly speaking, they needn't have worried: with a few reservations, the album was generally well received. In America, *Guitar* magazine were certain that the band could 'still make powerful arena anthem rock' but wondered 'is anybody listening?' *Metal CD* appreciated this was 'the first album of Jon Bon Jovi's musical adult life' and suggested that the band were 'by no means a spent force'.

In the UK, *Q* – at the more mature end of the market the band were hoping to appeal to – reacted cautiously, commenting on Jon Bon Jovi's penchant for writing about male bonding and the love of a good woman, comparing his consistency to a country music artist's. Offering three stars it concluded: 'No surprises but a decidedly pleasant way of treading water.' *Kerrang!* begrudgingly gave it only three stars but admitted it contained 'something for everyone; rock, ballads, pop, whatever' and concluded that it was 'perhaps the ultimate mainstream American rock record and with it, Bon Jovi are unstoppable.' *Raw*, on the other hand, went to the furthest extreme and gave it just one star and called it 'a last dance curtain call from a rich, comfortable man with no dreams left to fulfill . . .'

On its release, the band had lined up around eight months

of dates – beginning in Pensacola, Florida, on 13 January 1993 – vowing to take it steadily and see if the US was still interested in Bon Jovi. It certainly didn't look promising to begin with, as the combination of some harsh winter weather and the US's continuing economic recession made for some sobering ticket sales and part empty halls.

'It was a little hard,' Jon admitted, 'because everybody was watching, if truth be told. That's what this business is about. Anyone who says they aren't watching other people is lying . . . The real low point was Knoxville, Tennessee, where we walked out and all thought, "Keep your head down and do the best you can . . ." They weren't pretty shows. There were a lot of empty shows out there – but when we went back, we did twice as well.'

At the time, though, the band swallowed hard and decided to look into the possibility of exploiting other markets, not least that of South America where bands had only recently started to venture and the scarcity of supply meant demand was huge. In the UK the following May, caution limited them to announcing just six arena shows, including a brace of gigs at both Wembley Arena and Birmingham NEC. But within a month of the announcement, all their efforts seemed to have paid off and an extra night at each of the latter venues was added to the schedule. Nearly all European territories would come to repeat this kind of morale-boosting pattern.

So what of those long uncomfortable months when all anyone in the media seemed to want to hear about Bon Jovi was that they had split up?

'I was pissed off,' Jon admitted to Dave Reynolds of *Kerrang!* once everyone in Europe could see that the band were a living, breathing concern. 'I think *Kerrang!* could've approached me personally and got the true story, rather than print rumours and add fuel to the fire.'

But whilst the smoke signals might have been misread, the

fire had clearly been alight – and the band never once came forward with the offer of a clear-the-air explanation or even a cunningly worded press statement of denial. Unrepentant, Jon was still laying the blame squarely at the door of the UK press: 'There were some things said that might be viewed as English humour, but the rest of the world believed it. And there are other cans of worms in other areas connected with us that are just best left unopened . . .'

A veiled reference, almost certainly, to McGhee's court case and subsequent sentence . . .

For the US leg of the *Keep The Faith* tour, Jon buried the hatchet with former Ratt singer Stephen Pearcy and took Pearcey's new band Arcade along as the opening act. Arcade didn't survive long beyond the tour and for Bon Jovi the fruits of the trek were slow to ripen. In the US, the record made the *Billboard* top ten on release but was easily outsold by REM's *Automatic For The People* and even Pearl Jam's debut *Ten* – which by then had been on the charts for thirty-three weeks. But by the spring of 1993, the album sales at last passed the million mark, helped by the 'Bed Of Roses' single climbing into its respective top ten. Jon remembers those were anxious days.

'When it didn't come in at number one in America people were very quick to say it was over. Was I worried? Probably, yeah. But it was like, if it's done, it's been a pretty good ten years . . .' Jon was right. In ten years they had achieved the status of that implausible cliché – a household name. For every teenage Bon Jovi fan there was a parent who knew and possibly liked the music, too. By the same token, for every kid who still thought the band a bunch of pussies there was an adult *convinced* they were. Funniest among these was almost certainly American comic Denis Leary, who reflected on the band's decade in slightly more acerbic tones in his 'No Cure For Cancer' stand-up show.

'Stevie Ray Vaughan is dead and we can't get Jon Bon Jovi in a fucking helicopter? [pause for audience laughter] Tell him there's a fucking hairdresser in there . . .' That Leary had missed the news of Jon's new image was disconcerting. That he rated the late great Hendrix-inspired guitarist's death as a tragedy was no surprise. That he was unwittingly acknowledging and reflecting the impact of Bon Jovi was clear. But Jon had other things to think about, anyway. Like the album sales.

It was still a little early to order flowers or a wake. Two more singles eventually helped the album go double platinum in the States. This, though, was more of a relief than a cause for celebration as it showed Bon Jovi just how much ground they had lost in their home market in the wake of new rock acts like REM (whose *Automatic . . .* sold 3 million plus), Pearl Jam (8 million), Nirvana (6 million copies of *Nevermind*) and the red Hot Chili Peppers (2 million copies of *BloodSugarSexMagik*). If it was any consolation, *Keep The Faith* had at least matched the totals for Bruce Springsteen's twin releases *Human Touch* and *Lucky Town*.

If in their native North America, a new album by Bon Jovi was no longer a short-odds banker for chart-topping success, sales in Europe – a market still a year or so behind America's wholesale acceptance of the grunge phenomenon – were far more encouraging. The album went on to outsell *Slippery When Wet* in many European territories. In fact, even as they arrived to play their long scheduled arena shows, the band were confident enough to add further European shows, including some outdoor stadiums, in the autumn.

Back in April, at a show in Milan on the eve of the UK arena dates, Jon spoke of his motivations now that he was – at least in terms of Paul Korzilius' management – a man in control of his own destiny. 'If there's anything I've gotten out of this whole album and tour it is that I don't have anything to prove to anyone. We've sold 35 million albums. Compared to any of the other bands – I don't care who you wanna name – I'm sure we've sold as many, if not more, records than they have. There've been enough number ones, enough sold-out places, so there was nothing left to prove.'

Clearly, his position as the frontman of a phenomenally successful rock band was taking second place in his mind to something else. That something else was his then eight-month pregnant wife. For a week prior to the scheduled birth, with the band on tour in the UK, Jon had a seat booked on every available flight back to New York. In the event, Dorothea gave birth to their first child, a girl, a week later than planned, on 31 May. The couple named her Stephanie Rose and almost immediately took her with them to Europe for the next leg of the tour.

Germany was as keen for the band in 1993 as it ever had been, with sales of *Keep The Faith* outnumbering *Slippery . . .*'s by almost two-to-one as they reached the 1.2 million mark. In the UK, 500,000 copies sold were enough to prompt the band to book the 60,000 capacity Milton Keynes Bowl as a finale to the European tour on Saturday 18 September. Support was from special guest Billy Idol (Poison didn't make it as rumoured). Tickets, at £20, sold out so fast (and before any support acts apart from the fast fading Billy Idol were named) that there was little hesitation in adding a second show on the Sunday. The bill was eventually completed by Little Angels and Manic Street Preachers. From Europe, the band went to Japan then returned to tour the States, finding a much warmer welcome this time around. (Special guests on these US dates were Extreme, which afforded Richie the opportunity to play alongside their guitarist Nuno Bettencourt, a man he very much admired.)

But the tour didn't end there, and in November, ten months after their first date, the band were using their two private jets to fly them, their crew and equipment to stadiums in South America. From there they made their way back to New Jersey for what had become an almost annual Christmas charity show, played this year before around 4,000 people at Red Bank's Count Basie Theatre. Selling out in a matter of minutes, the event raised $300,000 for charities but also marked a milestone for the band. They had completed a tour organized in a way that left them not only better off financially but emotionally, too. Despite the initial plans to tour for just eight months they had stretched it for three more without needing to ressurect their old 'burned' cliché.

Something like 2.5 million people had seen the band play live in thirty-seven countries. Included among these were first time visits to: Taiwan, Thailand and The Philippines (these and other parts of the relatively new Asian market netted them a million sales of *Keep The Faith*); hitherto overlooked parts of Europe – Hungary, Austria, the Czech Republic and Turkey; as well as Guatemala, Costa Rica and Columbia in Central and South America.

As the tour wrapped up at the Count Basie, the above statistics were underlined by the fact that *Keep The Faith* had sold over 8 million copies. It was a million less than *New Jersey* but with 75 per cent of the sales overseas, the figure represented good business and, more importantly, good news for the future.

Quotes gratefully taken from:

Steve Mascord, *Kerrang!* 382, 7 March 1992; Paul Rees, *Raw* 107, 30 September–13 October 1992; Dave Reynolds, *Kerrang!* 412, 3 October 1992; Joe Mackett, *Riff Raff,* interview 16 October 1992; Paul Rees, *Raw* 109, 28 October–10 November 1992; Dave Reynolds, *Kerrang!* 412, 3 October 1992; Paul Elliott, *Kerrang!* 416, 31 October 1992; Mark Blake, *Metal CD,* November 1992; Johnny Walker, Radio 1, 7 November 1992; John Aizlewood, *Q* 75, December 1992; Pippa Lang, *Metal Hammer,*

January 1993; Dave Reynolds, *Kerrang!* 426, 16 January 1993; Malcolm Dome, *MF* issue 1, January 1993; Steffan Chirazi, *Kerrang!* 440, 24 April 1993; Steffan Chirazi, *Rip*, April 1994; Sylvie Simmons, *Kerrang!* 500, 25 June 1994; David Sinclair, *The Times*, 30 September 1994.

# CHAPTER SEVEN

# The Crossroads and Beyond . . .

*'The times when all I wanted to do was chase women and get laid are over. Now I've seen so many other things.'*
Jon Bon Jovi on where his head is at these days, 1995

*'Jon's very, very important to us. We like him very, very much . . .'*
PolyGram's chief executive officer Alain Levy on where his wallet is at these days, 1995

*'I like stadiums. Some people say it's not personal but those are the guys who can't play stadiums . . .'*
Jon Bon Jovi on entertaining the masses these days, 1995

UPON COMPLETION of the *Keep The Faith* dates, Bon Jovi did what they should have done on the four previous world tours: returned home and forgot about being a band. For a while. Predictably, Jon's powers of recollection were strongest and – within days of arriving in Mustique in the Caribbean for a holiday with his family, he had begun writing songs. At least this time he was doing so out of creativity rather than a sense of urgency forced on him by an unforgiving schedule. So, spotted leopards being what they are, he was soon on the phone to Richie inviting the guitarist to join him in a working vacation. Jon had no trouble recognizing his shortcoming, only curing it.

'My greatest problem is not sitting down and enjoying things more. I've got to sit back and catch a breath once in a while – smell the roses!'

The roses were smelling pretty good. Against all the odds, Bon Jovi's make-or-break 'comeback' album had sold 8 million copies. Although musical trends suggested otherwise, Jon and the band had got it right – again. And they could afford an air of confidence when in February 1994 they reassembled to discuss future plans. Although first and foremost among these was the follow-up album to *Keep The Faith*, it was also a question of when and what else? Jon – then a 32-year-old thinking about trying for a second child – was starting to view the future a little differently. For eleven years, his life had been almost exclusively as the singer in a hard-working rock band, now the dividends of that hard work were affording the time and space to do other things. He had secretly been having acting lessons and the music business was offering so many other ways of making a living.

Touring had become a much less stressful and far easier way to help sell albums, but it was no longer the only way. Jon no longer needed to answer the same questions in interview after interview because a promo video clip or a well-chosen guest slot on a networked TV show could tell the same story so much more effectively. For example, Jon and Richie flew to England to play at The Brit Awards show – backing UK solo artist Dina Carroll (formerly one of the band's labelmates at PolyGram) – and, however briefly, reached more people than they ever could by playing a string of dates around Europe.

Likewise the band saved themselves untold legwork by playing before the cameras at the MTV Music Awards, and later at a showcase in the Bahamas – where they further maximized their time by visiting a recording studio they were considering for possible future use. Live telecasts put Bon Jovi's faces and music direct into the homes of the casual music fan and therefore widely increased their potential catchment.

The band had played to 2.5 million people on their last tour, but 5.5 million more bought the album – people who might now like their music enough to purchase the record but perhaps wouldn't buy a ticket for one of the shows.

Jon recognized this fact and suggested to the rest of the band that in future Bon Jovi were going to be able to work in a different way. There was no need for the usual album-tour treadmill when they could rely on other outlets. As if by way of proof, they lifted one last single off *Keep The Faith* – a Bob Clearmountain remix of the album's least likely hit single, 'Dry County' – and watched it earn them a UK top ten placing in March 1994.

An album would follow, but when it suited Jon, who – because Bob Rock had opted to take a year's break – was considering recording it piecemeal, with the band trying out new locations, studios and producers until they struck upon one, or a combination, that suited them.

In May 1994, when the world's largest wooden building, the Todaiji Temple in Nara, Japan, played host to an East-meets-West music festival, Bon Jovi were represented. Co-organizers George Martin (the ex-Beatles producer) and Michael Kamen (the soundtrack composer/producer) wanted only the biggest names in rock and Bon Jovi's Jon and Richie were there to perform alongside Kodo drummers, Buddhist monks and the likes of Bob Dylan, Joni Mitchell, INXS and Ry Cooder. As the temple's Great Buddha statue looked down Jon quipped: 'I believe there is a supreme being out there, but I'm not sure whether it's Elvis, Buddha or Bruce Springsteen . . .'

Good soundbites like this had made Jon good copy. He had moved on from his days as a teen idol, to a gossip column regular, a rock star, a symbol of worldwide fame and riches.

He was still struggling to get into the men's lifestyle magazines, but he was working on it.

His band were not far behind either: both Richie and drummer Torres had been featured in *Hello!*, the former on his marriage to Heather Locklear and the latter upon his engagement to the traffic-troubling Wonderbra girl Eva Herzigova and again with a story on his horse-breeding ranch. It was all a far cry from the five youngsters performing watered-down heavy metal songs about 'lust not love'.

Titles bandied about for inclusion on the next album included 'Good Guys Don't Always Wear White' but this was subsequently donated to the soundtrack of the Kiefer Sutherland movie *The Cowboy Way*. The track broke fresh ground as the first new Bon Jovi song in a decade not to be recorded in Little Mountain Sound studios (admittedly undergoing a refit at the time the band needed it) and teamed the band with a new producer, Andy Johns. The track was mixed, like the 'Dry County' single, by Bob Clearmountain.

In the US 'Good Guys . . .' enabled Bon Jovi to enjoy the benefits of one of the music industry's fast rising phenomena: the synchronized release of film, record, promo clip, etc. (The European release of the movie and its soundtrack was later, and much more low key.) Ever since the soaring success of tracks from the 1986 *Top Gun* soundtrack album (which sold over 7 million copies in the US alone), compiling such albums had become big business. Few of the tracks assembled were ever intended to be heard in the movie score, but the album itself would be used by Hollywood as another spin-off promotional tool. Whitney Houston's phenomenal hit 'I Will Always Love You', the theme song to the 1992 blockbuster *The Bodyguard*, was directly linked to the success of that movie. The video promoted the song, the song promoted the soundtrack album and the film, while the film (and its trailer) in turn promoted album.

It was a kind of multi-media marketing approach that enabled bands to get in the faces of millions of MTV-watchers and cinema-goers – and Bon Jovi would have been happy for just a little more of the same when they set up in a Beatles-style Manhattan rooftop location to make a video. Neither 'Good Guys . . .' or *The Cowboy Way* (or indeed the promo clip) had quite the same impact as Ms Houston's – but the experience at least gave Bon Jovi a chance to experiment and learn. After his runaway success with *Blaze Of Glory*, using movies as a marketing tool for music was another option Jon was considering more and more. Not least because, following his Golden Globe for *Blaze Of Glory*, he was anxious to prove it wasn't a fluke.

'I've been wanting to do music for movies, to go back there ever since . . . I wrote 'Always' for [the 1993 movie] *Romeo Is Bleeding* . . . I loved the script and they told me Gary Oldman was in it and I said, "Please, I gotta write this song!" I was doing it as a solo thing for the movie but when I saw it, I didn't like the film so I pulled it. Great script but the film was terrible, fucking awful. I love Gary Oldman, just adore him, but they had problems. But we liked the song still, so as a band we re-recorded it . . . Too bad it wasn't a better film 'cause God knows I wrote a big enough song for them.'

Big enough, indeed. The movie soundtrack's loss was very much Bon Jovi's gain as the track (complete with strings added under the guidance of movie score veteran Michael Kamen) went on to become the band's biggest ever hit single – even without the cross-fertilizing support of movie and soundtrack support. Just prior to the track's release, Jon was in London with Richie, and suggested to PolyGram over dinner one night that it might be fun if the pair of them went out and tried their hand at a spot of busking. Yes it would, agreed PolyGram –

and from there the idea snowballed along to the morning of 7 September 1994, when the label spread the word . . .

But any one of the 3,000 or so who turned up that lunchtime at The Piazza in Covent Garden, expecting to find two anonymous figures strumming a couple of Bob Dylan tunes over an upturned hat, were sorely disappointed. Jon and Richie were there, all right, but so was a stage, a mini PA and mixing desk and cameras perched at every vantage point. What may have been a spontaneous idea had snowballed into a media event. Magazines and newspapers infiltrated a crowd comprising not just hardcore Bon Jovi fans but confused tourists and curious office workers taking their midday lunch hour. One and all heard Jon and Richie strum and croon their way through 'Sleep When I'm Dead', 'Livin' On A Prayer', new song 'Someday I'll Be Saturday Night', 'Wanted Dead Or Alive' and Simon & Garfunkel's 'Bridge Over Troubled Water' before being escorted through the crowd to their limo and back to the hotel.

Jon protested that it was not a coolly calculated move in the very week that 'Always' was released as a single. 'My original intention was to play on the steps of Tower Records in Piccadilly . . . then go in and buy a bunch of CDs. But my label got all excited and carried away, and things were drastically changed. I think it was a pity the whole gig was publicized in advance.' Not that he needed to lose any sleep over it. The event proved a massive coup, bringing Bon Jovi unprecedented media exposure – not least coverage in almost all the UK's national dailies, plus dozens of the regional papers. The single went to number two in the UK and was an equally big hit all over Europe. In the States, it spent an incredible thirty-two weeks in the *Billboard* top forty and went a long way to re-establishing the band as a singles act. Better still, 'Always' introduced the band to a whole new generation of fans that still thought 'Slippery When Wet' was a warning sign on a recently mopped McDonald's floor.


Not everything was going as Jon would have wished, however. Alec John Such had shot the video with the band for 'Good Guys . . .', but his working relationship with Bon Jovi was close to ending. Although to audiences all over the world he was little more than a sideman, to the band he was part of the brotherhood and to lose him would be a painful experience. Such flew to the UK in June to play at the Gibson Guitars Centenary Concert (where he joined the Paul Rodgers pick-up band alongside Slash for just one song, Bad Company's 'Bad Company') then announced that after fourteen years in the line-up, he would not be playing on the next Bon Jovi album.

'The guys are writing songs right now, but I'm not doing the next album with them. I will be touring with them, however . . . I'm still in touch with what's going on, they send me tapes to ask my opinion, but the thing is, I want time to do some stuff for myself like guitar clinics, and jam with a bunch of other people. At one time, Bon Jovi was the one, the only, the be all and end all, but I'm finding that there *are* other things . . .'

Other things like co-managing a band, setting up a Free-phone legal advice line for young musicians, running a company making turbochargers for Harley-Davidsons – and racing vintage cars. But Bon Jovi, he said, remained foremost in his plans: 'I'm as happy as I've ever been, I'm not quitting the band or anything like that . . .' Not yet, anyway. Such flew with them to the UK to support the 'Always' single on *Top Of The Pops* in September, but his time in Bon Jovi was rapidly running out. Whether he jumped or was pushed has remained the subject of speculation, but after a decade's service Jon certainly owed him the chance to say he quit even had the latter been true.

Initial guesses were that the sometime Todd Rundgren and Meat Loaf bassist Kasim Sultan might be his replacement in the studio, but it should have come as little surprise when the name of Jon's long term friend Hugh McDonald was announced. Indeed, even given McDonald's reputation as a studio-based session man, once his name was in the frame to record, it never really looked likely that Jon would follow up the plan to use Such for live work only. He never did . . .

Richie was certainly sorry to see him go, sighing as he reflected on the bassist's apparent loss of interest: 'I've known Alec for twenty-seven years, and we've been playing in bands together since we were kids . . . I think if your heart's not in it, you should be allowed to retire if you want. I hope he changes his mind . . .'

That possibility hung around for a while but was soon overshadowed by the news that the next Bon Jovi album was not to be a studio project after all, but a 'Best Of' set, including the monster hit 'Always'. Any idea that such a project meant that the band had run out of steam was quickly corrected by the news that they already had up to thirty songs written or demoed and under consideration for a studio album to follow – due for release early in 1995. It would take about three months longer than planned but the 'Best Of' album was about to take on a life of its own that would maintain the band's high profile for almost the whole year.

Jon oversaw the compilation of the album and video – which Richie tried to persuade him to call *Elvis Is Dead But We're Not* but he opted for the rather more enigmatic *Cross Road*. Compiling the record meant forcing himself to listen to some of the band's older material and watch promo clips that he had not heard or seen in years. Sonically, he was convinced much of the older material stood up well but watching the early videos proved quite a painful experience. The band's first single, 'Runaway', for instance, was still featuring in the live set but the video for it was not even considered for the VHS version. It was an embarrassment he joked about: 'Wouldn't it be a blessing to burn that . . . I did see a bit of that piece-of-shit video recently, and it nearly killed me.'

His reaction was an indication of just how much the band's visual image had changed. In 1994 only Dave Bryan's hair was still permed, and everyone else's was shorter and neater. The most flamboyant items in the touring wardrobe (aside from Jon's unfortunate choice of bandannas) was the odd brightly-coloured shirt or waistcoat and these were as often as not hidden beneath long, tailored, leather coats. The band were looking good in moody black-and-white and when it came to a shot for the *Cross Road* cover it was photographer Anton Corbijn (who had shot the images for *Keep The Faith*) who once again got the nod. Corbijn came up with a neat twist, too, parodying the five hands on the *Keep The Faith* cover with a shot of five boots on the inner sleeve of *Cross Road*. Jon's boot was the one on top, incidentally . . .

In October, on the eve of the release of *Cross Road*, Jon came up with the unusual idea of pushing Tico Torres into the media limelight to talk to magazines about the forthcoming album. It was a first for the band and a treat for Jon, who was increasingly coming to realize that Bon Jovi were well enough known for him not to have to act as their only spokesman.

As well as thirteen of the most popular songs from the band's back catalogue and 'Always', the *Cross Road* set contained one new song 'Someday I'll Be Saturday Night'. Once in the shops it was backed by a massive advertising campaign leading up to the traditionally busy, not to say lucrative, Christmas period.

Reviews of it in the rock press were mixed, but made

intriguing reading because they unwittingly provided not merely critiques of a new album, but almost definitive assessments of Bon Jovi's whole career and current standing. By now shifting ever closer to indie bands and the new generation punk acts like Green Day and Offspring, most magazines found themselves facing a dilemma. Bon Jovi were an anachronism they couldn't ignore. Long after their eighties contemporaries had been consigned to the scrapheap, Jon was still relevant and his face on the cover could still sell magazines.

Jon's one time premier supporters in the heavy metal magazines were still there with him. *Metal Hammer* said that whatever their relevance to the nineties, listening to the eighties hits 'makes you feel glad you went along with them for the ride'. *Kerrang!* bit the bullet and gave the compilation a four-K review, buttonholing the band in 1994 as pedalling a hard rock formula 'pitched somewhere between Bruce Springsteen and a soft drink ad'. But while the review was looking hard for weaknesses it ended up admitting that *Cross Road* was 'an impressive show of strength'. It was a typically guarded review from the section of the press which now saw Bon Jovi as a tolerable evil, one that was clearly not going to go away, and at least they weren't as bad as they used to be – in the old days when the same magazines were saying the band were wonderful.

At the less specialized and more trend-conscious ends of the market, the support was much weaker. *Melody Maker* said the band had moved 'from majestic flatulence to merely piss in the wind'. *Vox* criticized the album for a 'severe lack of substance'. Similarly, *Q* awarded the collection three stars whilst bemoaning the way the compilation merely underlined their lack of musical progress leaving the band in 'a mega-platinum rut . . .'

A measure of the depth of that rut was given in February 1995 when Bon Jovi's label's parent company published its annual accounts. The PolyGram group, with interests in both music and movies, is three-quarters owned by Dutch electronics giant Phillips. Whilst complaining bitterly about revenue lost to Chinese bootleggers who sold on pirate copies to the lucrative Far Eastern market, and graciously acknowledging the unprecedented revenue from the movie *Four Weddings And A Funeral*, they knew several slices of their bacon had been saved by Bon Jovi. With 68 per cent of PolyGram's sales accounted for by pop music, Bon Jovi's 'Best Of' set was listed as the highest seller (its 8 million copies approaching almost 1 per cent of PolyGram's turnover), a couple of hundred thousand ahead of Boyz II Men's *II* album. That 8 million figure was all the more impressive viewed alongside the same year's figures for Nirvana's first album since the suicide of Kurt Cobain – *Unplugged In New York* – which sold 7 million copies.

Meanwhile, the entire back catalogue of another of Seattle's alumni, Jimi Hendrix, had 'a very good year' when it sold 3.5 million albums. *Cross Roads*, which sold an astonishing 5 million copies during its first five weeks on release, ultimately went on to sell 12 million worldwide, making Bon Jovi the label's bestselling act. Not bad for an album the band were worried would be perceived as confirmation that they were all washed up and about to cash in their chips.

It was a point not lost on PolyGram's chief executive officer, Alain Levy, who abandoned his ivory towers to watch the band's 1995 gig in an Amsterdam football stadium. There he was heard to comment: 'Jon's very, very important to us. We like him very, very much . . .'

In December 1994, Jon took the unusual sideways step of releasing a Christmas single under his own name, featuring an assortment of festive-flavoured cuts from the vaults, and –

more significantly – backed by a headline-grabbing promotional video featuring himself and supermodel Cindy Crawford. 'She was available and agreed to be the love interest in the video. I said, "I get to kiss Cindy Crawford for seven hours? Fine!" She was a great kisser . . .'

The video proved to be a stroke of promotional genius as carefully selected stills of him in a clinch with Crawford earned column inches in tabloids all over the world. This free publicity was far more valuable to Jon personally than the record's actual sales as, having been originally recorded for a charity release, its profits were always destined to go to The Special Olympics (a body that organizes international meetings for disabled athletes and for which Jon had undertaken various fund-raising duties since 1987). When it became a hit, everyone was happy. The charity for the boost. Jon for the kudos. Crawford, who almost immediately but quite coincidentally announced her divorce from actor Richard Gere, for the MTV exposure. And Bon Jovi for bridging the profile gap between the 'Always' single and the release of the long-promised next studio album – whilst playing no small part in the continuing success of *Cross Road*.

On 14 December the band played its fifth (now annual) Christmas charity show at the Count Basie Theatre. The set, including the by now obligatory Beatles covers plus The Rolling Stones' 'Let It Bleed' and Tico Torres taking lead vocals on 'Waltzing Matilda', was the last before the band took a Yuletide break.

The studio record was *These Days*, originally to be called *Open All Night*. It was made chiefly at Bearsville Studios in upstate New York with English producer Peter Collins, who had achieved much success working with Queensrÿche. Collins' first sessions with the band, in Nashville, had resulted in the 'Always' and 'Someday I'll Be Saturday Night' tracks (on *Cross*

*Road*) and although the rest of these sessions were later abandoned, he had impressed Jon enough to get the thumbs-up when recording began again after Christmas 1994.

Jon – no one was surprised to learn – had spent some of the holiday season working on vocal tracks in his home studio, poetically christened Sanctuary. But work began in earnest in January 1995 when the band shifted to LA, in deference to Richie who wanted to be near to his new bride, Heather Locklear. Having previously been hitched to Mötley Crüe drummer Tommy Lee (himself then enjoying unprecedented publicity after his marriage to Pamela Anderson) Locklear was no stranger to rock'n'roll, but Richie wanted to spend as much time with her as possible before Bon Jovi's touring schedule kept them apart and Jon was happy to acquiesce.

By July '94, while working in three different Hollywood studios, Bon Jovi whittled the list of thirty contenders down to a shortlist of seventeen or eighteen songs. Amongst them were a couple that had been kicking around for years. One was a Prince-style song called 'Let's Make It Baby' (left over from the *New Jersey* sessions, said to be, according to Jon, a song about 'fucking . . . real nasty and moody . . . pretty wild') that wouldn't make the grade, and the other was 'Diamond Ring', which did. Back in 1990 Jon had described 'Diamond Ring' as being 'about what a wedding ring can do to you. It's like that song "Fever" by Peggy Lee. It's just slinky and quiet and spooky. It doesn't have a fully-fledged chorus, real different for us . . .'

'Diamond Ring' had been written originally for *Slippery . . .* and was re-recorded, unsatisfactorily for *New Jersey*. When the band had reconvened for the *Keep The Faith* tour they had played 'Fever' at the warm-up shows and in retrospect, 'Diamond Ring' did indeed owe the song a debt. For *These Days*, it was a case of third time lucky as Jon worked with Richie and Desmond Child and finally turned the song into something that he considered worth releasing, placing it as the haunting final cut on the album (before the addition of the bonus tracks). The 1995 take on 'Diamond Ring' would have sounded very out of place on *Slippery* . . . or *New Jersey* but it now illustrated perfectly how, in the intervening years, Jon had reinvented the band to the point where, stylistically, almost anything was acceptable.

For a while, it even seemed likely that 'In My Dreams', a ballad Jon wrote for Tico Torres to sing ('It makes my wife cry. It's just a sad song about somebody who died'), might also make the album. In the end Jon passed on it, not because he thought such a song might test the fans' loyalties – the drummer's singing voice, although tuneful, is pitched some-where close to Lee Marvin's in 'Paint Your Wagon' – but simply because he knew he had too many better options.

As with the *Cross Road* collection, *These Days'* smallprint included another credit to John Kalodner. The A&R guru was particularly impressed with the track 'Something For The Pain', a number which in its finished version certainly wouldn't seem totally out of place on any of Aerosmith's last three Geffen albums. (Ironically, Kalodner had followed Aerosmith to Columbia Records when they switched labels, but luckily for Bon Jovi had negotiated a contract that allowed him to work for artists on other labels.) Jon described the track as 'the hardest song on the album' and explained how Kalodner had helped change the number.

'We re-wrote it ten times and finally finished the song after six months of toil. John said, "Let's put an accordion on this song and a twelve-string Rickenbacker". The song was meant to sound like T. Rex but it's turned into something so incredibly unique that even we can't decide where it came from . . .'

Actually, it came from a demo called 'I've Been Lovin' You Too Long To Turn Back Now' and you didn't need to be a legendary A&R man to know that the title was the first thing that had to go. Notwithstanding this simple piece of advice, Jon paid tribute to the man's real talents. 'He's one of the smartest guys I've ever met, an old-style producer-type A&R guy [and] if he ever needs a favour for Columbia Records, I'll write him a song. That's just the way it is . . .'

One song on the album hinted at what Jon respected Kalodner for most – always having an idea. The song in question, 'My Guitar Lies Bleeding In My Arms', was Jon's painful description of his paranoia about losing the ability to write a song.

'It was the concept I'd learnt on "Bed Of Roses": If you can't come up with something, don't just put down the instrument. I had these visions of the scene in *Tommy* where he walks in and there's posters of him all over the wall. I had visions of me walking into a nightmare like that, posters of me staring down going, "Well, go on then, write a record!" It's cool to write that frustration down and admit the fear. It's a constant fear throughout the writing of every record. Every song on every record is like that. Will I ever write another song? Can I? Will I? You question yourself all the time . . .'

On a completely different tack came '(It's Hard) Letting You Go', a number featuring just Jon, Richie and a keyboard programmer called Robbie Buchanan. 'I wrote that song as a gift for one of the producers of *Moonlight And Valentino* (the movie in which Jon would make his acting debut). I didn't even want it in the movie, but they really wanted it . . . so slowly it got there. I'm very happy with how it turned out.'

Strange to think it started life as simply a 'thank-you' note on a cassette tape for having given Jon his break in the movie. Jon didn't even keep a copy of the song for his own sake. Ironic, too, that after turning down 'at least four or five' invitations to write songs for movie soundtracks whilst working on *These Days*, the one he did complete happened quite accidentally.

The sum of these and the other tracks was a record sonically and stylistically quite close to *Keep The Faith*, but lyrically altogether darker. 'It all comes with age and experience,' Jon explained. 'The times when all I wanted to do was chase women and get laid are over. Now I've seen so many other things.'

Amongst these was his perception of the inequalities in modern, particularly American society, a theme hammered home by the album's opening cut, 'Hey God'. The song spat out his vision of the problem with equal parts contempt and helplessness.

'I don't understand how I can walk down 57th Street in Manhattan and step over a guy who's sleeping in the street. It makes no sense to me. Why does America have to have this. You get the guilties, "Why not me?" '

Jon was not about to try to change the world but he was no longer gonna write songs like 'You Give Love A Bad Name' and ignore reality. And while he doubted he could do much to change things, he knew he might at least be able to make people think about them. Bruce Springsteen had once made him think about life, now the songs of Eddie Vedder and Kurt Cobain were talking to a new generation. Jon had long carried a torch for Vedder's Pearl Jam although they and Bon Jovi remained poles apart, even after Jon's lyrical improvements. Although 'Hey God' was a step forward, it hadn't really come close to Pearl Jam's 'Jeremy'. Jon could only shrug and acknowledge the fact: 'I never wrote a song about Jeremy blowing his head off in school because I never knew a kid that did such a thing . . .'

But there might yet be room for Jon to reach a few people – and he offered a theory as to what, other than simply age, separated him from so many of the new bands that had risen up of late.

'In the America I grew up in, we were still falling for Ronald Reagan's nonsense – believing that you could all still get a good, well-paid, job and do better than your dad. Kids in the nineties are given nothing like these expectations. They're told they can't achieve this and they can forget about doing that. Grunge is the voice of a disillusioned generation. I couldn't write those kinda lyrics, but Kurt did a fine job . . .'

The *These Days* tour began in Asia in May 1985. Following their groundbreaking visit as part of the *Keep The Faith* tour, and whatever their fortunes elsewhere around the globe, Bon Jovi could now rely on the burgeoning market of the Far East. Countries like Thailand, Indonesia and Vietnam were not exactly regulars on the worldwide circuit, but with the MTV subsidiary MTV Asia based in Hong Kong and set to be every bit as influential as MTV Europe, Bon Jovi were perfectly poised to make best use of the opportunities offered. Since the early nineties the area has grown ever more open to Western culture, and its youth have been embracing more and more rock bands, with Bon Jovi one of the most popular.

Evidence for this was provided by estimates of the number of pirate copies of their albums sold. PolyGram, keen to staunch this loss of potential revenue, geared up new marketing departments and wheeled in Bon Jovi to play dates in support. This is a trend likely to escalate since PolyGram bought a 50 per cent stake in MTV's Asian operations in April 1995 – and with it a chance to enter the potentially enormous Chinese market as and when satellite television captures the imagination of the long culturally isolated Chinese youth. Unsurprisingly then, MTV Asia was billed as 'exclusive tour presenter' when Bon Jovi began their 'Crossroads To The East' tour. A date in Bangkok was a 12,000 sell-out with 9,000 more locked outside. (Jon told John Aizlewood of *Q* that neither Pearl Jam or Janet Jackson had managed to attract more than 3,000 to the same venue.) The band's appearance in Jakarta, Indonesia, sparked a near riot as between 60,000 and 100,000 fans overcame 3,000 police to get into the Ancol Entertainment Centre.

As the band moved on to Europe, so *These Days*, their sixth studio album was released. *Kerrang!* awarded it the (by now) seemingly obligatory four-K review, the compliments flowing a little more freely this time and leading to the prediction that 'Bon Jovi are proving that classic hard rock is very much alive . . . the biggest rock record of 1995.' *Raw* went half a star better, saluting the band's 'cunning path between the same old same old and radical departure'. But other parts of the metal press were less impressed, *Metal Hammer* awarding only two stars and slamming it as 'surprisingly weak . . . devoid of the normal warmth'. The older readership of *Q* learned with relief that Jon had grown up enough to leave behind his 'mouth and trousers period' turning his hand instead to 'the kind of partial self-reinvention the longer career requires'. This, of course, was just the kind of review Jon would prefer to read . . .

Whatever the reviews, little gave Bon Jovi more pleasure than knowing that sales of *These Days* had raced ahead of the new album by one of the biggest names in the business. Its release coincided with Michael Jackson's album *History* – which represented something of a comeback for him after dismissing all the allegations of child abuse. *History* had cost a reputed $50 million to make and included initially a bonus greatest hits album. Even as they were on stage at Wembley Stadium on 25 June, Jon received the news that Bon Jovi had displaced Jackson at the top of the UK album chart. Better yet, they had outsold him two to one.

And well they might, because on top of the publicity generated by live shows was a concerted marketing effort by PolyGram. With *Cross Road* having established the band as one of the label's major earners, the campaign for *These Days* was the Mercury imprint's biggest of the year, the normal round of press ads being supplemented by leaflets at the shows, promotions at rock clubs, mobile 'ad vans' and posters.

On those posters was a line-up of just four people – Alec John Such had vacated the bass slot but Hugh McDonald hadn't been invited along to the photo sessions. McDonald had played on some of Jon's earliest demos and he, Jon and Richie had crossed paths many times since the early eighties and had even played alongside each other on a couple of tracks on Alice Cooper's 1989 *Trash* album. Many in the crowds perhaps didn't even notice that there had been a change in personnel – from a distance it was easy to assume that McDonald was merely Such wearing a beret. Jon, however, couldn't ever shake the feeling that while McDonald was more than equal to the task, by losing an original member, the whole was much weaker than the loss of just one part.

'Change is change and there's nothing you can do about it, but it is a major blow. We just have to accept it. I have nothing but the best to say about Alec, and I hope he's happy. Just because I want to constantly tour and make records doesn't mean that he should have to feel like that too.

'We miss him. His personality was wonderful and unique and he was a very loyal friend [but] as far as I'm concerned he left on good terms. I think he was surprised when it happened, but none of us were. He made his own bed so we told him, "Al, we're gonna get someone else" and that was that. But I still call him and leave messages. He sent gifts over when Jesse was born. It'll take time . . .'

Jon hinted further at the wrench when talking about getting in a replacement. 'First of all, I couldn't face the audition process. Hugh's a phenomenal bass player, a good man and I've known him my whole career – but he still can't be a full member of the band because I'm going through that "jilted romance" period.'

Which explained why his face wasn't on the posters. But McDonald fitted right in, anonymous yet dependable. The Rolling Stones had replaced Bill Wyman – maybe it was just a bad decade for long-time bassists.

The busking they had done the previous autumn had been such fun – and had won them so much publicity – that it was repeated again all over Europe when *These Days* was released. But because Britain had already seen it, the band (not just Jon and Richie) went one (or two) better and 'busked' in three cities in a single day, stopping traffic in Glasgow and Cardiff before returning to the capital on the evening of 14 June. All this in the middle of a twenty-five date stadium tour of continental Europe – a schedule which saw them take a midnight flight from Heathrow to Lisbon directly after the last acoustic set.

Elsewhere on that schedule were dates in Paris, where Jon opted to relinquish his band's headlining status and fulfil a lifetime's ambition. Enough people have asked him how on earth he pulled such a coup off to assume that the same simple answer is far more likely to be the truth than a carefully rehearsed answer. He got to play on the same bill as The Rolling Stones by bypassing managers, agents and the usual channels. Employing nothing more than a bit of detective work (for a number) and a bit of cheek (with a fax machine) . . .

'I wrote Mick Jagger a note and said, "Mick, I want to open for you". Honest to God! I said: "I'd carry your luggage for you any day of the week, you're the coolest. Let me open for you . . ."' Jagger said yes, it was that simple, and so Bon Jovi got to share the stage with The Rolling Stones in Paris – not once, but twice.

Watching The Rolling Stones during the US leg of their *Voodoo Lounge* tour, Jon couldn't help but catch a glimpse of the band's thirty foot high inflatable Elvis Presley. 'Jon liked it so much he said he wanted one too,' said its maker, Robin Harries of the English company Air Artists. Forsaking the Stones' fifties-style gold-suited Elvis, Jon's own preference was for a Vegas-style white-suited version – a little larger around the waistband, and with the extra attraction of two faces, devil's horns and – originally at least – a rather flaccid guitar neck.

'The stem of the guitar wasn't filling with air properly and was bending downwards,' smirked Harries. 'So we put another fan inside the guitar, up at the neck. It was great watching the crowd after that – suddenly it would jerk up and everyone would cheer . . .'

Suitably aroused, Elvis and his guitar went on to be a highlight of the tour, this despite the distractions of three other inflatables, two bizarre dragons and a naked woman with the head of a chicken. A couple of strong men on each inflatable, tugging rhythmically on guy ropes, saw to it that each night around £60,000-worth of plastic and fresh air briefly upstaged Bon Jovi as they danced along for the closing section of the main set.

But the £60,000 spent was small beer compared to the takings of even the UK dates. Three (almost) sold-out Wembley Stadiums, Cardiff Arms Park, Gateshead International Stadium and Sheffield Don Valley Stadium added up to something like a third of a million tickets sold. And at around £21 a throw, a conservative estimate of gate receipts would put the gross takings in the region of a cool £7 million. This was very big business by anybody's standards.

It was a big show, too. Yet the inflatables aside, many of those dancing at the back were unlikely to see anything of the band except in the form of their digitalized and giganticized images as projected onto the giant Jumbotron TV screens. Whilst many – bands and pundits alike – criticized any band who chose to play this kind of enormous outdoor gig, Jon was quick to defend his own choice.

'I like stadiums. Some people say it's not personal but those are the guys who can't play stadiums. Stadiums are a real fucking blast. They can be as personal as you want them to be. I'll talk to the guy in the hundredth row. If I see him, I'll go, "You with the Marlboro, what are you doing?" That's the magic.'

He would, too. As part of the attempt to get closer to the audience during this tour, small groups of people would be invited up onto the stage to dance or enjoy a free drink from 'bar' sets, or just to look out at the crowd and help share in a crude and approximate recreation of the times when Bon Jovi still played the bars. For sure, many of those standing awe-struck behind Richie or Dave Bryan were record company guests, media types or friends, but many others were competition winners plucked from magazines and radio audiences for a three song/fifteen minute slot of shared fame. Tokenism maybe, but a genuine effort on the part of the band to make a gig before tens of thousands of people become as close up and personal as possible.

For the British dates proper, Bon Jovi assembled an unmistakably heavy rock bill – an odd move given Bon Jovi's new found position towards the centre of the mainstream alongside the likes of The Rolling Stones, REM and U2. Jon claimed to have approached The Pretenders, Sheryl Crow, Soul Asylum, The Black Crowes, Collective Soul and Oasis but all were either unavailable or unprepared to sit third on the bill behind Van Halen.

The Wembley gigs were particularly poignant for Jon, falling as they did almost ten years to the day after he watched Live-Aid broadcast from there to his hotel room in the States where Bon Jovi were touring. Earlier on the European dates,

Bon Jovi had taken to playing 'Rockin' All Over The World' – the song written by former Creedence Clearwater Revival man John Fogerty, made popular by Status Quo and employed by them to open the Live-Aid event. But at Wembley, Jon had arranged another surprise. On the Sunday night, Bob Geldof joined them on stage for an encore rendition of his Boomtown Rats' classic 'I Don't Like Mondays'. Jon had hoped to persuade Geldof to sanction releasing the track as a charity single. But the Irishman, despite Dave Bryan's splendid piano work, was reluctant to go along with the idea and the live recording was therefore relegated to a subsequent B-side.

It was a small disappointment in light of the fact that the band had just played three shows at the UK's premier stadium, the same number booked a couple of months later for The Rolling Stones. In the nineties there were, estimated Live-Aid promoter Harvey Goldsmith, only twenty acts in the world who could sell out Wembley Stadium. There were far fewer who could (almost) sell out three. Bon Jovi now sat comfortably among the world's top drawing elite . . .

Jon, proud of this fact, had the third show filmed for release in October as the *Live From London* video. Released in October in time for the pre-Christmas rush, the marketing strategy for the tape was simple: maximum exposure. And so an independent publicist was ordered to aim for daily coverage in national newspapers every day before 25 December.

Bon Jovi in the 90s have learnt the difference between non-stop touring and carefully planned promotion. As the former becomes more measured, so the latter can ensure their longevity. After the European tour, dates in the US and Canada were followed by Central and Southern America shows then Bon Jovi's first ever appearance in South Africa at the start of December. Such schedules may look hectic but in reality are so much less intense than the tours of the late eighties.

Since then the band have learned many lessons, not least

that just as important as the dates played are the 'events' they slot in around the tour. In June, they were present at the MTV-featured *Kerrang!* Awards. In September, they were inducted into the Rock And Roll Hall Of Fame, the giant rock'n'roll museum in Cleveland, Ohio, and played a short set alongside the likes of Chuck Berry, Bruce Springsteen, The Kinks, Aretha Franklin, Little Richard (as well as Snoop Doggy Dog to remind Jon that not all recognized by the Hall Of Fame were of long-established musical credentials). That same month they stopped traffic in New York's Times Square on a stage built in the middle of the celebrated junction as a featured (but not nominated) act at the MTV Music Awards, a neat but not wholly original trick – violinist Vanessa Mae had done the same thing to great effect twelve months earlier.

As the 'Something For The Pain' single charted in the UK in October, the band were on tour in the States. *Top Of The Pops* beckoned and so the band booked ten minutes of satellite time, set up their gear in front of one of their jets, and lip-synched the tune from the airport tarmac. In November, they flew into Paris to pick up a trophy at the MTV Europe Music Awards – and to protest against French H-bomb tests alongside Bono of U2. December saw them named Best Rock Band in the *Smash Hits* Readers Poll and although they were in South Africa at the time, a video clip got their faces onto national television and a little closer to the hearts of the pop magazine's young readership.

The plaques and gongs for such events are one thing, but the media coverage is the real prize. Five minutes on MTV can go a very long way, being shown again and again all over the world. In the mid-nineties, a Bon Jovi tour will, as a matter of course, take in any major media events to maintain the profile of the band globally.

In 1995, a new approach to tailor-made clips for singles appeared to be evolving, too. For years, making a video was a chore to Bon Jovi. Although the medium served them well, they were never a band to employ technology to exploit its artistic possibilities. But the clip for 'Something For The Pain' – featuring lookalikes of Grunge stars Weiland (of Stone Temple Pilots), Courtney Love (of Hole), and Eddie Vedder of Pearl Jam plus an Ice-T clone all lip-synching the song – suggested Bon Jovi were at last trying a little harder.

Bon Jovi had clearly weathered the storm of competition from such bands when so many had predicted that these bands would wipe Bon Jovi out. It was really only a question of time before the cream floated to the surface and the rest sank without trace, as Jon observed.

'How many more alternative bands can you stand before you want to throw up? The good ones will survive and the bad ones will fade away. Pearl Jam will still be around because of what they are. But Eddie Vedder's Eddie Vedder and I'm me. I really do think a lot of these bands – like Therapy? and Tool and Nine Inch Nails – gave rock the kick it needed, with the chances they're taking lyrically and musically. I don't write those kinds of songs, but it sure makes you think. I just figure that fashion is fashion – and fashion comes and goes.'

Record labels, much in the way they had when Bon Jovi broke through with *Slippery* . . ., had fallen over themselves to sign bands exhibiting anything like the potential of Nirvana or Pearl Jam. But by 1995, although the world of rock music had been warped beyond all recognition, saturation point for the audience's capacity for new bands of short-haired angry young men was very close to being reached. Having watched what had happened to music tastes over the past two or three years, Jon could afford a smile, sure that, as ever, longevity was a direct function of quality. And although he would almost certainly never again sell as many copies of an album as with *Slippery* . . . there was at least room for Bon Jovi in the mid-nineties.

Quotes gratefully taken from:

Steffan Chirazi, *Kerrang!* 541, 15 April 1994; Dave Reynolds, *Kerrang!* 501, July 2 1994; Sylvie Simmons, *Kerrang!* 503, 9 July 1994; Paul Henderson, *Metal Hammer*, August 1994; Malcolm Dome, *Kerrang!* 512, 17 September 1994; Paul Elliott, *Kerrang!* 515, 8 October 1994; *The Economist*, 26 November 1994; Mick Wall, *Raw* 163, 23 November–6 December 1994; Kristina Estlund, *RIP*, December 1994; Steve Beebee, *Kerrang!* 526, 24/31 December 1994; *Guardian*, 22 February 1995; *The Times*, 20 April 1995; Steffan Chirazi, *Kerrang!* 543, 29 April 1995; *Guardian*, 3 May 1995; Jerry Ewing, *Metal Hammer*, July 1995; Paul Henderson, *Metal Hammer*, July 1995; Phil Sutcliffe, *Q* 106, July 1995; John Aizlewood, *Q* 106, July 1995; *Today*, 7 July 1995; David Hochman, *US*, August 1995.

# The Godfather Part III

*'I want us to be together because it's afforded me all these things.
It's really been my love and I feel a loyalty to those four guys that
I only feel toward my immediate family.'*
The paternal face of Jon Bon Jovi, 1990

*'If Eddie Vedder fucks up, runs into a wall, and crashes, I can't call
him up! He's not going to listen to me . . . I'm not trying to be a seer or
anything, I'm no old man, but there are times when you wish you could
say stuff to people . . .'* The caring face of Jon Bon Jovi, 1994

WE PICK UP the thread of Jon's parallel role as the Don of the
Jersey Syndicate in happier times. Following his conflicts with
Skid Row over the Underground deal, and with Richie over the
same matter, an undisclosed settlement brought the sorry affair
to a close. His fingers had been burnt but Jon was once again
free to, if not exactly rebuild the Jersey Syndicate, at least
spread a little goodwill. And unlike Michael Corleone's efforts
in the third part of Coppola's epic celluloid trilogy, this time
the family wasn't about to fall apart on him . . .

During 1990, his year out as a solo artist, Jon returned a
long-remembered favour to Hall & Oates – who had let him
support them years earlier, even before he was signed. Along
with his *Blaze Of Glory* co-producer Danny Kortchmar, Jon

stepped a little beyond the boundaries of rock music to write and produce a single for them. The track, 'So Close', was the lead-off cut on their *Change Of Season* album and became a top twenty hit in the States, denting the lower reaches of the UK listings also.

In 1991, after he and Richie agreed to dissolve The Underground, Jon decided to launch his own label, planning to give others the kind of break he had received at the start of his own career. With Richie making it plain that he had no interest in being involved in such a venture, Jon turned to his two younger brothers – both veterans of the Bon Jovi tour support team – and named the label Jambco: an acronym of Jon, Anthony and Matt Bongiovi Company.

Jambco's first release was Aldo Nova's comeback album, *Blood On The Bricks*, in June 1991. Nova was the Canadian-born guitarist who had produced and played on the 'Runaway' demo that had set the Bon Jovi ball rolling, and for Jon it was natural that Nova should be the first focus of attention for Jambco. He had been out of the limelight for five years but Jon wanted to change that. Together they co-wrote fifteen songs, which they planned to whittle down to an album's worth for recording during the spring of 1991. Nova was quick to acknowledge Jon's assistance.

'He got me out of my lethargy. Who knows where I'd be without Jonny? He really did work his heart out and played a big part on the album . . . He obviously has real clout at PolyGram. They will take notice of what he says and have to give this LP their best shot.'

But *Blood On The Bricks* was less than a hit and running Jambco proved to be the source of some frustration for Jon. The label's second release, *Pretty Blue World* by singer-songwriter Billy Falcon a few months later (co-produced by Jon and Danny Kortchmar) was lower key but similarly failed to set the charts alight.

Jon's intention was to keep Jambco cheap and simple – unlike, for example, Madonna, who ran her Maverick label as a full-time, fully-staffed business. 'If I stumble across something I like, I'll get involved,' he said later. 'I was gung-ho to sign Black 47 until I discovered they'd already gotten a deal. I'd love to unearth a budding Ice-T because I think the rap community is saying stuff that the whole of America – and certain sections of white society, especially – should be listening to.'

Disappointingly for Jon, record company politics meant Jambco turned out to be anything but simple. 'Your own record label is a difficult animal to run, because even though they give you the power to do what you want to do, you're always only a subsidiary to a major . . .'

'They' and 'a major' being PolyGram, of course. In short, it meant that no matter who Jon wanted to help promote, develop or release, his choices still had to be run by the same A&R departments that oversaw Bon Jovi's own releases (from *Keep The Faith* onwards also bearing an almost token Jambco logo) and the second Billy Falcon record has yet to surface. 'It isn't a pretty business . . .' he conceded.

To close the door on such frustrations, in late 1991 he went all the way back to his Jersey R'n'B/soul roots and fulfilled a lifetime's ambition by joining Southside Johnny And The Asbury Jukes, the band he had opened for way back and idolized for much longer, not just for a one-off jam as in the past, but for a whole twelve-date tour. After more than a year working as a solo artist, he rewarded himself with this ultimate busman's holiday, abandoning his accustomed touring luxuries for a humbling place alongside Southside's whole band in a tour bus as it motored between selected bars and small clubs in New Jersey. Jon was paid $75 a night but was richly rewarded spiritually.

'I had a roommate for the first time in my career!' laughed

Jon. 'John has ten guys in the band so he got his own room and I roomed with the other guitar player. We drove around in a van, stayed in [the flamboyantly named] Quality Inns. There were no wardrobe girls so what you wore in the van you wore in the club that night . . . No crew, so you loaded your own gear. It was pretty rough but it was great.'

The tour ended with a show in Asbury itself. 'That was cool. In Asbury with your hero and I'm just playing rhythm guitar and singing a little harmony. I felt like Keith Richards . . .'

And he still counts his blue satin Asbury Jukes jacket amongst his most prized possessions . . .

But rather than being the Don, that trip for Jon was perhaps more like kissing the ring of his *own* godfather. Truth to tell, benevolence was not his strongest suit in 1992 and 1993 – unless you count his dedication to Messrs Sambora, Bryan, Torres and Such in trying to regroup his immediate Bon Jovi family for the shit-or-bust *Keep The Faith* album and tour.

At the time he declared passionately: 'I want us to be together because it's afforded me all these things. It's really been my love and I feel a loyalty to those four guys that I only feel toward my immediate family.' Little wonder, perhaps, that it was only with that album and tour completed – and his and the band's future apparently restored – that his desire to help others could make itself evident once more.

Don't mistake Jon's opinion for an excuse. It's not intended as one. And there was no proper excuse given, either, for the surprise departure of bassist Alec John Such in 1995. This represented a major failing of Jon as Godfather of the brotherhood's most exclusive inner sanctum, shattering for ever the fraternal imagery of the five hands held together on the *Keep The Faith* artwork.

No attempt should be made to deify Jon Bon Jovi, but in the nineties, after more than a decade in the business, there is still plenty of evidence to suggest that, without being fawning or overly charitable, he still cares even when he doesn't need to. In him is apparently a deeply felt wish to help kindred souls advance or learn lessons more quickly and painlessly than he did. This has rarely been better illustrated than in 1994 when, musing on the painfully public discomfort Pearl Jam's Eddie Vedder seemed to be enduring, Jon was ruefully moved to say: 'If Eddie Vedder, with all his amazing talent – and, to me, he's a major superstar – fucks up, runs into a wall, and crashes, I can't call him up! He's not going to listen to me. Who am I to tell him? I'm just this rich rock'n'roll star, blah blah blah . . . I'm not trying to be a seer or anything, I'm no old man, but there are times when you wish you could say stuff to people . . .'

Onwards into 1995 and Jon was to be found trying to give a whole host of young bands a helping hand as Bon Jovi's world tour began. Foremost among these was Crown Of Thorns, the latest outfit fronted by his friend, the ex-Plasmatics and Little Steven bass player Jean Beauvoir. Jon arranged for Crown Of Thorns to open shows for Bon Jovi at stadium gigs all over Europe – even though their profile was no higher than most of the guys checking tickets at the turnstiles. Crown Of Thorns brought with them a special guest in the shape of Jon's old buddy – second only to Southside Johnny on the Jon Bon Jovi roll of honour – the permanently bandanna'd guitarist Little Steven. Although frequently taking the stage long before the venues were half full, having Crown Of Thorns along at least gave Jon another chance to repay a little of the debt he believes he still owes to Little Steven. To complete the supporting bill (topped by Van Halen) Jon even asked *Kerrang!* readers to elect their favourite up-and-coming band. And so a mixture of their votes – and more prosaic concerns such as agencies and availability – saw slots for fast-rising American heavy metallers Ugly Kid Joe and established UK favourites Thunder.

After they'd all been and gone, and Bon Jovi themselves had completed their main set, each night Jon insisted that Little Steven get up and play alongside him and the band during the encores, an appearance usually prefaced by Jon's introduction: 'If you look up the word "cool" in the dictionary, you'll find a picture of this man . . .' He had never forgotten Little Steven, when still the guitarist with Bruce Springsteen's E Street Band, had taken time to listen to and help Jon when he was being ignored by almost everyone else.

Little Steven's presence in the wings while the band played, coupled with various family members, friends, and the fans gazing on in awe from the on-stage 'bars', served to bring Jon closer to home, and with the memories of Bon Jovi's rocky times during the late eighties and early nineties now fading, allowed him time to sit back like the Don of a happy family once again. The departure of Alec John Such notwithstanding, Jon Bon Jovi's band were the band he always dreamed of. A band he could look upon and watch over as his immediate family.

'We know each other better than brothers because we've been together for twelve years,' he explained with pride. 'It's not a relationship where it's separate dressing rooms. I couldn't handle that. Show number four would be the end of the tour and we'd be at home watching TV. I only wish everybody in their lives could have friends like this . . .'

(To be continued? . . .)

Interlude quotes gratefully taken from:

Malcolm Dome, *Kerrang!* 127, 21 August–3 September 1986; Malcolm Dome, *Kerrang!* 128, 4–17 September 1986; Elianne Halbersberg, *Kerrang!* 224, 4 February 1989; Howard Johnson, *Mega Metal Kerrang!* 16,

# BON JOVI

1989; Alison Joy, *Kerrang!* 252, 19 August 1989; Steve Mascord, *Kerrang!* 263, 4 November 1989; Mick Wall, *Kerrang!* 265, 18 November 1989; Mick Wall, *Kerrang!* 301, 4 August 1990; Alison Joy, *Kerrang!* 313, 27 October 1990; Adrian Deevoy, *Q* 52, January 1991; Malcolm Dome, *Raw* 76, 24 July–6 August 1991; Toby Jepson, *Metal Hammer*, September 1993; Stuart Clark, *Hot Press*, 22 September 1993; Dave Reynolds, *Kerrang!* 426, 16 January 1993; Steffan Chirazi, *Rip*, April 1994; John Aizlewood, *Q* 106, July 1995; Paul Henderson, *Metal Hammer*, July 1995; Sylvie Simmons, *Kerrang!* 559, 19 August 1995.

# CHAPTER EIGHT

# The Movies

*'I can't see myself doing* Wayne's World *or something else where I'm basically playing myself. There's no challenge in that.'*
Jon Bon Jovi, 1993

*'I need to do this for the artistic freedom. It gives me the chance to be artistic without having to write it, in essence direct it, to market it and tour it for 250 shows.'* Jon Bon Jovi, 1995

*'I don't pretend to think I could be a great actor [just] because I've been in one movie. I'm going right back to lessons.'*
Jon Bon Jovi, 1995

JON BON JOVI'S fledgling career as a movie actor is one of the few things that have happened to him almost by accident. For years, people had been suggesting he had the looks of a matinée idol but if he harboured any ambitions of becoming one, then he did a very good job of keeping those thoughts private.

As a youngster, it wasn't all music music music for Jon Bon Jovi, but his passion for the cinema was certainly nothing like as consuming. Like many other teenagers, he'd catch up on the classics on TV and get taken by his father to check out the latest action movies in Hillsboro on a Saturday afternoon. His father also instilled in Jon a love of Clint Eastwood's man with no name and Westerns made before Jon was born like *The Magnificent Seven* and those of John Ford.

But with the band came touring commitments that tended to keep him away from the movies for months. Even so, he maintains that he always tries to catch up, suggesting that ever since his time in high school, he was the guy who on a Friday would run to the store to buy the newspaper to see what that week's new release was. Then he and Dorothea would often go straight from school into a matinée.

Acting was something he dallied with as a youngster – he admits to one 'itty bitty part' in a high school play called *Mame* – but he never really considered the stage (movie or theatre) as a career. The lure of rock'n'roll was stronger. Nevertheless, growing up so close to the bright lights and mean streets of New York City, he developed quite an interest in watching the works of Martin Scorsese up there on the big screen. Just as Southside Johnny and Bruce Springsteen wrote songs about places he visited, Scorsese and any number of world renowned film-makers were producing pictures based on places he knew almost as well.

Eschewing all the contemporary blockbusters made by the likes of Spielberg, Jon developed a taste for the more cosmopolitan films of Francis Ford Coppola, citing his favourite film as *The Godfather*, I and II. Ask him to name an actor and Al Pacino and Robert De Niro will come to his mind immediately.

Probe a little further into his appreciation of stars from Hollywood's classic Golden Age and his choice is no less controversial. 'I love Cagney because he could sing, he could dance and he could be the tough guy – all at the same time.' And of his contemporaries, he has no hesitation in giving his vote to Johnny Depp and, above all, Gary Oldman ('a genius, a wonderful actor').

These are discerning choices, of actors rather than movie stars, and while they may be far from radical, they at least convey that Jon has a sense of the movie as an artform rather than pure entertainment. And although such names are likely to be repeated by others all over the world, Jon views these actors as heroes rather than rôle models. He would hardly have claimed to have turned to movie acting because of a road-to-Damascus-type experience watching, say, Oldman's performance in *Prick Up Your Ears*. When Jon went over to Al Pacino and introduced himself after picking up the Golden Globe for 'Blaze Of Glory', he did so purely because he wanted to shake hands with a legend, not because he was after the name of Pacino's agent. Even then, a parallel career in acting was far from his mind.

That kind of schmoozing has never been his style and he's not naive enough to think that he could build a whole new career out of trading on his name as a rock'n'roll singer. 'I don't really like to mix with a lot of celebrities. If you're in those circles in Hollywood, you're in those circles, you know what I mean? I'm not. They're a lot of work. I'm from New Jersey and I stay at home.'

His trips to the Golden Globes and the Oscars when he was nominated for 'Blaze Of Glory' soundtrack taught him where he stood in the pecking order – and how much he'd need to change as a person to get himself ingratiated into studio circles. 'I mean, I was great. I loved every second. [But] I don't know very many people in the industry. I've met a few but I'm not in the loop, and you've got to be in the loop. You've got to go and work it. I'm not going to do that . . .'

It might actually be easier, he believes, if he were just plain old Jon Bongiovi, a wannabe actor, rather than Jon Bon Jovi the singer turned actor. In fact, even as he moved around the Golden Globes ceremony, still genuinely shocked and thrilled that he'd actually won something, shaking hands with tuxedo grins and glittering ball gowns, acting was very much the last thing on his mind. If the Golden Globes gave him any idea, it was that he might actually be able to make a go of writing movie *music*, to develop this new string to his bow as a sideline.

After seven years doing little else but eat, breathe and sleep Bon Jovi, the closest he'd ever come to acting was endless hours spent hamming it up in any number of boring and frustrating promo video shoots. Not for him the long format videos that Axl Rose had spent multi-million dollar budgets making for the Guns N' Roses singles 'Don't Cry', 'November Rain' and 'Estranged'. Certainly not. A movie was strictly something he watched – in a darkened room as a paying customer, or at home pushing a tape into a VCR.

The only time he seriously considered dabbling in the medium was in early 1984, a few months before the first Bon Jovi album came out. Paramount were still looking to cast the lead in *Footloose* but were struggling to find a suitably attractive young dancer. They got desperate enough to consider re-writing the script to make its central figure an aspiring rock singer instead, and so Jon was auditioned. Jon then made a wise decision, as he told Mick Wall later that year.

'I turned down the chance because what I really wanted to be known for was making records. If I made a movie first, then for ever more I would be labelled as an actor that wanted to be a rock star . . .'

Rick Springfield would certainly agree with that. Ironically, Richie Sambora did appear in that movie as part of a nightclub band – after the producers went back to their original story plan and cast Kevin Bacon in the lead role, as a dancer.

And so it was not until February 1990 that a phonecall set him on the way to facing a camera in the hands of someone other than a video crew or magazine photographer.

At the time, having just completed their *New Jersey* world tour amidst no small amount of bad feeling, the band were preparing to take a lengthy break from each other. Jon was facing a few months in an editing suite listening to tapes of concerts recorded over the previous months and mixing them down into a live album. A month earlier it had seemed like a great idea, but when his phone rang and his friend Emilio Estevez was on the other end, Jon had instant second thoughts.

Jon had been friends with Estevez, son of Martin Sheen (whose real name is Ramon Estevez), for some time. The two were of the same generation and got on well socially. Like Jon, Estevez was born in 1962 and had begun his career in earnest at the age of twenty. While Jon was signing to Mercury and Doc McGhee, Estevez was debuting in *Tex*, although it would not be until 1984's *Repo Man*, alongside Harry Dean Stanton, that he would really make his mark.

In 1990, however, Estevez was about to film *Young Guns II* and suggested that Jon come along, hang out in the desert with him, watch the movie being made, hire a motorcycle, blah blah blah. Estevez's description of the location and the good time to be had proved more than persuasive and Jon found himself ditching thoughts of tape reels and mixing desks in cramped and darkened rooms, exchanging them for wide open spaces, rocky canyons and the wind in his hair.

'The one thing on my mind was, if something comes up that you don't do every day of your life, do it this time. For the first time when you say you're going to do something – go out and fucking do it. If you finally want to go somewhere where there isn't an arena, then go there, you know? Like, I always say I wanna go to Utah and ride motorcycles and I never fuckin' do . . .'

He never did make it to Utah, but New Mexico seemed like the next best thing. But as he later admitted, doing something on his own – travelling without the band, a road manager, his family and even Dorothea – was a big step. As confident and self-assured as he may have been, he was more a team player than a free spirit.

'It's a big deal for me to come to New York City, an hour

and a half from my house, without picking up my dad on the way and saying, "Hey, you wanna take a ride?" I'm not used to doing anything by myself. I just don't do it.'

But do it he did. And, quite quickly, like it he didn't. 'I was freezing my ass off in Santa Fe, New Mexico, in February, dressed the way you would dress your three-year-old kid. You know, snowsuit, gloves, feetwarmers, just freezing my ass. I was thinking, why am I out here with these idiots? I was miserable.'

It wasn't made any better watching Estevez, who was putting him up in a rented house off the set, and the other stars of the movie, running around in T-shirts and jeans, having the time of their lives riding horses, and shooting guns. After four or five days, Jon had seen enough and said so.

'I'm going, "Fuck this, I'm a spoilt brat, I wanna go home!" ... The crew finally said, as a joke, "C'mon, dress up, you can be one of the extras" and I said, "Okay, I'll do it, it'll be fun." And as I did it, they made fun of me. They all sang, "Shot through the heart . . ." as I got shot and the blood thing spurts. One take, three a.m.'

His role wasn't much more glamorous than an innocent bystander, but at least he got to briefly feel a little warmer. He took solace in the fact that alongside him was the movie's scriptwriter, John Frusco, meeting a similar fate. But although Jon claimed his scene lasts about half a minute, his actual screen time is closer to a mere sixteen seconds, occurring as a band of captives escape from a jail – in the movie merely a pit dug in the ground topped with a cage lid.

'We were locked up in this pit, a bunch of extras jumped out of the pit and I'm one of those guys. There's a whole screen shot of me getting shot and falling back into the hole.

'The sheriff sees me and loads up his gun and I take one hit to the chest and there's blood everywhere. It's in slow motion and in close-up. And that's it. It took me longer to explain than it did for it to happen . . .

'My own grandmother went to see the movie and she said to me, "It was very good but I didn't see you in it!" Don't mistake this for an acting career . . .'

Nevertheless, it got him started on one. Quite a turnaround in such a short time. 'I just watched Emilio and Kiefer [Sutherland] and all those guys, and I was intrigued by it but not enough that I was gonna quit my day job, so I went home and I started to talk to him about it whenever I'd be in California, then I took up lessons. I read a couple of books first to see about it then I went to lessons in New York and I never told anybody. I never told the band, I never told Emilio, I never told anybody. [And it was] three years before I considered doing anything.'

Three years is a long time to keep a secret, unless that secret is something you either desperately want to impress with or are especially scared of failing at. A long time, too, for a man coming from one industry alive with gossip and moving into another perhaps even more deeply permeated with rumour and scandal. Comparing acting with singing in a rock'n'roll band is a perilous practice, but it seems reasonable to assume that Jon was merely exercising the same quality control that had steered him through the rest of his personal life.

'I'd rather be in a cult movie than some big blockbuster which takes its $40 million budget and uses car chases and explosions to plaster over the cracks in the plot. Look at Quentin Tarantino – he was given loose change to make *Reservoir Dogs* and it's a classic. Another favourite of mine is *State Of Grace* starring Gary Oldman and Sean Penn, which doesn't do anything fancy but has brilliant dialogue.'

An alternative and more cynical definition of 'cult' has always been 'unsuccessful', but Jon clearly prefered to be true to whatever talent he could muster rather than take the easy route. 'I can't see myself doing *Wayne's World* or something else where I'm basically playing myself. There's no challenge in that.'

He had plenty to gain if he could equal the challenge and make a success of acting, but much more to lose if he flopped. His critics would have been queuing up to take a swipe if he announced his intention prematurely, then flunked out – or worse, if he tried to run before he could walk and made a fool of himself. Jon wasn't planning on doing either. He was well aware of the stigma attached to rock'n'rollers with thespian ambitions.

'I never took it for granted that because I was a singer in a rock band I could act. But I wouldn't give a microphone to even Robert De Niro because there's no way he could do Wembley Stadium. The theory behind it was always that I wanted to be an actor in a film not a rock star in a movie. I am very serious about what I am pursuing . . .'

There was no doubt that his is the kind of face the camera loves and even if he wasn't serious he would at least look good having a half-hearted go. In magazines and on posters he's rarely looked like a man beaten as a child with the ugly stick. Watch a promo video or catch a glimpse of him smile, his face ten metres wide on a Jumbotron screen in concert, and the impression is reinforced. But rock stars turned actors is not a topic that would take much of an evening to discuss.

'Hopefully, if I ever get out of my depth, someone will say, "Jon, that sucks!" – but it'll probably happen too late and I'll make a fool of myself. Just because you can sing, it doesn't necessarily mean you can act.'

Jon himself nominates perhaps only David Bowie and Sting as occasionally deserving of the tag 'great', clearly aware that for their every respective success like *Merry Christmas Mr*

*Lawrence* or *Brimstone And Treacle* there lurks a *The Man Who Fell To Earth* or a *Dune*. Others that have made the transition with any distinction are indeed rare, among them Cher, Tom Waits and Madonna, but look much further and you'll be forced to include Mick Jagger and Phil Collins. Elvis Presley, even . . .

So Jon took the prospect seriously. Seriously enough to get himself an acting tutor. In Hollywood studio movies, there are broadly two kinds of actors: there are film stars and actors. 'Film stars' may be the tip of a very large iceberg who have headed out west to Hollywood and worked their way through all manner of often thankless walk-on rôles and TV parts until they got themselves noticed. The casting couch is an over-used cliché but very often a winning smile and a face that the camera loves can go a long way to gloss over the lack of any real acting talent.

The other kind, 'the actors', may drift into Hollywood only reluctantly. They consider movies an end rather than a means and tend to start out in New York, training as a stage actor. As a New Jersey-ite, this was geographically an easier option for Jon, but a nonetheless admirable one. He could easily have used his name and good looks to get himself into any number of (probably) straight-to-video TV movies, but instead he hooked up with a New York tutor called Harold Guskin.

Something of a celebrated figure on the NY acting scene, Guskin had a client list that included Kevin Klein, Sally Field, Michelle Pfeiffer – and certainly impressed Jon: 'You name it, he's done them all through the years.'

Guskin, who as well as coaching had acted and directed, worked with his clients in a one-room apartment, putting them through his exercises and their paces on a one-to-one basis on and around his furniture. Jon is full of admiration for his help and no nonsense attitude: 'He's just a great New York kinda guy who'll call "Bullshit!" everytime you do something, so he's great!'

When Jon felt he was ready, and Guskin had begun calling 'Bullshit!' a little less convincingly, Jon decided it was time to let the secret out, but then only on something like a need-to-know basis. 'I finally told a couple of people at the record company. I changed agencies and I got an acting agent. We just said, "Let's do the *Keep The Faith* album and tour and we'll just start considering reading things..." Then after the tour was over, it took me a year of meeting people and stuff before I got to the first rôle.'

One he did try for was that of Lt Peter Ince – or 'Weps' – in 1995's surprise smash submarine thriller *Crimson Tide*, directed by Tony Scott. Jon met and felt he got on well with Scott (whose previous credits included *Top Gun* and *Days Of Thunder*) but thinks that in the end, the director was reluctant to entrust such a pivotal part to a newcomer and chose the more experienced Viggo Mortensen, who had starred opposite Al Pacino in *Carlito's Way*, instead.

Jon's first serious role, then, came in *Moonlight And Valentino*, directed by David Anspaugh (formerly director of the hit TV series *Hill Street Blues*). 'I got involved maybe a year before it went to film. I saw a rough draft of the script and thought, this could be the one ... It's a great rôle. Regardless of who did it, had I gone to see the film I would've gone, this is the rôle. Even though you're not in a scene or talking about the character, it's a great rôle ... So I waited for the script revision and went through the process. I thought I was definitely the *last* guy they wanted to cast but, um, through persistence ...'

When the movie had finally wrapped, the film's producers admitted to him that his persistence had been a major factor and that they met him initially only out of courtesy. But it was an opportunity he predicably grasped with both hands. 'I was very prepared for it, I got a callback and at the callback I flew over to Toronto and won the rôle.'

Odd to think, then, that he almost didn't bother to go. 'I was in Cleveland with my friend, who's the head coach of the Cleveland Browns [NFL football team] and they were going to have a scrimmage game and I was in Cleveland. I had practised with the team the day prior and I was going to sit on the bench. That was more thrilling to me than being turned down in a movie audition. I asked my agent and said, "Listen, am I being a jerk, I'm leaving a football game for this?" And he said, "Well, if you don't go, you're definitely not going to get it."'

And so the Cleveland Browns missed out. Speaking of the film at the time of Bon Jovi's Wembley Stadium shows in June 1995, he was clearly under no illusions as to *Moonlight And Valentino*'s place in the celluloid cosmos, describing it as 'an okay film' and 'a girlie movie, like *Steel Magnolias*', or rather more obliquely, 'a hip movie not a hick movie'. The experience, though, had been priceless.

'Those actresses were *awesome*. All of them. And as far as I'm concerned, David Anspaugh is Francis Coppola because he took a shot on me. He went against the odds and said, "Okay, I'll do it." I mean, I know I could do better now because that was almost a year ago. I know I'd be much better but again, I'm sure I write better songs than I would a year ago, too. Yeah, but for a first shot . . .'

It was a first shot where, despite only ever having worked opposite his tutor in a single room, never with another actress, he was given no quarter by the crew. If anything, they were actually uninterested in the step he was about to take, due to the outside influence of his sometime contact, Mick Jagger. 'I got up to the rehearsal and The Rolling Stones were on tour and I go, "Half those guys work for me, too". Everybody puts the script down and goes, "Take us to The Stones!" And I'm like, "Hey! I came up here to rehearse!"'

Unable to persuade any of the cast and crew otherwise, he was left with no choice but to pull a few strings, get them invited and accept Anspaugh's assurances that he would be fine because he knew everything and wouldn't need to rehearse. With The Stones gig out of the way, he came onto the set the first day, and was thrown in the deep end with a take almost immediately. On the way there, though, he recalls feeling a strange urge.

'After I'd gone through the whole process, the years of studying, I got the rôle, the callback, I went there and I did it – I was in the van and I go to myself, "Well, you've accomplished this, in theory, why don't you try to leave now? Why don't you get back on the plane . . ."'

Whether this was last minute nerves or a warped sense of pride in his achievement, or possibly both, he decided to go through with it. The results are there for all to see. Jon's role is the leading male, a house painter called Valentino, playing opposite Whoopie Goldberg, Kathleen Turner, Gwyneth Paltrow and Elizabeth Perkins. Perkins, who previously made a name for herself as Wilma in *The Flintstones*, was cast as the newly-widowed character with whom Valentino had a romantic interlude.

After all the time spent working in Guskin's apartment, *Moonlight And Valentino* at last gave him the chance to work with others and put his fledgling acting skills to the real test. He relished the opportunity but regretted that there was only one scene where he was together with all the actresses – but that scene taught him an instant lesson.

'Kathleen Turner said to me, "Hey! I want you to come here . . ." And I'm like, "What?" "What do you see?" And she pulled me over like this. "Now what do you see?" "A shadow." "And that shadow is on me. Don't let it happen again!" And the point about what she was doing was, here I was blocking this light that was supposed to be on her while she was saying,

"Hey, nice ass!" or something. And the great part about it was that the way she did it, in her stern comedic way, was educational. It was hip and I certainly wasn't flustered by it – and I certainly won't forget it!'

His scenes with Elizabeth Perkins were, incidentally, shot within days of his appearance opposite Cindy Crawford in the 'Please Come Home For Christmas' video. It was, he observed, 'tough being me that week'. At the very least, 'it didn't suck', he joked. But the passing pleasures of such moments are hardly enough to inspire him to embark on a different career. In the rock world he is undoubtedly among those at the top of the tree, a huge star selling millions of records. To start again at the bottom in a completely different field might be viewed as either incredibly brave or slightly foolhardy. Recognizing it as a mixture of the two, Jon sees his prime motivation as, simply, 'the challenge . . . the freedom that it leads to.'

Just as well, then, that he wasn't in it for the glory. For *Moonlight And Valentino*'s US release, the distributors decided that Jon's estimation of the film as 'a girlie movie' was spot-on and marketed it as such – airbrushed artwork was commissioned featuring the faces of the four actresses. An expensive and extravagant promotional pack was produced, too, featuring studies of all the women, once more making only this passing reference to Jon's character in the synopsis:

'The single girl, the divorcee and the wife reconvene a few months later bearing gifts for Rebecca's birthday. Alberta's present is characteristically the most ostentatious. She's hired a house painter – a very handsome house painter – to spruce up Rebecca's siding and possibly lift up her spirits. The painter, however, holds their attention much better than he holds a brush. For all four women, his mere presence conjures up shared feelings and fantasies and, almost like magic, brings about a change in each one of them . . . a change in the course of their search for the perfect life.'

No mention of Jon at all. His involvement in *Moonlight And Valentino* was earlier kept discreetly under wraps in case people came to perceive the film as a vehicle for him rather than a serious work on the part of its whole cast and crew. Now he knew why. If he felt insulted, worse was to come because the company that was distributing the movie which had overlooked his involvement was PolyGram International, an affiliate of his own record label.

The film's UK release was designed to coincide with the frustrations of thousands of housewives 'widowed' by television coverage of the European Championship soccer finals: a movie with a feminine flavour and Jon there as a bonus to look at. Word of mouth from America and early UK screenings produced very favourable reports from many who had been expecting to damn him. Much to people's surprise (and, occasionally, dismay) Jon Bon Jovi may yet get his wish for a second career. Financially, of course, he hardly needed to worry. He didn't have to undertake any kind of work again. He could and does live comfortably, but not extravagantly, on his own terms on the riches Bon Jovi has already brought him. But whilst admitting that kind of security is wonderful, it was never his motivation. In rock'n'roll or, now, with film acting.

'I was never in this for money, for gain. I was in this because I loved making records and writing songs. Now, thank God it's gotten this big, and it's a lot of fun, but that wasn't ever why. I didn't do it to pull women. I did it to be in The Asbury Jukes, hahaha!

'But now I need to do *this* for the artistic freedom. And in a great way, too, because the way I looked at it, I thought, "Why am I so obsessed? Why do I really want to do this so bad?" And I realized what it was: it gives me the chance to be artistic without having to write it, in essence direct it [by producing the records], to market it [by coming up with album covers and videos and doing the press junkets] because I don't

**252**

have to go out here and tour it for 250 shows. All I do is show up on the set. You live in one great hotel room for five or six weeks or rent a house, or whatever you care to do . . . You just show up, be artistic and leave.'

If only it were that simple. In reality, fitting in movie shoots around Bon Jovi's recording and touring schedules is never going to be easy. For *Moonlight And Valentino*, he spent five weeks on set in Canada. But then the *Cross Road/These Days* world tour began and he soon had to turn down two other rôles. One of them was offered to him by Australian writer-director John Duigan whose best known films include *The Year My Voice Broke*, *Flirting* and *Sirens*. Jon was 'broken hearted' that he had to pass on the opportunity, but knew that his commitments to Bon Jovi would put acting off limits until a break in the tour. 'I'm not gonna quit my day job, but I would love, in a perfect world, to do this tour, do a film . . . juggle them.'

It was a tall order but one Jon was keen to fulfil. One of the first rôles he was reported to have been offered was that of the lead in the sequel to *The Crow*, taking on the part originally filled by the late Brandon Lee, who was killed filming the first. But the rumours reached Jon before the script did and the rôle eventually went to French actor Vincent Perez. Besides, some reports suggested Jon was far keener on a part in *Mission Impossible* and had been seen having lunch with its star, Tom Cruise. A little later in 1995, Emilio Estevez also spoke to Jon about the possibility of him appearing as his brother, in an unnamed movie which the world can only hope is not another in *The Mighty Ducks* ice hockey series . . .

His second movie turned out to be 'an erotic thriller' called *The Leading Man*, filmed in England in early 1996. When asked if he was afraid of performing sex scenes Jon was quick to respond: 'It's basically what I do for a living.'

Moves into serious acting may eventually involve much

more serious choices, not least a change of image, according to the parts he plays. *Moonlight And Valentino* required his hair to be cut shorter and dyed, but he also volunteered to grow a moustache. Clearly no resemblance to Kevin Kline was deemed necessary but he insists he would not have been afraid of this or more drastic changes. Indeed, when he tried for the part of a naval officer in *Crimson Tide*, he was so keen he promised director Tony Scott he would 'get a crew cut tomorrow'.

That kind of enthusiasm will get him far, but only if mixed with the all-important talent and word of mouth. Just as John Duigan saw and was impressed by him in *Moonlight And Valentino* so, he hopes, will others feel the same. After the movie opened in the States, the word went around that Duigan was not alone and that no lesser personage than Robert De Niro had been impressed enough to suggest Jon do a screen test for the role of his buddy in *Heat*.

But Bob De Niro or no Bob De Niro, Jon is happy to start gently, appear in small low budget movies, and is not naive enough to stop taking acting classes. 'I don't pretend to think I could be a great actor [just] because I've been in one movie. I'm going right back to lessons and I'm not going to jeopardize what David Anspaugh did for me by jumping into something else stupid.'

Stupid is a word never likely to be used to describe Jon Bon Jovi.

Quotes gratefully reproduced from:

Mick Wall, *Kerrang!* 300, 28 July 1990; Adrian Deevoy, *Q* 52, January 1991; Stuart Clark, *Hot Press*, 22 September 1993; George Wayne, *Vanity Fair*, October 1995; Mark Salisbury, *Empire*, interview 24 June 1995; David Hochman, *US*, August 1995.

# CHAPTER NINE

# The Man, The Family, The Future

*'Success can drive you down sometimes. It's a lifeforce when you first pick up a guitar and get that rush . . . but when the machine comes down and tries to eat you up, it can kill you.'* Jon Bon Jovi, 1994

*'I could be very happy not doing it. I could live, no problem. I'd play bars when I wanted to, make records when I wanted to. I don't need the roar of the stadium, I'm not a celebrity junkie.'* Jon Bon Jovi, 1995

*'I want to be like my wife. She's incredibly focused and intelligent, and she's cooler than anybody I know.'* Jon Bon Jovi, 1995

ALTHOUGH HIS IS one of the most recognised faces of modern times, and certainly in the entertainment industry, Jon Bon Jovi remains a largely private person between his intensely high profile bouts of touring or self-promotion.

Unlike Kurt Cobain or the increasingly unhappy Eddie Vedder, he is able to cope with the pressures his fame and success has inevitably brought him – a price Jon considers to be a small one to pay for seeing almost all his personal and professional ambitions realized.

An almost ever-present constant, supporting his personal happiness and professional success, has been Dorothea Hurley. Although married as recently as 1989, they met while they were both at school. Her name was there in the special thanks list on the band's 1984 debut album and it's there over a decade later, in the dedication on *These Days*. Their relationship today is stronger than ever, probably because of, rather than despite, the fact that while they have not always been partners, they have almost always been best friends.

While Richie Sambora has taken full advantage of Bon Jovi's position in the public eye to court a succession of high profile women, Jon has always been happiest with the girl he met at school.

Dorothea aside, Jon's teenage lovelife was little more than a succession of meaningless flings. In public since, throughout his years with the band, flirting has been an almost full-time occupation. But it was only during the first couple of overseas tours that his and Dorothea's relationship ever wholly broke down. After his time spent looking for clues with the rock'n'roll set in Hollywood, he found the answer he needed when he returned to New Jersey in 1985 and set up home with her. It is perhaps no coincidence that having made that commitment and gained that security (and after making little more than a promising start with the first two albums), he then went on to write and record the worldwide success that was *Slippery When Wet* . . .

Jon has valued Dorothea's friendship even more than those he has made within the band, not least because she understands his need to throw himself so wholeheartedly – and so often – into his work. Clearly she has learned when to support and when to stand back and cut him loose.

Perhaps because he was afraid of altering that bond, he fell shy of marrying her until 1989. And when he did, it was an oddly light-hearted (not to say light-headed) occasion. Fresh from a show at the Los Angeles Forum, he and Dorothea boarded an aeroplane and flew the 150 miles north-east to Las Vegas. Telling the story of what, for other couples, might have been the highlight of their lives together, Jon seemed anxious to make it sound like a no-big-deal spur-of-the-moment decision. Which it probably was.

'We went out and got very drunk, went to a tattoo parlour and got myself a new tattoo, went gambling in a casino and won lots and lots of money and I said, "Hey, let's get married!" So we went and we did that and we got back to the hotel before the bar closed . . .'

The service would have remained private had an employee at the commerically-run Graceland Chapel not sold a copy of the wedding licence to the press. The Xerox showed that Jon and Dorothea were married at 11.45 p.m. on Saturday 28 April 1989. No friends or family were present and the venue was chosen purely for its fame as a mecca for Elvis Presley fanatics like Jon. After each service the happy couple are serenaded by an Elvis impersonator – Vegas-era, naturally, with aviator shades – strumming a guitar and crooning the song of their choice.

When news of their marriage got out, Jon appeared concerned that it might harm his career. How else to explain his explanation that: 'The band is still the first thing I'm married to, you know. It's just like me and my best friend went out and did something one night. No one was there, no one knew about it, it was a big secret until someone sold the marriage licence . . . I don't need to hide it, but there's nothing left in my life that's private any more. I can't sit in my house without [shades over] the bedroom windows because somebody's taking a picture of my bedroom window. There's always somebody hanging out in front of my house. People are wonderful, mind you, but I can't do anything in private.'

Friendship and privacy were clearly a winning combination.

Since their marriage, his infidelity has often been pondered over but never backed by any evidence. The blame for most of the suggestions can be laid, if you'll excuse the pun, directly at the door of Jon himself. As the object of lust for thousands of women every night on tour, a marriage licence was never likely to make him break the habit of the lifetime and turn into a shrinking violet on stage. It's an act though, isn't it?

'No way! I'm hitting on every one of those women every night!' he has boasted, in a manner that suggests that even if he wasn't kidding, Dorothea would understand. She very obviously does, because he seems to kid about it often.

On a gruelling solo promotional visit to the UK in 1991, speaking to writer Adrian Deevoy, he cursed her for packing his suitcase ('She packed a fucking suit for me. My wife, what can I tell you? . . .') then boasted: 'Hey, I'm in London, I'm going to try my best to get drunk tonight, to get laid and steal as much money from my record company as I can . . . And tomorrow night I'm going to try it again in Sweden. Then Rome . . .'

It was a remark he said he would deny if it made it into print, but it was one he knew that Dorothea – even if she ever read it – would not take seriously. His insistence on maintaining the image of a lust-fuelled sex maniac since his marriage seems to be a deliberate move to stress, rather than test, the strength of his personal life. He appears so convinced of the permanence of his and Dorothea's relationship that he is purposefully trying to belittle it by keeping it out of the public eye. Just as he attempted to do, initially, with their marriage. These days, however, he will reflect more maturely on the matter.

'I read in an article somewhere that in relationships, when you get beyond that initial sexual attraction, you realize that you sort of want to be like the other person. And I thought, yeah, I want to be like my wife. She's incredibly focused and intelligent, and she's cooler than anybody I know. She's very, very together. Probably a lot of that has to do with her martial arts background. [Dorothea is a black belt in karate] At the heart of martial arts is a focus. I'm one who sometimes says things before he thinks, and she thinks before she says things. That's a talent, and I learn from her all the time.'

Although in the eighties Jon denied it, he has been learning from her for years. And profiting: Dorothea has long been the inspiration behind many of Bon Jovi's songs. For years his lyrics were inherently escapist, but as he has matured they rely increasingly on real life for inspiration and sometimes, therefore, on Dorothea. 'Without Love', 'I'd Die For You' and 'Never Say Goodbye' from *Slippery* . . . all hint at his personal life – but could just have easily been written to appeal to the young couples in Bon Jovi's audience. But 'Living In Sin' on *New Jersey* in which he defended their (pre-nuptial) relationship whilst criticizing the pressures, real or imagined, of his Catholic background, is more personal.

On its release in 1988 he admitted: 'It's about where I am in my life right now. Where I find the misconceptions of what life, love and trust are all about, and that it's hard sometimes.' 'I'll Be There For You', from the same album, stressed the importance he placed upon loyalty . . .

The very crux of Bon Jovi's success is almost certainly his ability to transfer the personal nature of such songs to a wider audience. Hits like 'Livin' On A Prayer' on *Slippery When Wet* were written as the story of two kids, Tommy and Gina. 'Born To Be My Baby' from *New Jersey*, picked the couple up a few years down the line

'It's maybe Tommy and Gina grow up, but maybe it's more than that,' he said at the time. 'It's about being friends within a couple. Being friends is more important . . . You can get laid anywhere, you know what I mean?'

It doesn't take a genius or psychiatrist to see that Jon was

once again talking about times in his relationship with Dorothea. He was doing it again with 'Bed Of Roses' on *Keep The
Faith* and once more on 'Lie To Me' from *These Days*. By then,
several years older and wiser, he could speak of the lyric with
greater confidence and candour. 'It's Tommy and Gina growing
up, saying, "I can't make ends met, but don't walk out on me
'cause I'm in deep shit. So if you can't tell me you love me, lie
to me!" This didn't come from fiction . . .'

Generally, though, he disguises anything intensely personal
to maintain the privacy not only of his and Dorothea's lives,
but now their children's. And that's because these days, Jon
Bon Jovi is primarily a married man in his mid-thirties with
two children and no money worries. His primary concern is
making the time to live his private life as he wants it, with the
recording studio, the concert hall – even the movie set – places
he goes to only when it suits him and his family. Being a father
has, predictably, changed him a lot.

Although he doesn't remember what he was doing on 8
April 1994 when the world heard that Kurt Cobain had shot
himself, Jon recalls instead a sense of concern. 'I think what
followed bothered me more – the reasons why he did it and the
various implications for his daughter, his family . . .'

When his first child, daughter Stephanie Rose was born in
May 1993, she arrived on the eve of a European tour. Three
months later he and Dorothea had got her a passport and were
taking her on the road, giggling at the thrill of it all and telling
the press too. 'I don't sleep a lot. It's a lot of fun, though. She's
wonderful. I told her the morning before we flew to Europe, to
Germany, that when you get off the plane they're gonna say,
"*Achtung*, baby!" and you can reply, "Ah-goo!"'

There spoke a man who saw more important things in life
than maintaining a cool public image. A couple of years later
he and Dorothea had a baby boy to think of also, Jesse James

Louis, born in March 1995. Shortly afterwards he laughed as he told of the further effect young Stephanie Rose was having on his life. 'It is very important for me to spend time with her. She says, "Sack of potatoes" when I'm on the phone which means, "Get off the phone and carry me like a sack of potatoes!" So I say, "Gotta go", hang up and have fun.'

His children are now very clearly and very properly the most important thing in his life. It's hard to imagine him, before they arrived, hanging up the phone – even if the house was burning down – if the call was of a business nature.

When Bon Jovi tour, they tour as a family as big as Don Jon could wish for. As well as Dorothea, Stephanie Rose and Jesse James, Dave Bryan takes his wife April and their twins, a boy and a girl (born July 1994). The Bon Jovi tour jet is packed with a lot more gear than it ever used to carry. Much of it coloured pink and sky blue . . .

'You bring little pieces of home with you,' Jon said while touring Europe in 1995. 'I've had the same band for twelve years, my guitar handler has been working with me since I was sixteen. I've had the same friends all my life. I've been with my wife for fifteen years . . .

'Families are the only thing that makes it worthwhile. I wouldn't be here if they weren't out here.'

Touching sentiments from a man who spent the early hours of many nights on that tour not propping up some bar but being woken up by the cries of his five-month-old son. But as much of a new man as he appears to be (at least by rock'n'roll standards) he would still boast that, although he knew how to, he hadn't changed a single diaper in three and a half months.

Generally, his wife and children wait at the hotel and don't go to the shows but Stephanie Rose attended her first in Europe. Jon had her sit at the front of the stage, from where she got an extraordinary glimpse of the extraordinary world she had been born into. Afterwards, having been part of a 60,000 audience had left her speechless except for the bewildered phrase: 'Daddy . . . sing . . . microphone . . . lights . . . people clappy.'

Except for his wife and children, Jon has never retreated to an ivory tower and cut himself off from the world. He remains in touch. He still worships the NFL's New York Giants. He remains a fan of The Stones. Of Southside Johnny. Of Bruce Springsteen. Of Little Steven – 'so I still have my heroes that I get to play with'. Hero worship has both driven him personally and motivated his fans and experience has taught him the power of that force.

'Heroes are important. What would we do without them? If there was no Bruce, there'd be no me. And if there was no Bob Dylan, there'd be no Bruce. If there was no Jimmy Page, there'd be no Richie Sambora . . .'

Returning to England after the Moscow Music Peace Festival, Jon learned that another of the guests at Mayfair's expensively exclusive St James Club (where the band prefers to stay whilst in London) was one Clint Eastwood.

'We had a bunch of caviar so I thought, I'll send him some up and a little note saying I really love his work. Then he called my room and said, "Hi, it's Clint. Do you want to meet down in the lobby?" He had no idea who I was but he was very friendly and polite and cool. He's talking, being real nice, and I'm just standing there thinking, "This is fucking Clint!"'

Yet Jon could not grow fat on the plaudits of his fellow musicians. His endorsements are nearly all from the masses – and so when Elvis Costello was quoted as saying that he believed 'Bad Medicine' to be 'the best song on the radio' in 1988, Jon was ecstatic.

'Hallelujah! Fucking flattered like you wouldn't believe,' he told David Cavanagh. 'I can't tell you how flattered that somebody I admire so much would think something of what I did.'

Jon, who listed Costello alongside Tom Waits and Bob Dylan as 'the greatest living lyricists' even contacted Costello with a view to writing together. That possibility, for the time being at least, remains unfulfilled. Whether a similar one arose after Tony Mortimer of East 17 proclaimed Bon Jovi to be 'the best rock band around' when listing *Cross Road* as one of his top ten CDs is unlikely. If only because Mortimer described Jon's untrained ('but soulful') voice as that of 'a pub bloke who's sort of developed it to a really high standard. I think people who can't sing could sing like Bon Jovi one day . . .'

Jon, of course, had heard that one before – and said with malice – but he never let it bother him. As he once said: 'It was blind faith that got me here because everyone told me, "You can't write, you can't sing . . ."' Jon is no fool, he knows that Bon Jovi have survived due to the support of their fans.

'We were never critics' darlings, but the people cared. And that was what really mattered because it gave us the opportunity to tour when and where we wanted. Now that critics seem to be coming around you go, "Well, that's nice," but it's no big deal. And as long as people still like it, we'll be able to take it out on the road . . .'

The road. With Bon Jovi, everything always returns to it. It's hard to imagine them existing as a purely recording band, their get togethers limited to a few sessions in some dimly lit and expensively furnished studio. They are, however, easing off. Although the shows are getting bigger and some of the destinations more remote, the dates are fewer and stretched over less demanding schedules in each territory. These territories are grouped into legs of world tours, but may be separated by weeks at home to break up the routine and avoid the nightmare of the late eighties.

'Between 1986 and 1990 I never unpacked my suitcase,' Jon recalls. 'That killed me. Everybody thought I was happening, but when I look back at pictures from that time, I look beat up. Now there's a new picture: getting on a plane with my family and coming here. I'm going to remember these days. In the past I would have blocked them out. I'd get uptight. I'd worry about everything. But I'm here to enjoy the ride this time. I told the guys I'd stay out as long as there's not something better to do that night. As long as every day is fun fun fun, I'm there . . .'

He returns to this idea often, clearly relieved that as master of his own destiny, rather than a tool of Doc McGhee, he can finally call the shots. 'I could be very happy not doing it. I could live, no problem. I'd play bars when I wanted to, make records when I wanted to. I don't need the roar of the stadium, I'm not a celebrity junkie.'

But he is a celebrity, and one who can breathe a sigh of relief that the bad hair days at the start of his career seem light years away. 'Everybody's going to have their baby pictures to regret. For me, looking at the eighties is like looking back at pictures from the disco era. I think maybe I should have stuck to a pair of Levi jeans and not been the king of long hair,' he now candidly admits. 'But that's how things worked out. You survive it and move on.'

Jon may not have moved on a million miles, but he is certainly a survivor.

Along with Dorothea, the main reason for his survival must surely be that he has remained true to his New Jersey roots. Although he has a house on America's West Coast, at Malibu (purchased during a fit of hedonism in the mid-eighties) *home* remains at Rumson, a leafy town forty miles from New York but very much in the state of his birth.

The house, replete with a basement studio where *Blaze Of Glory*, *Keep The Faith* and *These Days* were all demoed, is something of a monument to his success. Sparsely but expensively furnished, it is also decorated with countless gold discs, photographs and artefacts that bear witness to one young man's dream becoming a reality. The house is only a short drive from another he once naively offered to buy for Dorothea when, as teenagers, they drove around the area open-mouthed in the way some of the more persistent Bon Jovi fans do today, looking for a glimpse of their hero.

If he goes out for a jog he'll wait until they've gone rather than go out surrounded by a pack of musclemen. (Then again, if, as he reckons, he can run fifteen miles in under two hours, any fans would be hard-pushed to keep up with him.) On tour, security guards are needed purely for personal saftey when he is close to large crowds that might pull him in and crush him, but bodyguards are an affectation he has no time for in his private life.

And while the house may be a lot larger and the cars parked in the drive include a Ferrari, it's a car he rarely uses and wishes he could sell. When he drives, he prefers the more modest comfort of a Mercedes.

In Rumson, he still mixes socially with the other guys in the band and the management and touring set-up. He can still count Richie Sambora as one of his neighbours and is also close enough to pop round to Bruce Springsteen's for a cup of sugar. (Pausing to reflect, no doubt, that Bruce, with his veritable portfolio of property in the same area, is still and probably always will be The Boss.)

The trappings of success are not things a New Jersey boy would flaunt, although he did take the unusual step of inviting journalists into both his homes during 1994. In a way, though, he did it almost naively in an attempt to prove that success had not changed him, rather than to exhibit how it had. Even in doing so he sighed and reflected upon this.

'Success can drive you down sometimes. It's a lifeforce when you first pick up a guitar and get that rush, that aspiration to take on the world and conquer it. There's no greater feeling for me than to write songs that people like. But when the machine comes down and tries to eat you up, it can kill you. Even if you survive, it can still fuck you up.'

If anything keeps him awake at nights, notwithstanding the kids, it might be his personal demons. The lounge in his home in Malibu is dominated by a collection of crucifixes. For years, he never spoke of his guilt at having abandoned Catholicism as a child but now in interviews – and in songs like 'Something To Believe In' and 'Hey God' – he speaks of it more and more.

'I'm a recovering Catholic. Daily. My whole head is completely fucked with what you're brought up to believe in . . .' His solution is practical, even if it doesn't ease his torment. 'I just feel you've got to do right by yourself and other people.'

Yet such concerns aside, in so many ways Jon Bon Jovi remains an embodiment of the American Dream. He saw what he wanted, reached out and took it. These days few would blame him for sitting back and enjoying it. His biggest problem remains his inability to do just that.

'Im working a sixteen-hour day, every day, three different projects at the same time. And that's when I'm happiest, that's when I realize I'm a psychopath. I should be a little more like Richie, he should be a little more like me. He can miss his flight to lay in bed . . . I'm at the airport banging on the plane to open the door.'

Success has changed Jon and he wouldn't attempt to deny it. Success changes everybody. Especially when it means having a Boeing 737 *and* a DC–8 with your name painted on the side. But through it and despite it all, Jon has retained much the same energy and enthusiasm levels he had as a youngster. He may be a lot more cynical these days, but he still has the youthful zest that so many of his contemporaries have lost along the way. 'In rock'n'roll you can get a lobotomy without realizing what's happening. People have had the life and soul sucked out of them. It does happen . . .'

But not to him. He prefers to make the time to play with his children, sit and watch TV and be a slob – all the 'normal kind of shit' as he puts it. He has been known to swing a golf club in the name of charity but he's no Arnold Palmer (or even Alice Cooper) and prefers his home life and refuses to do anything resembling business once a tour has ended.

He'll maybe have a drink but will do nothing to excess. 'I have four glasses of wine and I call it drinking too much. I drink a bottle of wine and any good Italian would say you *should* drink a bottle of wine a night for your blood! I push my escape door to the point where I can relax – and also hit the notes the next night . . .'

Ah yes, the day job. Something he knows how to appreciate. 'My life has been a dream, a charmed life. There's no doubt about it. But I don't take it for granted and I don't think that it's more than it is, either. We were a lucky garage band who wrote songs that people liked. I'm not Kurt Cobain – who I greatly respect as a writer – and I wouldn't want to be. I'm pretty happy when I write songs and the pains I have are simple emotional things.'

A man from New Jersey who has become a star the world over. A star with simple tastes.

'I'm blessed with a loving family, loving band, loving parents and I don't take them for granted . . .'

Quotes gratefully taken from:

Alison Joy, *Kerrang!* 204, 10 September 1988; Personal File, *Smash Hits*, 9 August 1989; Steve Mascord, *Kerrang!* 264, 11 November 1989; Adrian

## BON JOVI

Deevoy, *Q* 52, January 1991; Steffan Chirazi, *Kerrang!* 513, 24 September 1994; Andrew Collins, *Q* 98, November 1994; Steve Beebee, *Kerrang!* 526, 24/31 December 1994; Tom Doyle, *Q* 103, April 1995; Steffan Chirazi, *Kerrang!* 543, 29 April 29 1995; Paul Henderson, *Metal Hammer*, July 1995; David Hochman, *US*, August 1995.

# The Discography

1. The Albums
2. The Singles
3. The Videos
4. The Rest

(All details as for UK releases unless otherwise specified.)

## 1. The Albums

**BON JOVI (Vertigo) April 1984**
*Tracks:*
Runaway, She Don't Know Me, Shot Through The Heart, Love Lies, Burning For Love, Breakout, Come Back, Get Ready.
*Available as:*
(814 982–2) CD
(VERLC 14) cassette
(VERL 14) vinyl
Entered the UK Top 75 for one week only at Number 68.

**7800° FAHRENHEIT (Vertigo) April 1985**
*Tracks:*
In And Out Of Love, The Price Of Love, Only Lonely, King Of The Mountain, Silent Night, Tokyo Road, The Hardest Part Is The Night, Always Run To You, To The Fire, Secret Dreams.
*Available as:*
(824 509–2) CD

(VERLC 24) cassette
(VERL 24) vinyl
Spent twelve weeks on the UK chart peaking at Number 28.

### SLIPPERY WHEN WET (Vertigo) September 1986
*Tracks:*
Let It Rock, You Give Love A Bad Name, Livin' On A Prayer, Social Disease, Wanted Dead Or Alive, Raise Your Hands, Without Love, I'd Die For You, Never Say Goodbye, Wild In The Streets. (Keyboard intro to 'Let It Rock' is sometimes titled 'Pink Flamingos'.)
*Available as:*
(830 264–2) CD
(VERHC 38) cassette
(VERH 38) vinyl
(VERHP 38) limited edition UK picture disc with poster, released 10 August 1987 to commemorate headlining Donington Monsters Of Rock Festival.
(Mercury PHCR 6003) Japanese CD version with original, later withdrawn, sleeve featuring a close-up of a woman's chest in a slightly torn yellow T-shirt.
Spent 122 weeks on the UK chart, peaking at Number 6.

### NEW JERSEY (Vertigo) September 1988
*Tracks:*
Lay Your Hands On Me, Bad Medicine, Born To Be My Baby, Living In Sin, Blood On Blood, Stick To Your Guns, Homebound Train, I'll Be There For You, 99 In The Shade, Love For Sale, Wild Is The Wind, Ride Cowboy Ride.
*Available as:*
(836 345–2) CD, released November 1988
(VERHC 62) cassette
(VERH 62) vinyl
(VERHP 62) picture disc, released January 1989
Spent forty-five weeks on the UK chart, peaking at Number 1.

### KEEP THE FAITH (Jambco/Mercury) November 1992
*Tracks:*
I Believe, Keep The Faith, I'll Sleep When I'm Dead, In These Arms,

Bed Of Roses, If I Was Your Mother, Dry County, Woman In Love, Fear, I Want You, Blame It On The Love Of Rock & Roll, Little Bit Of Soul, Save A Prayer.
*Available as:*
(514 197–2) CD
(514 197–4) cassette
(514 197–1) vinyl
The CD version was re-issued, as a strictly limited edition version with a bonus 'Live 1989–1993' CD and a mini poster in 1993. The live tracks featured were: Keep The Faith, In These Arms, Lay Your Hands On Me, Blaze Of Glory, I'll Be There For You, Bad Medicine, Bed Of Roses (Acoustic) and Never Say Goodbye. Spent seventy weeks on the UK chart, peaking at Number 1.

## CROSS ROAD – THE BEST OF BON JOVI (Mercury)
## October 1994
*Tracks:*
Livin' On A Prayer, Keep The Faith, Someday I'll Be Saturday Night, Always, Wanted Dead Or Alive, Lay Your Hands On Me, You Give Love A Bad Name, Bed Of Roses, Blaze Of Glory, In These Arms, Bad Medicine, I'll Be There For You, In And Out Of Love, Runaway, Never Say Goodbye.
*Available as:*
(522 936–2) CD
(522 936–4) cassette
(522 936–1) vinyl
(522 936–5) DCC
'Someday I'll Be Saturday Night' and 'Always' were two new tracks produced by Peter Collins. Spent fifty-seven weeks on the UK chart, peaking at Number 1.

## THESE DAYS (Mercury) 19 June 1995
*Tracks:*
Hey God, Something For The Pain, This Ain't A Love Song, These Days, Lie To Me, Damned, My Guitar Lies Bleeding In My Arms, (It's Hard) Letting You Go, Hearts Breaking Even, Something To Believe In, If That's What It Takes, Diamond Ring, All I Want Is Everything, Bitter Wine.

*Available as:*
(528 248–2) CD
(528 248–4) cassette
(528 248–1) limited edition double vinyl
'All I Want Is Everything' and 'Bitter Wine' listed as 'bonus tracks' on the CD, cassette and original double vinyl versions.
At time of writing has spent twenty-four weeks on the UK chart, peaking at Number 1.

## 1 (b)   Jon Bon Jovi solo

**BLAZE OF GLORY/YOUNG GUNS II (Vertigo 846 473 1, 2 and 4) August 1990**
*Tracks:*
Billy Get Your Guns, Miracle, Blaze Of Glory, Blood Money, Santa Fe, Justice In The Barrel, Never Say Die, You Really Got Me Now, Bang A Drum, Dyin' Ain't Much Of A Livin', Guano City.
Jon wrote all 10 songs for the album 'inspired by the film *Young Guns II*', except the 60 second closing number, 'Guano City' which was composed, conducted and produced by Alan Silvestri. Much of the rest of this soundtrack album is not included in the movie despite performances by the likes of Elton John, Jeff Beck, Little Richard and Tom Petty's keyboard player Benmont Tench, Keith Richards' guitar player Waddy Wachtel and the *Young Guns* actor Lou Diamond Phillips (on backing vocals). Jon co-produced the record with guitarist Danny Kortchmar and Also Nova was on hand to play guitar and keyboards, too.Charted August 1990, spent twenty-three weeks on the charts, peaking at Number 2. In the US, it sold over 2 million copies and reached Number 4.

## 1 (c)   Richie Sambora solo

**STRANGER IN THIS TOWN (Mercury 848 895 1, 2 and 4) September 1991**
*Tracks:*
Rest In Peace, Church Of Desire, Stranger In This Town, Ballad Of

Youth, One Light Burning, Mr Bluesman, Rosie, River Of Love, Father Time, The Answer.

Richie's album featured a band comprising himself, David Bryan on keyboards, Tico Torres on drums and sometime Peter Gabriel bassist Tony Levin. Eric Clapton played the guitar solo on 'Mr Bluesman'. Richie wrote, or co-wrote all the tracks. 'Rosie' was credited to R. Sambora/J. Bon Jovi/D. Child/D. Warren. Japanese version includes the bonus track 'The Wind Cries Mary', originally recorded for the *Ford Fairlane* movie soundtrack.

## 2. The Singles

**SHE DON'T KNOW ME**
Released: May 1984
Formats: two
She Don't Know Me/Breakout (Vertigo VER 11) 7″
She Don't Know Me/Breakout (Vertigo VERX 11) 12″
Did not chart.

**RUNAWAY**
Released: October 1984
Formats: two
Runaway/Breakout (Live) (Vertigo VER 14) 7″
Runaway/Breakout (Live)/Runaway (Live) (Vertigo VERX 14) 12″
Live tracks from BBC 'In Concert' broadcast. Did not chart.

**IN AND OUT OF LOVE**
Released: May 1985
Formats: three
In And Out Of Love/Roulette (Live) (Vertigo VER 19) 7″
In And Out Of Love/Roulette (Live) (Vertigo VERP 19) picture disc
In And Out Of Love/Roulette (Live)/Shot Through The Heart (Live) (Vertigo VERX 19) 12″
Live tracks from BBC 'In Concert' broadcast. Did not chart.

## THE HARDEST PART IS THE NIGHT
Released: August 1985
Formats: four
The Hardest Part Is The Night/Always Run To You (Vertigo VER 22) 7″
The Hardest Part Is The Night/Always Run To You/Tokyo Road (Live) (Vertigo VERX 22) 12″
The Hardest Part Is The Night/Always Run To You/Tokyo Road (Live)/Shot Through The Heart (Live) (Vertigo VERDP 22) 7″ gatefold doublepack
The Hardest Part Is The Night/Tokyo Road (Live)/In And Out Of Love (Live) (Vertigo VERXR 22) 12″, red vinyl, limited edition of 5,000 released September 1985
Live tracks from BBC 'In Concert' broadcast. Entered the Top 75 on 31 August for one week at Number 68.

## YOU GIVE LOVE A BAD NAME
Released: August 1986
Formats: four
You Give Love A Bad Name/Let It Rock (Vertigo VER 26) 7″
You Give Love A Bad Name/Let It Rock/Borderline (Vertigo VERX 26) 12″
You Give Love A Bad Name/Let It Rock (Vertigo VERP 26) 10″ London Transport logo-shaped pic disc, limited edition of 5,000, released September 1986
You Give Love A Bad Name/Let It Rock/The Hardest Part Is The Night (Live)/Burning For Love (Live) (Vertigo VERXR 26) 12″ blue vinyl, limited edition of 7,500, released September 1986
'Borderline' is a 'Slippery When Wet' out-take unavailable elsewhere. Live tracks recorded on the previous American tour. Charted 9 August for 10 weeks, peaking at Number 14.

## LIVIN' ON A PRAYER
Released: October 1986
Formats: six
Livin' On A Prayer/Wild In The Streets (Vertigo VER 28) 7″
Livin' On A Prayer/Wild In The Streets/Edge Of A Broken Heart (Vertigo VERX 28) 12″

Livin' On A Prayer/Wild In The Streets (Vertigo VERPA 28) 7" with free patch, limited edition of 5,000, released November 1986
Livin' On A Prayer/Wild In The Streets (Vertigo VERP 28) picture disc, limited edition of 5,000, released November 1986
Livin' On A Prayer/Wild In The Streets/Only Lonely (Live)/Runaway (Live) (Vertigo VERXG 28) 12", green vinyl, limited edition of 10,000, released November 1986
Livin' On A Prayer/Wild In The Streets/Edge Of A Broken Heart/ Livin' On A Prayer (Remix) (Vertigo VERXR 28) 12", released November 1986
'Edge Of A Broken Heart' is a 'Slippery When Wet' out-take unavailable elsewhere. 'Runaway (Live)' is different to that on VERX 14, two years earlier.
Charted 25 October for 15 weeks peaking at Number 4, it would remain the band's biggest hit until 'Always' eight years later.

## WANTED DEAD OR ALIVE
Released: March 1987
Formats: five
Wanted Dead Or Alive/Shot Through The Heart (Vertigo JOV 1) 7"
Wanted Dead Or Alive/Shot Through The Heart/Social Disease (Vertigo JOV 112) 12"
Wanted Dead Or Alive/Shot Through The Heart/Social Disease (Vertigo JOVCD 1) CD
Wanted Dead Or Alive/Shot Through The Heart (Vertigo JOV S1) 7" with free 'metal' stickers
Wanted Dead Or Alive/Shot Through The Heart/Social Disease/Get Ready (Live) (Vertigo JOVR 112) 12" silver vinyl released April 1987
Charted April 11 for seven weeks peaking at Number 13.

## NEVER SAY GOODBYE
Released: August 1987
Formats: five
Never Say Goodbye/Raise Your Hands (Vertigo JOV 2) 7"
Never Say Goodbye/Raise Your Hands/Wanted Dead Or Alive (Acoustic Version) (Vertigo JOV 212) 12"
Never Say Goodbye/Raise Your Hands/Wanted Dead Or Alive (Acoustic Version) (Vertigo JOVR 212) 12" yellow vinyl, PVC sleeve

Never Say Goodbye/Raise Your Hands (Vertigo JOVC 2) cassette
'Wanted Dead Or Alive (Acoustic Version)' is unavailable elsewhere.
Charted August 15 for five weeks peaking at Number 21.

## BAD MEDICINE
Released: September 1988
Formats: five
Bad Medicine/99 In The Shade (Vertigo JOV 3) 7"
Bad Medicine/99 In The Shade (Vertigo JOVS 3) 7" with '3-D' wraparound sleeve
Bad Medicine/99 In The Shade/Lay Your Hands On Me (Vertigo JOV 312) 12"
Bad Medicine/99 In The Shade/Livin' On A Prayer (Live) (Vertigo JOVR 312) 12"
Bad Medicine/99 In The Shade/Lay Your Hands On Me (Vertigo JOVCD 3) CD
Charted 24 September for seven weeks peaking at Number 17.

## BORN TO BE MY BABY
Released: November 1988
Formats: five
Born To Be My Baby/Love For Sale (Vertigo JOV 4) 7"
Born To Be My Baby/Love For Sale/Wanted Dead Or Alive (Vertigo JOV 412) 12"
Born To Be My Baby/Love For Sale/Runaway (Live)/Livin' On A Prayer (Live) (Vertigo JOVCD 4) CD
Born To Be My Baby/Love For Sale (Vertigo JOVS 4) 7" special version, released December 1988
Born To Be My Baby/Love For Sale/Wanted Dead Or Alive (Live) (Vertigo JOVR 412) 12" special version
Charted 10 December for seven weeks peaking at Number 22.

## I'LL BE THERE FOR YOU
Released: April 1989
Formats: six
I'll Be There For You/Homebound Train (Vertigo JOV 5) 7"
I'll Be There For You/Homebound Train/Wild In The Streets (Live) (Vertigo JOV 512) 12"

I'll Be There For You/Homebound Train/Borderline (Live)/Edge Of A Broken Heart (Live) (Vertigo JOVCD 5) CD
I'll Be There For You/Homebound Train (Vertigo JOVPB 5) 7" special version
I'll Be There For You/Homebound Train/Wild In The Streets (Live) (Vertigo JOVR 512) 12" special poster sleeve version
I'll Be There For You/Homebound Train (Vertigo 872 564 4) cassette, released May 1989
Charted 29 April for seven weeks peaking at Number 18.


## LAY YOUR HANDS ON ME
Released: July 1989
Formats: nine
Lay Your Hands On Me/Bad Medicine (Live) (Vertigo JOV 6) 7"
Lay Your Hands On Me/Bad Medicine (Live) (Vertigo JOVMC 6) cassette
Lay Your Hands On Me/Bad Medicine (Live)/Blood On Blood (Live) (Vertigo JOV 612) 12"
Lay Your Hands On Me/Bad Medicine (Live) (Vertigo JOVS 661) 7" red vinyl version, released August 1989
Lay Your Hands On Me/Bad Medicine (Live) (Vertigo JOVS 662) 7" white vinyl version, released August 1989
Lay Your Hands On Me/Bad Medicine (Live) (Vertigo JOVS 663) 7" blue vinyl version, released August 1989
Lay Your Hands On Me/Bad Medicine (Live)/Blood On Blood (Live) (Vertigo JOVCD 6) CD, released August 1989
Lay Your Hands On Me/Bad Medicine (Live) (Vertigo JOVP 610) 10" shaped picture disc
Lay Your Hands On Me/Bad Medicine/Blood On Blood/Born To Be My Baby (Acoustic) (Vertigo JOVG 612) special 12", released September 1989
Charted 26 August for six weeks peaking at Number 18.


## LIVING IN SIN
Released: November 1989
Formats: five
Living In Sin/Love Is War (Vertigo JOV 7) 7"

Living In Sin/Love Is War/Ride Cowboy Ride (Vertigo JOV 712) 12″
Living In Sin/Love Is War (Vertigo JOVMC 7) cassette
Living In Sin/Love Is War/Ride Cowboy Ride/Stick To Your Guns (Vertigo JOVR 712) 12″ special version, released January 1990
Living In Sin/Love Is War/Ride Cowboy Ride/Stick To Your Guns (Vertigo JOVCD 7) CD, released January 1990
Charted 9 December for six weeks peaking at Number 35.

### KEEP THE FAITH
Released: October 1992
Formats: four
Keep The Faith/I Wish Every Day Could Be Like Christmas (Jambco JOV 8) 7″
Keep The Faith/I Wish Every Day Could Be Like Christmas (Jambco JOVMC 8) cassette
Keep The Faith/I Wish Every Day Could Be Like Christmas/A Little Bit Of Soul (Jambco JOVCD 8) CD 1
Keep The Faith/I Wish Every Day Could Be Like Christmas/Living In Sin (Live) (Jambco JOVCB 8) CD 2
'I Wish Every Day Could Be Like Christmas' includes guest appearances from Jon's solo co-producer Danny Kortchmar and Tom Petty's keyboard player Benmont Tench. Charted 24 October for six weeks peaking at Number 5.

### BED OF ROSES
Released: January 1993
Formats: four
Bed Of Roses/Starting All Over Again (Jambco JOV 9) 7″
Bed Of Roses/Starting All Over Again (Jambco JOVMC 9) cassette
Bed Of Roses/Lay Your Hands On Me (Live)/Tokyo Road (Live)/I'll Be There For You (Live) (Jambco JOVCD 9) CD
Bed Of Roses/Starting All Over Again/Lay Your Hands On Me (Live) (Jambco JOVXP 9) 12″ picture disc
'Starting All Over' was a track written when Jon and Richie first reunited after their time apart making solo records. Added to the *Keep The Faith* album in the Far East as a bonus cut. Charted 23 January for six weeks peaking at Number 13.

### IN THESE ARMS
Released: May 3 1993
Formats: four
In These Arms/Bed Of Roses (Acoustic) (Jambco JOV 10) etched 7"
In These Arms/Bed Of Roses (Acoustic) (Jambco JOVMC 10) cassette
In These Arms/Blaze Of Glory (Live) (Jambco JOVMB 10) cassette,
limited edition of 10,000 boxed with 'souvenir tour pass'
In These Arms/Keep The Faith (Live)/In These Arms (Live) (Jambco
JOVCD 10) CD
Charted 15 May for seven weeks peaking at Number 9.

### I'LL SLEEP WHEN I'M DEAD
Released: July 1993
Formats: four
I'll Sleep When I'm Dead/Never Say Goodbye (Live Acoustic)
(Jambco JOV 11) 7"
I'll Sleep When I'm Dead/Never Say Goodbye (Live Acoustic)
(Jambco JOVMC 11) cassette
I'll Sleep When I'm Dead/Blaze Of Glory (Live)/Wild In The Streets
(Live) (Jambco JOVCD 11) CD 1
I'll Sleep When I'm Dead/Blaze Of Glory (Live)/You Give Love A
Bad Name (Live)/Bad Medicine (Live) (Jambco JOVD 11) CD 2
Charted 7 August for five weeks peaking at Number 17.

### I BELIEVE
Released: September 20, 1993
Formats: four
I Believe (Clearmountain Mix)/I Believe (Live) (Jambco JOV 12) 7"
I Believe (Clearmountain Mix)/I Believe (Live) (Jambco JOVMC 12)
cassette
I Believe (Clearmountain Mix)/You Give Love A Bad Name (Live)/
Born To Be My Baby (Live)/Living On A Prayer (Live)/Wanted Dead
Or Alive (Live) (Jambco JOVCD 12) CD 1
I Believe (Clearmountain Mix)/Runaway (Live)/Living On A Prayer
(Live)/Wanted Dead Or Alive (Live) (Jambco JOVD 12) CD 2
Live version recorded at Count Basie Theatre, Red Bank, NJ December 1992. Charted 2 October for six weeks peaking at Number 11.

## DRY COUNTY
Released: March 1994
Formats: four
Dry County (Clearmountain Mix)/Stranger In This Town (Live) (Jambco JOV 13) 7″
Dry County (Clearmountain Mix)/Stranger In This Town (Live) (Jambco JOVMC 13) cassette
Dry County (Live)/It's Only Rock 'N' Roll (Live)/Waltzing Mathilda (Live) (Jambco JOVCD 13) CD 1
Dry County (Clearmountain Mix)/Stranger In This Town (Live)/ Blood Money (Live) (Jambco JOVBX 13) CD 2
'Dry County (Live)' recorded at Milton Keynes, 'It's Only Rock 'N' Roll (Live)' and 'Waltzing Matilda (Live)' recorded at Count Basie Theatre, Red Bank NJ 20 December 1993 – the latter features Tico Torres on vocals! Charted 26 March for six weeks peaking at Number 9.

## ALWAYS
Released: September 1994
Formats: four
Always (Edit)/Always (Full Length Version) (Jambco JOVMC 14) cassette
Always (Full Length Version)/Always (Edit)/The Boys Are Back In Town (Jambco JOVG 14) 12″ coloured vinyl
Always (Edit)/Always (Full Length Version)/Edge Of A Broken Heart (Jambco JOVCD 14) CD 1
Always (Edit)/Always (Full Length Version)/Edge Of A Broken Heart/ Prayer '94 (Jambco JOVCX 14) CD 2
'Prayer '94' is a new mix of 'Livin' On A Prayer'. Charted 24 September for eighteen weeks peaking at Number 2.

## PLEASE COME HOME FOR CHRISTMAS
(Credited to Jon Bon Jovi but given a Bon Jovi band catalogue number)
Released: December 1994
Formats: three
Please Come Home For Christmas/Back Door Santa (Jambco JOVP 16) 7″ picture disc

Please Come Home For Christmas/Back Door Santa (Jambco JOVMC 16) cassette

Please Come Home For Christmas/I Wish Every Day Could Be Like Christmas/Back Door Santa (Jambco JOVCD 16) CD

All proceeds to the Special Olympics disabled athletes charity. A-side originally released on 'A Very Special Christmas 2' in 1992 (see p.287). Track two originally a B-side of 'Keep The Faith'. Track three originally on 'A Very Special Christmas' in 1987 (see p.286). Single charted 17 December for ten weeks peaking at Number 7.

## SOMEDAY I'LL BE SATURDAY NIGHT

Released: 13 February 1995

Formats: four

Someday I'll Be Saturday Night/Always (Live In Montreal) (Jambco JOVP 15) 7" picture disc

Someday I'll Be Saturday Night/Always (Live In Montreal) (Jambco JOVMC 15) cassette

Someday I'll Be Saturday Night/Good Guys Don't Always Wear White/With A Little Help From My Friends (Live In Montreal)/Always (Live In Montreal) (Jambco JOVCX 15) CD 1

Someday I'll Be Saturday Night/Good Guys Don't Always Wear White/Always (Live In Montreal)/Someday I'll Be Saturday Night (Live In Montreal) (Jambco JOVDD 15) CD 2

Charted 19 February for seven weeks peaking at Number 7. (Single originally scheduled for late 1994.)

## THIS AIN'T A LOVE SONG

Released: May 1995

Formats: three

This Ain't A Love Song/Lonely At The Top (Jambco JOVMC 17) cassette

This Ain't A Love Song/Lonely At The Top/The End (Jambco JOVCD 17) CD 1

This Ain't A Love Song/When She Comes/Wedding Day/Prostitute (Jambco JOVCDX 17) CD 2

Released 29 May charted 4 June for nine weeks peaking at Number 6.

### SOMETHING FOR THE PAIN
Released: September 1995
Formats: three
Something For The Pain/This Ain't A Love Song (Live)/I Don't Like Mondays (Live) (JOVCD 18) CD 1
Something For The Pain/Livin' On A Prayer (Live)/You Give Love A Bad Name (Live)/Wild In The Streets (Live) (JOVCDX 18) CD 2
Something For The Pain/This Ain't A Love Song (Live) (JOVMC 18) cassette
Live tracks recorded at Wembley Stadium 25 June 1995. Charted 24 September for seven weeks peaking at Number 8.

### LIE TO ME
Released: November 1995
Formats: three
Lie To Me/Something For The Pain/Hey God (Live)/I'll Sleep When I'm Dead (Live) (JOVCD 19) CD 1
Lie To Me (Edit)/Something For The Pain (Live)/Always (Live)/Keep The Faith (Live) (JOVCDX 19) CD 2
Lie To Me/Something For The Pain (Live) (JOVMC 19) cassette
Live tracks recorded at Wembley Stadium 25th June 1995. Charted 19 November. Peaked at Number 6.


## 2 (b)  Jon Bon Jovi solo

### BLAZE OF GLORY
Released: August 1990
Formats: four
Blaze Of Glory/You Really Got Me Now (Vertigo JBJ 1) 7",
Blaze Of Glory/You Really Got Me Now/Blood Money (Vertigo JBJ 112) 12"
Blaze Of Glory/You Really Got Me Now (Vertigo JBJMC 1) cassette
Blaze Of Glory/You Really Got Me Now/Blood Money (Vertigo JBJCD 1) CD
Charted 4 August for eight weeks peaking at Number 13.

**MIRACLE**
Released: November 1990
Formats: five
Miracle/Bang A Drum (Vertigo JBJ 2) 7"
Miracle/Bang A Drum (Vertigo JBJMC 2) cassette
Miracle/Dyin' Ain't Much Of A Livin'/Going Back (Live) (Vertigo JBJP 212) 12" picture disc
Miracle/Dyin' Ain't Much Of A Livin'/Going Back (Live) (Vertigo JBJCD 2) CD
Miracle/Dyin' Ain't Much Of A Livin'/Eight Minute Interview (Vertigo JBJ 212) 12" with poster
Charted 10 November for five weeks peaking at Number 29.

## 2 (c)  Richie Sambora solo

**BALLAD OF YOUTH**
Released: August/September 1991
Formats: four
Ballad Of Youth/Mr Bluesman (Mercury MER 350) 7"
Ballad Of Youth/Mr Bluesman (Mercury MERMC 350) cassette
Ballad Of Youth/Mr Bluesman/Wind Cries Mary (Mercury MERCD 350) CD
Ballad Of Youth/Mr Bluesman/Wind Cries Mary (Mercury MERX 350) 12" poster bag
Charted 7 September for one week at Number 59.

## 3. The Videos

**TOKYO ROSE – LIVE IN JAPAN '85 (Mercury) 1985**
11 songs including: Breakout, Silent Knight, In And Out Of Love, Runaway, Hardest Part Of The Night. These five also broadcast by BBC's *Whistle Test* as a 30-minute set on 10 September 1985.

**BREAKOUT – VIDEO SINGLES (PolyGram 041 386 2) June 1986 (27 minutes)**
*Tracks:* In And Out Of Love, Only Lonely, Silent Night, She Don't Know Me, Hardest Part Is The Night, Runaway.
*Also available as:*
Betamax (PolyGram 041 386 4)
re-release VHS (Channel 5 CFV 06112) October 1988

**BAD MEDICINE (PolyGram Music Video 080 566 2) September 1988 (CD video single)**

**SLIPPERY WHEN WET – THE VIDEOS (Channel 5 CFV 04002) June 1988 (41 minutes)**
*Tracks:* Wild In The Streets, Livin' On A Prayer (Live), You Give Love A Bad Name, Never Say Goodbye, Livin' On A Prayer, Wanted Dead Or Alive.
*Also available as:*
CD video (PolyGram Music Video 080 296 1) October 1988

**LIVIN' ON A PRAYER (PolyGram Music Video 080 042 2) October 1988 (CD video single)**

**WANTED DEAD OR ALIVE (PolyGram Music Video 080 052 2) September 1989 (CD video single)**

**NEW JERSEY (Channel 5 CFV 08892) November 1989 (60 minutes)**
Featuring the singles Bad Medicine, I'll Be There For You, Born To Be My Baby and Living In Sin plus Blood On Blood (Live), Lay Your Hands On Me, Bad Medicine (version two) and Bon Jovi 'home videos'.

**ACCESS ALL AREAS – A ROCK 'N' ROLL ODYSSEY (PolyGram Music Video) December 1990**
90 minute 'rockumentary' video of the Jersey Syndicate (*New Jersey* album) world tour.

### KEEP THE FAITH – AN EVENING WITH BON JOVI (PolyGram) 1992

'An MTV presentation' recorded 25 October 1992 at New York's Kaufman Astoria Studios as part of the channel's *Unplugged* series. An 85 minute, 15 song set with the tracklist: With A Little Help From My Friends, Love For Sale, Lay Your Hands On Me, Blaze Of Glory, Little Bit Of Soul, Brother Louie, Bed Of Roses, Livin' On A Prayer, Fever, It's My Life/We Gotta Get Out Of This Place, Wanted Dead Or Alive, I'll Sleep When I'm Dead, Bad Medicine, Keep The Faith.

Also available on LaserDisc and double CD-i.

### KEEP THE FAITH – THE VIDEOS (PolyGram) July 1993

A 60 minute, 11-song collection of interviews, other footage and promo clips for the album's singles. Tracklist: Keep The Faith, Bed Of Roses, In These Arms, If I Was Your Mother, I'll Sleep When I'm Dead, I Believe, I Wish Everyday Could be Like Christmas, Cama De Rosas (Bed Of Roses, Spanish Version), Ballad Of Youth, Dyin' Ain't Much Of A Livin', I'll Sleep When I'm Dead (Acoustic Version).

### CROSS ROAD – THE BEST OF BON JOVI (PolyGram) October 1994

An 80 minute, 16-song version of the album with a slightly different tracklist: Livin' On A Prayer, Keep The Faith, Wanted Dead Or Alive, Lay Your Hands On Me, You Give Love A Bad Name, Bed Of Roses, Blaze Of Glory*, In These Arms, Bad Medicine, I'll Be There For You, Dry County*, Living In Sin, Miracle*, I Believe, I'll Sleep When I'm Dead, Always*.

(All tracks marked * were listed as previously unavailable.)

### LIVE FROM LONDON (PolyGram) October 1995

A 90-minute edit of the set recorded at Wembley Stadium on Sunday, 25 June 1995. Tracklist: Livin' On A Prayer, You Give Love A Bad Name, Keep The Faith, Always, Blaze Of Glory, Lay Your Hands On Me, I'll Sleep When I'm Dead, Bad Medicine/Shout, Hey God, Wanted Dead Or Alive, This Ain't A Love Song plus a promo clip for *These Days*.

## 3 (b)  Plus

KERRANG! KOMPILATION 1 (PMI MVP 99 1077 2) July
1985 (various artists, included: 'Runaway')

KERRANG! KLASSIKS (PMI MVP 99 1191 3) October 1989
(various artists, included: 'Livin' On A Prayer')

SMOKE ON THE WATER (Virgin VISION VVD 636)
November 1989 (Rock-Aid Armenia charity compilation, various
artists, included 'Livin' On A Prayer')

MOSCOW MUSIC PEACE FESTIVAL (Warner Music Vision)
1991
Bon Jovi featured (alongside Cinderella and Skid Row) on volume
one of two tapes of the Make A Difference Foundation shows in
August 1989. Various members (but not Jon) featured in the jam
with Gorky Park that closes volume two.

## 4. The Rest

## 4 (a)  Rare tracks

A VERY SPECIAL CHRISTMAS (A&M 393 911–2) 1987
Various artists compilation of Christmas songs to raise funds for
Special Olympics International – a disabled athletes charity. Bon Jovi
contributed one song, a live version of 'Back Door Santa' recorded at
Nassau Coliseum, NY on 8 August, 1987.

STAIRWAY TO HEAVEN: HIGHWAY TO HELL (Vertigo)
December 1989
Various artists charity collection to raise funds for the Make A
Difference Foundation. Bon Jovi cover Thin Lizzy's 'The Boys Are
Back In Town'. Tico Torres plays on cover of Led Zeppelin's 'Moby
Dick', part of 'Drum Madness'. Members of Bon Jovi also perform

on 'Hound Dog' and 'Blue Suede Shoes', with David Bryan featured in 'Long Tall Sally', all parts of 'Jam', the all-star closing track recorded live at Moscow World Music Peace Festival, Lenin Stadium, 12–13 August 1989.
*Available as:*
(Vertigo 482 093–2) CD
(Vertigo 482 093–4) cassette
(Vertigo 842 093–1) vinyl

**NAVY SEALS (Atlantic) 1990**
Movie soundtrack including Bon Jovi's cover of Thin Lizzy's 'The Boys Are Back In Town' originally recorded for the Make A Difference Foundation 'Stairway To Heaven... Highway To Hell' album.

**A VERY SPECIAL CHRISTMAS 2 (A&M 540 003–2) 1992**
Second various artists compilation to raise funds for Special Olympics International. Jon Bon Jovi contributed 'Please Come Home For Christmas' featuring a one-off band including Tom Petty's keyboard player Benmont Tench (who had played on his *Blaze Of Glory* soundtrack album).

**THE COWBOY WAY – MUSIC FROM THE MOTION PICTURE (Epic Soundtrax 476822–2) 1994**
Soundtrack includes the (then) previously unreleased Bon Jovi track 'Good Guys Don't Always Wear White' alongside contributions from Blind Melon, The Allman Brothers, En Vogue etc. Film starred Jon's friend Kiefer Sutherland.

## 4 (b)  Richie Sambora solo

**THE ADVENTURES OF FORD FAIRLANE (Elektra) 1990**
Various artists soundtrack to movie starring Andrew Dice Clay. Richie Sambora plays Jimi Hendrix's 'Wind Cries Mary'.

## 4 (c)  Dave Bryan solo

**THE NETHERWORLD (PolyGram) 1992**
Instrumental film soundtrack album. ('It was scary to do things away from the band but it helps you grow as a person . . .' – Bryan.)

**ON A FULL MOON (PolyGram) 1994**
Instrumental album of new and re-worked soundtrack material. Released only in Japan.

## 4 (d)  Bon Jovi guest appearances

**with Surgin'**
**WHEN MIDNIGHT COMES (Music For Nations/EMI America) 1985**
Jon sang backing vocals on 'Shot Through The Heart', a new version of the track co-written by Jon and Jack Ponti and included on Bon Jovi's debut album. Surgin' was Ponti's band. Album credits list Jon by his real name, 'John Bongiovi'.

**with Paul Dean**
**HARD CORE (Columbia) 1989**
The debut solo album by the Loverboy guitarist. The track 'Under The Gun' – credited to P. Dean, M. Reno, J. Bon Jovi, R. Sambora – features Jon on harmonica. Jon met Dean through Bruce Fairbairn and Bob Rock. The latter engineered this album at Little Mountain Sound studios in Vancouver.

**with Alice Cooper**
**TRASH (Epic 465130)1989**
Jon and Richie co-wrote 'Hell Is Living Without You' with Alice and his producer Desmond Child. Richie plays guitar on the same track. Jon sings back-up vocals on the title-track and single, 'Trash'. Bassist throughout the album is Hugh (aka Huey) McDonald.

288

## with Cher
### CHER (Geffen) 1987

Cher's first solo album after a long sojourn out of the musical limelight. Jon, Richie and Desmond Child produced on a reworking of her sixties hit 'Bang Bang'. Also co-wrote and produced the album's 1988 Number 11 Stateside hit 'We All Sleep Alone' (which peaked at Number 47 in the UK) with Desmond Child. All of Bon Jovi played on the album. Richie later played the song live during his 1991/92 solo tour.

### HEART OF STONE (Geffen) 1989

Follow-up to *Cher*. Jon and Richie co-wrote (with Desmond Child and Dianne Warren) the track 'Does Anyone Really Fall In Love Anymore?' Huey McDonald plays bass on this track and two others.

## with Gorky Park
### GORKY PARK (Vertigo 838 628–2) October 1989

Jon and Richie co-wrote, produced and played on one track, 'Peace In Our Time', on the Russian band's Western debut album.

## with Hall & Oates
### CHANGE OF SEASON (Arista) 1990

Working mid-1990, after the *Blaze Of Glory* soundtrack Jon co-wrote and co-produced (with Danny Kortchmar) the single 'So Close', the first track on the duo's album. Single spent one week on the UK chart at Number 69 in September.

## with Ratt
### DETONATOR (Atlantic 7567 82127 2) September 1990

Jon sings backing vocals on one track, 'Heads I Win, Tails You Lose'.

## with Desmond Child
### DISCIPLINE (Elektra) July 1991

Richie among the guest musicians.

**with Stevie Nicks**
**TIMESPACE – THE BEST OF STEVIE NICKS (EMI CDP 797623–2) 1991**
Jon co-wrote the album's one new track 'Sometimes It's A Bitch' with Billy Falcon. He and Danny Kortchmar produced the song and in addition to a number of the musicians who also featured on the *Blaze Of Glory* soundtrack, Jon played acoustic guitar and Tico Torres played drums.

**with Aldo Nova**
**BLOOD ON THE BRICKS (Jambco/Mercury 848513–2) June 1991**
Jon co-produced and arranged the album with Aldo, got a co-writing credit on 9 of the album's 10 tracks, and sang backing vocals on all tracks bar one. Aldo used the same rhythm section Jon used on some tracks on the *Blaze Of Glory* soundtrack. In addition, Jon arranged for the album to come out on his Mercury subsidiary Jambco, and his cousin Tony Bongiovi is even credited with 'project coordination (USA)'. At least five tracks co-written with Bon Jovi were omitted from the final sessions.

**with Billy Falcon**
**PRETTY BLUE WORLD (Jambco 848 800–2) August 1991**
Album produced by Danny Kortchmar and Jon Bon Jovi. Musicians include many also featured on the *Blaze Of Glory* soundtrack. Jon credited with guitar and backing vocals on various tracks.

**with Rockhead**
**ROCKHEAD (EMI EMC 3649) March 1993**
One-off band led by Bon Jovi engineer/producer Bob Rock. Richie Sambora played guitar on one song, last track 'House Of Cards'.

**with Larry Adler**
**THE GLORY OF GERSHWIN (Mercury) 1994**
Jon and Richie played on one song, 'How Long Has This Been Going On', credited to 'Jon Bon Jovi (featuring Richie Sambora)', on this all-star tribute to the music of George Gershwin – 1994 was his

centennial year – each track featuring legendary harmonica player Larry Adler, celebrating his eightieth birthday.

**with Little Steven**
**NINE MONTHS (Milan/BMG) 1995**
Soundtrack includes the track 'The Time Of Your Life', 'written performed and produced by Little Steven'. Little Steven is, however, backed by Richie Sambora, David Bryan, Hugh McDonald and Tico Torres. Special thanks are offered to 'Jonny Bon Jovi'.

NB: Jon and Richie have also written (or have been reported to have written) songs for Gary 'US' Bonds, Jennifer Rush, Charlie Sexton, Ted Nugent, Billy Squier, Bonnie Tyler, Belinda Carlisle, Loverboy, etc., etc.

## 4 (e)  Promo singles

Runaway/Shot Through The Heart/Breakout (Vertigo BON DJ 12) 12″, 250 copies, February 1984

She Don't Know Me/Breakout (Vertigo VER DJ 11) 12″, different pic sleeve to commercial version, 600 copies, April 1984

In And Out Of Love/Roulette (Live) (Vertigo VERR19) Radio edit, 300 copies, May 1985
In And Out Of Love/Only Lonely (Vertigo BON DJ 212) 12″, white label, May 1985

The Hardest Part Is The Night/In And Out Of Love (Vertigo BON DJ 312) 12″, 250 copies, July 1985

Silent Night (Stereo)/Silent Night (Mono) (Mercury PRO 381/1) American 12″, in gatefold black-and-white sleeve, only 75 originally sent to UK DJs, 1985

# BON JOVI

Let It Rock/You Give Love A Bad Name (Vertigo BON DJ 412) 12″, August 1986

Livin' On A Prayer/Wild In The Streets (Vertigo VER DJ 28) Radio edit – omitting synthesizer intro – 1,000 copies, September 1986

Livin' On A Prayer (Vertigo BON DJ 512) Unreleased – possibly un-pressed – one-sided 12″, 1986

Wanted Dead Or Alive (LP Version)/Livin' On A Prayer/You Give Love A Bad Name (Vertigo JOV CD 1). Limited edition, first ever UK promotional Bon Jovi CD, March 1987

## 4 (f)  Non-UK releases

**LIVE TOUR EP (Mercury) October 1987**
*Tracks:*
Breakout, Runaway, Tokyo Road, Wanted Dead Or Alive.
*Available as:*
(Mercury 888820) Live EP recorded in Japan. 26 minutes of music on two 7″ discs, gatefold sleeve. Released only in Japan and Australia.

**LIVIN' ON A PRAYER (Mercury) November 1987**
Livin' On A Prayer/You Give Love A Bad Name/Edge Of A Broken Heart
(Mercury 888 2311) 12″ Germany-only single

**BURNING FOR LOVE (Mercury) December 1988**
(Mercury 15 PP44) 12″ Japan-only single

**BORDERLINE (Mercury) December 1988**
(Mercury 15 PP56) 12″ Japan-only single

## 4 (g)  Various artists compilations

**SHOUT (Vertigo) 1984**
CD-only various artists collection including 'Runaway'.

**THE KERRANG! KOMPILATION (Virgin) June 1985**
Various artists collection including 'Runaway'.

**THE DISORDERLY (label unknown) 1987**
Soundtrack album including 'Edge Of A Broken Heart'.

**ROCK CITY NIGHTS (PolyGram) October 1989**
Various artists collection including 'You Give Love A Bad Name'.

**GLORYLAND USA (Mercury) 1994**
Jon Bon Jovi's 'Blaze Of Glory' appears alongside tracks by Queen, Fleetwood Mac and Santana on an album to celebrate the USA's hosting of the 1994 World Cup Finals.

plus a host of others

## 4 (h)  Miscellaneous

**BON JOVI CD BOX SET (Vertigo 838 605 2) October 1989**

**BON JOVI INTERVIEW PICTURE DISC (Baktabak BAK 2022) April 1988**
Also available as: CD (Baktabak CBAK 4004)

**BON JOVI INTERVIEW PICTURE DISC, VOL 2 (Baktabak BAK 2106) August 1988**
Also available as: 7″ set (Baktabak BAKPAK 1007)

**CHRIS TETLEY INTERVIEWS BON JOVI (Music & Media CT 1001) October 1987**

**VERTIGO INTERVIEW (Vertigo WAX-JOV 10) 1988 (12″ pic disc)**

If you've read this far, you must be pretty keen. And if you haven't already, why not join the official Bon Jovi fan club?

## BON JOVI

Send cheque or money order in US funds only ($20 for US addresses, $30 rest of world) to:
Backstage With Jon Bon Jovi
PO Box 326
Fords NJ 08863
USA
(Prices correct as of 1995)

Bon Jovi's Internet address is: http://www.polygram.com/polygram

# Index